Global Community Policing

Problems and Challenges

International Police Executive Symposium Co-Publications

Dilip K. Das, *Founding President-IPES*

PUBLISHED

Global Trafficking in Women and Children
By Obi N.I. Ebbe and Dilip K. Das, ISBN: 978-1-4200-5943-4

Contemporary Issues in Law Enforcement and Policing
By Andrew Millie and Dilip K. Das, ISBN: 978-1-4200-7215-0

Trends in Policing: Interviews with Police Leaders Across the Globe, Volume Two
By Dilip K. Das and Otwin Marenin, ISBN: 978-1-4200-7520-5

Criminal Abuse of Women and Children: An International Perspective
By Obi N.I. Ebbe and Dilip K. Das, ISBN: 978-1-4200-8803-8

Urbanization, Policing, and Security: Global Perspectives
By Gary Cordner, AnnMarie Cordner and Dilip K. Das, ISBN: 978-1-4200-8557-0

Global Environment of Policing
By Dilip K. Das, Darren Palmer, and Michael M. Berlin, ISBN: 978-1-4200-6590-9

Trends in Policing: Interviews with Police Leaders Across the Globe, Volume Three
By Otwin Marenin and Dilip K. Das, ISBN: 978-1-4398-1924-1

Police Without Borders: The Fading Distinction between Local and Global
By Cliff Roberson, Dilip K. Das, and Jennie K. Singer, ISBN: 978-1-4398-0501-5

Effective Crime Reduction Strategies: International Perspectives Enhancing Law Enforcement Profesionalism, Effectiveness and Leadership in the 21st Century
By James F. Albrecht and Dilip K. Das, ISBN: 978-1-4200-7838-1

Strategic Responses to Crime: Thinking Locally, Acting Globally
By Melchor de Guzman, Aieteo Mintie Das, and Dilip K. Das, ISBN: 978-1-4200-7669-1

FORTHCOMING

Policing Neoliberal Societies
By Allison Wakefield, Bankole Cole, and Dilip K. Das, ISBN: 978-1-4398-4135-8

Terrorism, Counterterrorism, and Internal Wars: Examining International Political Violence
By Austin Turk, Dilip K. Das, and James Ross, ISBN: 978-1-4398-2104-6

Justices of the World: Their Views, Opinions and Perspectives
By Chandrika M. Kelso and Dilip K. Das, ISBN: 978-1-4200-9978-2

Cross Cultural Profiles of Policing
By Dilip K. Das, Osman Dolu, and Bonnie Mihalka, ISBN: 978-1-4200-7014-9

International Police Executive Symposium Co-Publications

Dilip K. Das, *Founding President-IPES*

Interviews with Global Leaders in Policing, Prisons, and Courts Series

PUBLISHED

Trends in Policing: Interviews with Police Leaders Across the Globe, Volume Three
By Otwin Marenin and Dilip K. Das, ISBN: 978-1-4398-1924-1

Justices of the World: Their Views, Opinions, and Perspectives
By Chandrika M. Kelso and Dilip K. Das, ISBN: 978-1-4200-9978-2

FORTHCOMING

Trends in Corrections: Interviews with Corrections Leaders Around the World
By Jennie K. Singer and Dilip K. Das, ISBN: 978-1-4398-3578-4

Trends in Policing: Interviews with Police Leaders Across the Globe, Volume Three
By Bruce F. Baker and Dilip K. Das, ISBN: 978-1-4398-8073-9

Global Community Policing

Problems and Challenges

Edited by
Arvind Verma
Dilip K. Das
Manoj Abraham

International Police Executive Symposium Co-Publication

CRC Press
Taylor & Francis Group
Boca Raton London New York

CRC Press is an imprint of the
Taylor & Francis Group, an **informa** business

CRC Press
Taylor & Francis Group
6000 Broken Sound Parkway NW, Suite 300
Boca Raton, FL 33487-2742

First issued in paperback 2019

ISBN-13: 978-1-4398-8416-4 (hbk)
ISBN-13: 978-0-367-86676-1 (pbk)

Library of Congress Cataloging-in-Publication Data

Global community policing : problems and challenges / [edited by] Arvind Verma, Dilip K. Das, and Manoj Abraham.
p. cm.
Includes bibliographical references and index.
ISBN 978-1-4398-8416-4
1. Community policing. 2. Police. I. Verma, Arvind. II. Das, Dilip K., 1941- III. Abraham, Manoj.

HV7936.C83G56 2012
363.2'3--dc23 2012005403

Visit the Taylor & Francis Web site at
http://www.taylorandfrancis.com

and the CRC Press Web site at
http://www.crcpress.com

Contents

IPES Preface

The International Police Executive Symposium (IPES), established in 1994, seeks to address one major challenge: The two worlds of research and practice remain disconnected even though cooperation between the two is growing. A major reason is that the two groups speak in different languages. The research is published in hard-to-access journals and presented in a manner that is difficult for some to comprehend. On the other hand, police practitioners tend not to mix with researchers and remain secretive about their work. Consequently, there is little dialogue between the two and almost no attempt to learn from one another. The global dialogue among police researchers and practitioners is limited. True, the literature on the police is growing exponentially, but its impact upon day-to-day policing is negligible.

The aims and objectives of the IPES are to provide a forum to foster closer relationships among police researchers and practitioners on a global scale, to facilitate cross-cultural, international, and interdisciplinary exchanges for the enrichment of the law enforcement profession, to encourage discussion, and to publish research on challenging and contemporary problems facing the policing profession. One of the most important activities of the IPES is the organization of an annual meeting under the auspices of a police agency or an educational institution. Now in its 17th year, the annual meeting, a five-day initiative on specific issues relevant to the policing profession, brings together ministers of interior and justice, police commissioners and chiefs, members of academia representing world-renown institutions, and many more criminal justice elite from over 60 countries. It facilitates interaction and the exchange of ideas and opinions on all aspects of policing. The agenda is structured to encourage dialogue in both formal and informal settings.

Another important aspect of the meeting is the publication of the best papers presented, edited by well-known criminal justice scholars and police professionals who attend the meetings. The best papers are selected, thoroughly revised, fully updated, meticulously edited, and published as books based upon the theme of each meeting. This repository of knowledge under the copublication imprint of IPES and CRC Press–Taylor & Francis Group chronicles the important contributions of the International Police

Executive Symposium over the last two decades. As a result, in 2011 the United Nations awarded IPES a special consultative status for the Economic and Social Council (ECSOC) honoring its importance in the global security community.

In addition to this book series, the IPES also has a research journal, *Police Practices and Research: An International Journal* (PPR). The PPR contains research articles on police issues from practitioners and researchers. It is an international journal in the true sense of the term and is distributed worldwide. For more information on the PPR visit http://www.tandf.co.uk/journals/GPPR.

Community-oriented policing and police-citizen cooperation is now the accepted framework for all progressive police departments. Yet, the practices and even some of the principles guiding this framework vary across the globe. The IPES Kerala, India, conference brought together a large number of academics and police practitioners from all continents, and this book is an outcome of their deliberations. From the design and implementation of community policing in the United States to the evaluation of Police e Mardumi, an indigenous system of community policing in Afghanistan, this book provides a fascinating perspective on this subject. The ambitious and highly successful Janmaitri Suraksha project in Kerala, India; the Mahila Dakshata Suraksha in Maharashtra, India; the weed and seed project in Connecticut; the problem-solving models used by police and partnership agencies in Great Britain to the caution required in dealing with road blocks, such as predatory leadership in Gambia, all provide different insights into the development and implementation of community policing in different regions. The book provides not only lessons in the design, implementation, and administration of community policing, but also various ways in which such programs can be evaluated. For any serious scholar and interested practitioner this book is a must-read.

IPES advocates, promotes, and propagates that policing is one of the most basic and essential avenues for improving the quality of life in all nations, rich and poor, modern and traditional, large and small, as well as peaceful and strife-ridden. IPES actively works to drive home to all its office bearers, supporters, and admirers that, in order to reach its full potential as an instrument of service to humanity, policing must be fully and enthusiastically open to collaboration between research and practice, global exchange of information between police practitioners and academics, universal disseminations and sharing of best practices, generating thinking police leaders and followers, as well as reflecting and writing on the issues challenging to the profession. Through its annual meetings, hosts, institutional supporters, and publications, IPES reaffirms that policing is a moral profession with unflinching adherence to the rule of law and human rights as the embodiment of humane values.

Dilip K. Das
Founding President, International Police Executive Symposium, www.ipes.info

Book Series Editor, Advances in Police Theory and Practice, CRC Press, Taylor and Francis Group

Book Series Editor, Interviews with Global Leaders in Criminal Justice, CRC Press, Taylor and Francis Group

Book Series Editor, PPR Special Issues as Books, Routledge, Taylor and Francis Group

Founding Editor in Chief, Police Practice and Research: An International Journal, PPR, http://www.tandf.co.uk/journals/GPPR

Foreword

Valedictory Speech

V.S. Achuthanandan, Chief Minister–Kerala

Police was generally considered a part of the repressive machinery of the state, in colonial times. After independence and the country becoming democratic, there was rethinking on the role of police in the society. This happened not only in states like India, but countries like Britain as well. Since then policing continuously underwent changes along with the developments on democratization.

It is in this background, one has to study initiatives like community policing, which have begun to spread far and wide. All over the world, community policing is found extremely beneficial in improving public confidence in the police. In this era of globalization, security of private or public places and public order depends largely upon a police-citizen relationship. There cannot be true social and economic progress, unless the quality of law enforcement improves and a people-friendly police is set up.

All over the globe, the need for police-public partnerships is widely discussed today. It is undoubtedly one of the foundations for good governance. The citizen's expectation of freedom from crime and violence cannot be met by any government without a good police-public partnership. It is in this context that the government of Kerala decided to introduce community policing in the state, as a government project.

A police force exhibiting friendly disposition and empathy towards the public is a long-cherished dream of the society and any democratic government. Community policing has helped the state of Kerala to come nearer to that dream. To sustain and to spread the same is our next responsibility. To carry out this huge responsibility, we still have miles to go.

Our interest in community policing has prompted us to think about learning more lessons from the models existing all over the world. It is in this context that the government of Kerala decided to hold a Global Community Policing Conclave in Kochi. I am sure that this has indeed benefited the practitioners from our state by exposing them to the various global models of community policing. These include the challenges of various kinds, encountered in different countries.

The community of practitioners and researchers mutually benefit from interaction with one another and this must be promoted. Against the grave backdrop of growing threats of terrorism and globalization of crimes, ensuring community participation in the maintenance of public order and bringing about reduction in crimes are the major challenges faced by any government. We do require police-community partnership in the forefront, not only for the success of our democracy, but also to achieve the mission of global peace.

This book contributes to a better understanding of community policing and the area of police public interface. I am sure both the researchers and practitioners will benefit immensely from the labor of scholars and police officers who have contributed to this work.

Preface

While the "police are the public and the public are the police" has been expressed for several decades, the concept and implementation of community policing still remains elusive. Every police officer expresses the need to work with the community and considers it essential to win the trust of the citizens. There is no dispute that without the cooperation of the citizens, no police function can succeed. Moreover, in a democratic society it is imperative the police work with the citizens and remain accountable for their actions. Yet, as seen across the globe, these themes play out in different ways. The police find it difficult to remain neutral in conflict-prone situations and officers' behavior leaves much to be desired. The citizens demand a police that responds to every small and insignificant incident and yet the residents do not wish to be involved with the police. The demand for a ubiquitous police that patrols and prevents crime at every nook and corner, at every moment, does not translate into hiring more officers and providing adequate resources. The gap between the ideal of police-citizen relations and the actual mutually suspicious relationship remains unbridgeable.

This book is an attempt to go beyond the common rhetoric and examine both the theory and practice of community policing around the globe. Bringing a wide variety of case studies and examples from different parts of the world, the book brings new scholarship and attention to police-citizen relations. The chapters are largely based upon the conference presentations made at the widely attended International Police Executive Symposium (IPES) annual gathering at Kerala, India. Other contributions have come from special topics covered by eminent scholars working in the field of policing. Together, the effort is an excellent documentation of new insights into community policing and a critical appraisal that questions its conceptualization.

Apart from the geographical reach of these contributions a number of specific contributions are made herein. In the rugged war-torn mountains of Afghanistan a form of community policing called Police e Mardumi is being practiced with considerable promise, which may surprise many scholars. A case study from West Africa cautions that the support of leadership and political masters remains crucial in any effort to implement citizen-oriented policing reforms. But special methods like emotional intelligence can be applied to overcome historical antipathies and are illustrated by other studies from the same continent. Significantly, historically discredited police, such as that in India, can transform itself to strengthen democracy and work to address long-standing citizen problems, suggesting that given the will, change is possible. The Janmaitri Suraksha and Mahila Dakshat Suraksha schemes in India introduce a framework that most police practitioners will find attractive. Furthermore, the Dutch experience suggests that community policing principles and practices need constant evaluation and modifications to serve the community better.

The book also provides valuable information about ways of measuring success of police policies. A case study from Sweden suggests an innovative form of citizen surveys to evaluate police efforts. An evaluation of a weed and seed program suggests that targeted public funding can be a productive strategy and can help to leverage efforts that seek to develop increased resilience at the community level. This may happen at a bigger scale too, as evident from Japan, where a national comprehensive crime reduction campaign resulted in measurable success. Additionally, a variety of problem-solving projects are presented that could be customized by many forces around the world. Clearly, the book will be a valuable resource for any researcher or practitioner of community-oriented policing.

Arvind Verma
Dilip K. Das
Manoj Abraham

About the Editors

Manoj Abraham is a senior officer of the Indian Police Service and has served in various capacities as chief of police of the cities of Cochin, Trivandrum, and Quilon. His community policing initiative was recognized with a special award in 2009 by the IACP. He has also been decorated with the Man of the Decade Award 2011 for the Success in Community Policing in Kochi City. Presently he is working as commissioner of police, Thiruvananthapuram City. Address: Commissioner of Police, Thiruvananthapuram City, Kerala, India. manojabraham05@gmail.com

Dilip K. Das, PhD, a former member of the Indian Police Service, is the founder and president of the International Police Executive Symposium (IPES), www.ipes.info, and author or editor of a large number of books on police-related subjects. He is also the editor in chief of *Police Practice and Research: An International Journal* (PPR). Professor Das is also editor in chief of two book series, *Advances in Police Theory and Practice* and *Interviews with Global Leaders in Police, Courts and Prisons.*

Arvind Verma is a former officer of the Indian Police Service and currently teaches at Indiana University, Bloomington. He has a large number of publications and is the author of several books. His most recent book is *The New Khaki: The Evolving Nature of Policing in India.* His research interests are in policing in India and computational criminology.

About the Contributors

V.S. Achuthanandan is the former chief minister of Kerala and a senior member of the Communist Party of India (Marxist). He is known for promoting free software in the state, particularly in the public education system.

A. Oyesoji Aremu is a correctional psychologist and an associate professor at the Department of Guidance and Counseling and also the deputy director (academic), Distance Learning Centre, University of Ibadan, Nigeria. Address: Deputy Director (Academic), Distance Learning Centre, University of Ibadan, Nigeria. sojiaremu@yahoo.co.uk

Meeran Chadha Borwankar is a senior officer of the 1981 batch of Indian Police Service and has a PhD from Pune University. She has served in various capacities in different districts of Maharashtra and as a DIG in the Central Bureau of Investigation. She is currently the commissioner of police, Pune—the first lady officer to hold this post. Address: Commissioner of Police, Pune, Maharashtra India. mcborwankar@gmail.com

S.E. Costanza holds a PhD from Louisiana State University in sociology with an emphasis in criminology. He has published in *Security Journal*, *Police Quarterly*, *Criminal Justice Review*, and the *Journal of Crime and Justice*. His specialty areas are crime mapping and policy analysis. He is coauthor of a book on halfway houses entitled *Salvation City: Halfway House Stories*. He is currently at the University of Alabama. stevecostanza@comcast.net

Setlhomamaru Dintwe is a graduate of University of South Africa, majoring in forensic investigations and policing. He has worked for the South African Police Services, later as manager of Investigations at the Independent Complaints Directorate. Currently, he is a senior lecturer at the University of South Africa. Dintwsi@unisa.ac.za

Kjell Elefalk holds a master's degree from the National Defence College in collaboration with Uppsala University, Sweden, and has studied European Law at the University of Leiden (the Netherlands). He is the chairman and cocreator of International Reflection Group, which promotes best practices in management inside the public sector around the world. His key experiences lie in developing, theoretically and in practice, management and budget reforms for police effectiveness, and he is an internationally recognized expert in performance management. marina_elefalk@hotmail.com

Ronald Helms holds a PhD from the University of Oregon. He is currently a professor of sociology at Western Washington University. His teaching and research emphasizes political sociology explanations for crime, social control, and punishment. He has published in *American Journal of Sociology, Social Forces, Social Science Research, Journal of Criminal Justice, Criminal Justice Review, Policing and Society*, and *Police Quarterly.*

Taisuke Kanayama is the director of Police Policy Research Center, National Police Agency of Japan, as well as a visiting professor of public safety policy at Hitotsubashi University. He served as the commissioner of police of Tochigi and Yamanashi prefecture. kanayama-t@smrj.go.jp

Wook Kang is an instructor at the University of Central Oklahoma. He has served as a captain in the Korean Police Force and is completing his doctoral studies at Michigan State University. He has published in *Policing: An International Journal of Police Strategies and Management* and *Asian Journal of Criminology.* Address: School of Criminal Justice, University of Central Oklahoma, Edmond, Oklahoma. kangwook@msu.edu

John C. Kilburn Jr. is associate dean of research and professor of sociology and criminal justice at Texas A&M International University. His research focuses on urban crime and health issues. He is coauthor of a book on halfway houses entitled *Salvation City: Halfway House Stories.*

Susan Vendetti Koski holds a doctorate in law and policy from Northeastern University with a concentration in crime theory and gender studies. She is an assistant professor at Central Connecticut State University in New Britain, Connecticut. Her research specialty areas are qualitative research methods and issues in female reentry.

Doel Mukerjee worked in Afghanistan for UNDP in 2009–2010. For a long period she has worked on justice sector reforms, with specialized work in human rights, judicial reforms, informal justice sector, police reforms, and gender justice with grassroots organizations and international development agencies. Currently she heads the Promoting Access to Justice and Human Rights Project for UNDP Bangladesh. doel.mukerjee@undp.org

Mahesh K. Nalla is professor and interim director of the School of Criminal Justice at Michigan State University. Currently he is exploring the relationship between organizational and work culture on police job satisfaction in developed, emerging, and transitional economies; citizen confidence and trust in private police and related issues; and risk and safe communities. His publications have appeared in the *Journal of Research in Crime and Delinquency*, *Justice Quarterly*, *European Journal of Criminology*, and *Journal of Criminal Justice*, among others. nalla@msu.edu

Stephen B. Perrott, professor of psychology at Mount Saint Vincent University, Nova Scotia, Canada, is a former police officer and current volunteer firefighter for the Halifax Regional Municipality. He has acted as a lecturer for the Halifax Regional Police, Royal Canadian Mounted Police, and Canadian Police College, consulted with the Philippine National Police on a five-year sex tourism-focused project, and was project director of the six-year community-based policing in the Gambia. stephen.perrott@msvu.ca

Prateep V. Philip is a senior officer of the Indian Police Service and is currently director of the Tamil Nadu Police Academy. He is the recipient of the prestigious inaugural British Queen's Award for Innovation in Police Training and Development, 2002. He is well known for the Friends of Police movement and has overseen the training in community policing of more than 100,000 police personnel and volunteers. He has a book titled *The Friends of Police Movement: A Roadmap for Proactive People Protection.* prateep.philip@gmail.com

David W. Purdy has 32 years in law enforcement in the United States and 10 years in international policing. He was the police chief in three U.S. cities and second to the Jamaica Constabulary Force Commissioner's Office. During his tenure he implemented community policing in all four jurisdictions. Currently he works for the U.S. Department of State serving as a senior police advisor. PurdyDW@state.gov

Mushtaq Rahim has worked for over four years focusing on peace building, disarmament, reintegration, police development, and reforms in Afghanistan. He is currently working for UNDP Afghanistan as head of the Crisis Prevention and Recovery.

B. Sandhya is a senior officer of the Indian Police Service holding the rank of inspector general of police. She is a prolific writer and painter and contributes to local media outlets. She is currently working as the nodal officer for the Community Policing program in Kerala state, and her work has been widely reported in the press.

Dr. Arie van Sluis is an assistant professor at the Faculty of Social Sciences of Erasmus University. **Dr. Lex Cachet** is associate professor at the Faculty of Social Sciences of Erasmus University. Commissioner **Peter van Os** is program manager of Community-Oriented Policing for the Dutch Board of Chiefs of Police at the Dutch Police Academy. **Ruth Prins** is a PhD student at the Faculty of Social Sciences of Erasmus University. **D. Peter Marks** is an assistant professor at the Faculty of Social Sciences of Erasmus University.

Community Policing
Theoretical Problems and Operational Issues

1

DAVID W. PURDY

The Creating, Caring, and Feeding of Community Policing

Community policing is not the panacea of all ills, but very close if properly developed, implemented, and cared for by all stakeholders. We have often heard that history repeats itself. Is it true? This researcher believes history does repeat itself, and also firmly believes that we have an obligation to learn from history and arm ourselves with the best weapons available as we look toward the future. History holds answers to prevention and cures for future events when we really study it correctly. For example, the United States does not want any more terrorist attacks, but there still exists a high probability the United States will be exposed to attempts. History also reveals a style of policing that may effectively address the future threats and challenges—community policing.

This chapter addresses how to design, implement, and support community policing based on lessons learned from history. There is discussion on responding to changes in our social, cultural, economic, technological, political, and global environments. Each environment impacts our policing philosophy, operational activity, and organizational responses, and modifications should be based on lessons learned from history. The perspective also changes depending on the particular position or role played in the organization. Capturing these various perspectives provides clues for solutions and the development of a high-performance organization. The author/presenter's experiences in implementing community policing in three U.S. cities and one international country are shared throughout the chapter. Upon its conclusion there is both clarity and the stimuli for more discussion.

There is reflection and sharing of personal and professional lessons learned by the author during his career of 40 years in law enforcement, with special attention to the development of community policing. As a police chief in three U.S. cities, he has established community-oriented policing. He then took his expertise to Jamaica where he assisted in a project putting community policing into practice and reality on international soil.

Community policing is a natural extension of the process of reform and modernization for any police service agency. It does not matter where in the world the process is initiated, the principles that follow still apply. Failure to follow the building instructions may result in failure or at best lack-luster performance. This would not be an acceptable outcome for the citizens.

What is community policing? This is an appropriate point to explain what community-oriented policing is and the key components that make it so effective. It is called community policing, community-oriented policing, and community-oriented policing and problem solving all interchangeably. Community policing is not a specific program, but rather a philosophy. It becomes an organizational strategy that has partnerships as its cornerstone. There is no "one size fits all" community policing formula. Community policing must be designed and tailored for each specific community. The community policing this police commissioner initiated in Nebraska was different than the strategy used in Washington, which was modified for the plans applied in Michigan, and different yet again in the community policing designed in Jamaica.

Remembering that community policing is not an exact program where one size fits all is important throughout the process of establishing it in your communities. The analogy of buying a business suit or new uniform is helpful. The need for a new suit or uniform is recognized by either yourself or someone else—internal or external. Some source has noticed or assessed the present condition of your suit or uniform and found it ill-fitting, in need of repair, perhaps soiled or stained from excessive work, or faded to a totally unrecognized color. Accepting the fact one needs a new suit or uniform moves us to another process. An assessment determines the type or style of the suit that satisfies the intended and articulated purpose. Then one shops for a tailor—an engineer to design and build the specified suit. Finally, one will try the suit on for size and the tailor makes the last adjustments to confirm a good fit. In the case of a community the process is the same. The need is recognized by either the government or the citizens complaining and demanding changes in service delivery. The government finds a partner to complete an assessment of what is needed and how to create the product. Another body is contracted to design the program and build the new model. Final adjustments are made during implementation, and it is presented publicly. The point is: Community policing must be individualized and tailored to the individual community based on the needs and uniqueness of the community involved. One size does not fit all communities.

Any tailored article requires proper care and attention in order to fulfill the original intention. Periodic adjustments and cleaning are important to keep it looking its best. Over time we all find that the tailored business suit begins to not fit properly. It may become too small or too loose, or perhaps worn out in places. Any of these conditions may result in a new assessment that major repairs are necessary or even a reengineered new suit. The same is true for our community policing models. They must be given what is referred to as proper care and feeding, and evaluations performed periodically to ensure proper functioning and satisfactory performance.

Community policing has gained prominence over the past two decades, but in the United States the reality is we have actually returned to a more traditional style of policing that predates most of us. This is a reference to what was known as the "old beat cop" who policed the American cities of yesteryear. The beat officer knew everyone and everyone knew the beat officer. That was a time when citizens truly liked and supported their police officers. With that type of relationship between the police and the people the information was free flowing. It is important to note that community policing does not suggest or equate to "community spies," as it is so translated in some countries. But rather, community policing is a partnership between the citizens and the police working toward safety and an enhanced quality of life for all. Going back to the example of fighting terrorism via community policing, the exchange of communication produces information and intelligence that may prevent an incident or protect the community. Keeping in mind that the terrorists may actually live among us prior to inflicting their wrath upon us, the knowledge and awareness of the community police officer becomes our likely early detection point. With proper training and the community policing partnerships, our fight against terrorism is strengthened.

Many people view community policing as merely a soft-on-crime approach to policing, and this could not be further from the truth when properly embraced, implemented, and empowered. The logical question in the United States is: If the beat cop was so effective, why did American police departments move away from it? Frankly, the benefits and effectiveness were not recognized at the time. Police administrators were looking for ways to use technology and more modern response methods. The new technology of the era included two-way radios and police squad cars. No longer did police officers walk to calls and utilize police call boxes on street corners, thus removing the officers from opportunities for frequent contact with the people.

Sure officers could respond quicker and air-conditioned police cars were more comfortable. But the police became robotic in their daily patrols. The dispatcher would tell them where to go, when to go, and what they should do when they arrived. Then the dispatcher would even tell them when they should be finished because another call was holding. They didn't have portable radios, so they were relegated to staying inside their cars because they would be disciplined for missing radio calls. The end result was less time on the street and reduced public contact. The cars became barriers to public interaction.

Another realization was the fact that crime rates continued to climb year after year. It didn't matter how many police cars we had or even whether we had portable radios. We were obviously very adept at taking calls from the public, dispatching police officers, completing reports, and documenting crime.

It became apparent across the country that something different had to be done. What we were doing we were doing very well, but we were having no impact on the runaway crime affecting every region of America. Progressive, forward-thinking police and social experts reinvented traditional policing, giving birth to modern-day community-oriented policing.

As we discuss the components of community policing you will see the similarities to the previously discussed traditional beat officer. Today's community policing creates partnerships with stakeholders in the community and then works on problem-solving efforts. It is essential that the community is clearly defined and police officers are specifically assigned to long-term involvement with a specific community, enabling them to become very knowledgeable of people and problems in that community.

Community policing, in order to be most effective, needs to be the philosophy and strategy for the entire police agency. Many departments have established community policing units that become specialty units within the department and assigned to specific service calls. With this model the public can become confused over differing responses. In some agencies the police officers are classified as first responders, or patrol units assigned to answer primary calls for service in beats, and a second classification is the community police officer who handles the "other" calls for service. Too often this creates an "us versus them" mentality and an avenue for the first responder police officer to decline dispatched calls for service, stating they are community policing type calls. Then the community policing officer throws a call back indicating it sounds more like a first responder or normal patrol call. This game discredits the department and many calls actually go unanswered, thus doing a disservice to the public. This is not acceptable.

As a police chief, this practitioner has implemented community policing in several police departments. Each was based on a department-wide, jurisdiction-wide basis where every police officer was a community policing officer. They all respond to every type of call for service. Such a shift in a service delivery model required a significant effort in training, orientation, public education, political support, and decentralization of police operations.

Now let us discuss the building of this new policing model. The logical place to start is, of course, at the beginning. The caution at this point from past experience is to take your time and do it right! Many have probably heard the saying "Measure twice and cut once, instead of measuring once and cutting more." This is so true in this process, yet we often make haste in the beginning and actually set the process on the path of failure. The first step is to build a solid foundation that will help guarantee success and sustainability. Because of its basic core components and flexibility, the U.S.

model of community policing has a wide range of applicability and can be adopted in diverse international communities.

Building the infrastructure and community support takes time. A good, solid foundation is required to make community policing a successful venture. On average this practitioner dedicated three years to the process of fielding a community policing model. And it was well worth the wait to ensure it was built correctly. If done correctly, the police agency benefits, as does the community, from community policing.

Our analogy of the need for a new business suit started with a recognition of the need for a new suit of clothing. Awareness came from some event or perhaps an in-depth study. But there must be a detailed analysis to guide and support the process. Identifying a great solution for the wrongly identified problem does not produce satisfactory results. It is essential to analyze so we know where we are and what we are heading into and why. Basically, what is the climate?

There is a reason you are looking at this option—we call that a clue! Follow up on it and do what police do well—investigate. Explore via every resource available to ensure a correct answer. Simply put, the problem is the key to the solution. Possibly citizens feel oppressed or abused by police/government, citizens don't report crimes or about being victims, or they are isolated. Look for answers based on lessons learned from history. Possibly services have shifted out of reach or there has been a return to previous political or abusive issues.

Some basics need to be dealt with early in the process for an orderly development of community policing. Obviously, the geographic boundaries need to be established. Use logical, recognized boundaries, considering natural barriers and obstacles that might impede service delivery. Also consider political alliances, ethnicity, gang or criminal territories, and religious groups that may impact policing and community interaction. There is nothing wrong with diversity, but if the situation is at a conflict stage it will be more difficult to perform community building. The boundaries limit the workload and help narrow problems to a manageable size. The clearly defined boundaries also provide for better accountability, as areas of responsibility are known by all and specific officers and community leaders are assigned to specific areas.

Ideally, the community and political leaders will come together and search for the total picture of the current situation and conduct a thorough assessment with representatives of all groups, parties, diversities, and political persuasions. The police executive must demand this type of process and become the catalyst for change. Most importantly, there needs to be a sincere desire to succeed in the best interest of the people.

Early warnings are strongly advised! Let us now break the discussion down into what this executive calls the "three spirits" associated with establishing community policing. Experience has demonstrated that they each can take on a life of their own—thus the term *spirits*—and will make or break the program.

Spirit number one is the police. It is vitally important to openly discuss the assessment or reason that has led to the recognition of needed change or concern. They need to know the real picture and have a clear understanding of the situation. Depending on where in the organization the person is stationed, he or she will have different views or concerns. He or she will react differently. The results of this candid discussion may also suggest the need for more research or additional surveys of the community, the total community. It is critical to correctly identify the issues and problems in order to respond effectively.

What would you expect the reaction to be from the staff? Be prepared by thinking through all the possible scenarios before the meeting. They will run the range of reactions from minimal to the extreme. There will be confusion and disbelief because this may be the first time they actually recognize that the public might not respect them in their professional role. This will be difficult for some who take it personally, and management needs to be prepared for the various reactions in order to address damage control.

The most common reaction will be the fear of change. This will impact the most numbers and is a fact in all organizations. People just do not easily embrace change. They will often fight it and refuse to accept the reality of the situation. This can impair forward progress and should be dealt with immediately, with sincerity and positive posturing. Some police personnel will argue that we should not trust the public and stay the present course. Being in denial is counterproductive. Employees will rally around any hope of maintaining the status quo. This will divert their attention from the task at hand. Along with this reaction is the belief that the public is not adequately informed and unable to assess the police services. Other members of the police agency just won't care what the public thinks. This is very revealing while providing insight into the real problems between the police and the public they are sworn to serve. Many will even view the public as "criminals" in an attempt to discredit them. Denial is one more common reaction, much like deflecting criticism.

Do not be surprised if officers display a lack of self-confidence and a fear of being exposed. Part of this may be associated with fear of losing their job or facing exposure for possible corruption. This is fear of the unknown, and let's face it—police officers can be very paranoid at times. The "everyone's out to get us" syndrome is real. One summary of reality often discovered is that the public doesn't trust the police and the police don't trust the public. This may actually be the heart of the problem. Each of these reactions is very telling, suggestive, and confirming. A careful review of their reactions will directly correspond to the public's view.

Different members of the organization will also develop preconceived notions about the impact of the change process. The work faced by each level of the organization will be assessed differently, depending on where they are in the agency. The executive level will see this as a great opportunity, while the administrative staff interprets it as a tremendous amount of new work coming their way. And the new tasking may be very unfamiliar to them, causing anxiety. The progressive, proactive executive will embrace the new mission as an excellent time to rebuild or reengineer the police service. This would include new positions, rotations, promotions, demotions, growth or reduction in staff, staff development, mentoring opportunity, new tools and technology, building public support, gaining respect from political leaders and the community, and pride in service to the community. All of these are real outcomes and not necessarily bad for any organization.

The level just below the executive has different perspectives on the impact. Whether real or perceived, they must be planned for and adequately addressed very early in the process. Failure to properly prepare the agency at all levels may prove disastrous. Middle managers will view this change as increased work they may not be prepared for, a chance for individual promotion, a fear of being replaced or eliminated from the organization, internal turmoil and friction between management and line employees running up and down the chain of command and across the organizational chart, conflict among subordinates and labor groups, and opportunity to enhance service delivery or failure to thrive.

The first-line supervisors will find themselves in the middle between management and street-level police officers. They will be encouraged to support management while struggling with personal conflict and friendships within their subordinates. These are some of the most critical players in the entire process from start to finish to aftercare. Support personnel like clerks, records workers, radio communication personnel, and secretaries will feel overloaded at times, and minimized or marginalized at other times. They may feel involved and fully engaged or totally left out.

As one may easily see from this discussion, there are significant challenges and issues requiring quick and certain action. Missteps at this stage can derail the shift toward community policing. The key is education, education, and more education. Educate the entire police body. Leaving any employee at any level out of this process creates a weakness in the end product. Everyone in the organization should receive a thorough explanation of the proposals, the issues, the goals, and the importance associated with this movement. Employees will need reassurance, support, and even "grieving" time as the agency transforms. The grieving process is often omitted, and it may be the one essential step that could bring success or failure. Change is hard on people and affects them differently, the same as a death might. They are moving from a comfort zone into the unknown zone.

Along with education there are extensive training requirements for all personnel. Each will gain new responsibilities, and this mandates good training so as to properly equip them for success. Give them the tools to succeed. In order to maintain the expectations communicated through community outreach and programs, police will require ongoing training and support. We must prepare them for success.

Ways to provide keys to success are by developing effective police training programs after identifying appropriate training needs. Remember the catalyst for this change is the clue! This may involve such things as on-site assessments, community meetings to acquire local issues and knowledge, talking to police officers, and talking with personnel throughout the ranks and in civilian positions as well as in different agency units. Look for basic training in police skills and tactics since good street-level policing is essential to building public trust. Then seek to identify community policing-specific training, such as public relations, communications skills, collaborative processes, problem-solving models, and community intervention techniques.

Another key to success is the provision of solid support from top down and across all lines. Some of this will be expanded later in this discussion, but this pertains to changes, updated, modified, and new policies that reflect the revised method of conducting business. Good policy acts as a guide to employee performance. It creates a means to explain, train, and hold employees accountable. All of these are important to the implementation of positive community policing. New organizational configurations may be helpful in deployment, assignment, and management of personnel and programs.

Ensure top- and mid-level support for new policing strategies, techniques, and training. Though leadership support is critical, mid-level personnel must also be willing to ensure the project goals will be carved out. Without ownership and commitment to community policing from this group, a vacuum is created that will have serious consequences. There have been attempts at community policing that were developed and rolled out at the top without the buy-in of other ranks. The opposite has also occurred, where the street-level officers start their own version of community policing without management approval. These do not survive for obvious reasons. The successful endeavors empower all levels of the agency to take action and responsibility for their respective parts in the police operation. The executive officer, the middle manager, the first-line supervisor, the street-level police officer, the support staff, the training academy, and the human resource personnel all must support community policing.

Ongoing assistance, once officers are trained, becomes an essential task as you oversee the implementation of their newly acquired skills by offering mentoring and guidance to ensure the skills are adopted and applied properly. We do this by observing the officers in action and debriefing them afterward.

Further, having the officers demonstrate new skills reinforces what they have learned and helps to embed these new skills into sustainable practice.

The shift to community policing does not require a complete redo of the organization, but sometimes it is the best time to make major changes. This discussion includes the extremes that may surface with a full-scale overhaul of an agency to ensure everyone has a sense of the potential for accomplishments and pitfalls.

Perhaps you have seen the motto written on the side of American police cars, "To Protect and To Serve." This police chief applied the following words to all police vehicles, business cards, literature, and stationary—"Deeds Speak"—as a reminder to both the public and the police that our actions speak for us. The implementation of community policing must bring about visible changes in the service delivery and interaction between the public and the police. The public needs to recognize a difference in action, not just words. "To change a culture, show people results; it's easy to wow locals with promises of what could be, but when you do the things they want done, that's when people notice." The author of this quote is unknown, but the message is very telling for all in the police services.

Of course, there are some common barriers facing the police leaders designing and implementing community policing. They must be identified and addressed in order to support the process. The most common include several already mentioned, communications, political pressure and interference, fear of the unknown, lack of training, costs, and supervision.

The simple answer to communications is to be totally transparent and, if anything, overcommunicate. It cannot hurt you to constantly remind the police agency employees, the politicians, and the public that you are building a changed service delivery model to better meet the needs of the community. Establishing boundaries and roles for the politicians in the beginning phases is important, as is reminding them constantly throughout the process. They may attempt to influence or rush the process. Appropriate consideration in a transparent process showing impartiality and neutrality is the proper posture to exhibit. The training issue includes training the public, which will be discussed in a few minutes. The actual transition cost to our budget is often the greatest fear or impediment to attempting the adoption of community policing. Experience will demonstrate minimal increases in budgetary expenditures. But this will vary from agency to agency, country to country, mostly depending on original police service expenses.

Additional tactics to overcome barriers include applying the same problem-solving skills we want to use in the community interaction. Assess where they are today and where they need to be in the final picture. This applies to the police and the public equally. Involve and empower employees by challenging them to produce and letting them actually participate. The ground-level employees generally have the view of reality and may provide the most essential solution. They have the best street-level knowledge and understanding, so when you develop their ownership in the process they will become committed employees. Engaging them in the process makes them more committed to success and creativity. Along the same lines, creating engaged first-line supervisors is just as important. Command officer interaction within the department and out in the community will fill gaps in the total communication and education process.

A major organizational transformation item associated with community policing that now deserves some attention is the planning and policy challenge. In order for community policing to be supported there must have been well-constructed strategic planning and the creation of policies that define and mandate certain actions and reactions. A number of obvious ones come to mind and will trigger others as this discussion continues. It is essential to survey your employees and community members for input during this assessment in order to gain a complete picture. Policies are a means of solidifying community norms and best practices for police and community interaction.

Sustaining success will require embedding the community policing philosophy and the new programs that support it into daily practice. It also requires maintaining relationships that will continue to support efforts that advance the community policing vision. This must be accomplished through ongoing outreach, training, and technical assistance that will institutionalize this new policing philosophy.

A significant topic requiring serious thought and planning is the authority issue. Typically our police agencies have been highly centralized. All commands come from headquarters and everything flows down from the top. In many agencies decision making is only at the top and strictly prohibited at the bottom. The backbone of community policing rests on the street-level police officer being empowered to make daily decisions in his or her area of responsibility. For problem solving to be effective and responsive to the public demands it needs to be quick. Any time a decision request goes up to the top for a decision valuable time is lost in seeing the change we promise in our community policing model. American policing has become extremely decentralized and proves very effective in the delivery of police services and problem solving.

Decentralized control mortifies many and appears impossible. But there are many ways to control it without inhibiting it. This takes us directly to a discussion on personnel hiring, training, and supervision; for they are keys to powerful, successful decentralized police services. The agency should look at the recruitment process to clarify what qualities your police service desires. Then you must target those groups that possess the profile you have determined best capable of service delivery under your model of community policing. Then the hiring process should support the recruitment efforts and bring to employment those who meet the established criteria of ethics, intelligence, interpersonal skills, logical thinking, decision making, psychological suitability, and maturity. Of course, this all requires the implementation of a fair pay and compensation package that attracts and retains the quality candidate desired.

The next step in the personnel process is training. We have already mentioned specific community policing training, but here we are talking about basic police skills related to human rights, proper police tactics and techniques, and understanding of the law. Decision making and discretion are two vital areas that directly impact decentralization. Police officers should be taught how to make good decisions, identify applicable issues, weigh the degree of impact, measure against policy and administrative guidance, and produce a safe or low-risk decision. Then permission to use police discretion may be granted as long as the police officer has received good training on the exercise of discretion that is supported by good policy and mentored via good supervision.

Once these issues are resolved and the quality of personnel is elevated, the fear of decentralization is reduced because there is confidence the police officer will exercise sound decision making. The deployment of personnel will reflect the commitment to community policing. Police officers need to be assigned to the same geographic community for an extended period of time in order to learn, know, and start to own the problems within that geographic community. That is when the officer will become most effective in making changes and solving problems. Fear of corruption from being in one location too long is countered by an effective, proactive disciplinary policy. Officers will be monitored, supervised, and held accountable regardless if assigned to a particular post for one week or one year. Again, this speaks to the need to have high standards in our recruitment, selection, and hiring process; a good pay package to discourage the corruption temptation; and sound supervision and policy that proactively address misconduct.

Now satisfied with the orientation of spirit number one, let us move on to the elected officials, or spirit number two. This is included for obvious reasons, but we will not consume too much time discussing the political issues. Frankly, if you do not include, inform, and involve your elected officials you will most likely be shooting yourself in the foot when it comes to anything you do, especially community policing. The elected officials can make or break a program, and this should be an early stop in your process of partnership building. Educate them early and regularly. Highlight how good community policing will be for the total community in dealing with much more than crime—enhancing the quality of life. What politician would not support a winning opportunity? Politicians need to see how much community policing can help them before they really adopt and support the effort. This is a fact of life, so use it to your advantage. Don't hold back any of the pluses and minuses, as they don't want to be surprised later in the process.

Of course, there is also the need for resources. The elected officials are the ones controlling the purse strings. It is difficult to assess the true cost of community policing because so much depends on the actual starting point for your agency. Some may require large amounts of funding, while for others minimal impact will be experienced. Remember, if we shortcut the funding now we will suffer elsewhere. But on the other side, don't use this change as a golden goose opportunity. Taking advantage of your elected officials is suicidal.

Informing and updating the officials is critically important. They need to know what each step is and when it is completed. They should be involved in the celebrations along the way as different milestones are reached. This keeps them engaged and in the public eye. Having the elected officials in the public eye sends a message of support, solidarity, and commitment to the implementation of community policing. The public will recognize this, and it acts to energize them as well. And be sure to include the opposition parties, as things do change in politics. The police need to be impartial and neutral, which is challenging in the political world.

Enough said about spirit number two. But don't view this brief discussion as suggesting politicians are minimal in the process. It is time to focus on spirit number three—the community. Much like the analogy of the old suit or uniform needing to be replaced, something in the community has identified the need for a change. Therefore, a complete assessment is imperative and it must be executed properly, thoroughly, and transparently. In order for community policing to start, survive, and thrive, the community must embrace the new model. Their involvement is essential and requires the careful building of consensus about issues, problems, differences, needs, wants, and definitions of quality of life. Input from the collective community via their various leaders serves as notice to the police agency on what they wish community policing to look and feel like once implemented.

A reality that requires attention is that often the long-term conflict between the public and the police has developed an intolerance and resistance to assistance. Trust building is of absolute importance. This can only be accomplished through sincere efforts over time. Adequately addressing this major obstacle will yield many positive benefits. The tactic most successful in establishing credibility for the police is to reach out to all the citizens in a nonthreatening, consensus-building process, which takes time, patience, and determination to succeed. Who comes to the consensus building is as important as the process itself. There must be a complete representative collection of community views and voices. Seek out first the community members, local business owners, clergy, government authorities, schools, and elected leaders. This is the group that will define the meaning of community policing in that community and what they expect it to look like in reality. In other words, they will identify the new role of the police in their community.

One can see the importance of engaging community leaders by keeping them informed and involved constantly. The partnerships we wish to form include police, other government agencies, community members, civic groups, nonprofit organizations, private businesses, and the media. We tend to underestimate what the media can do for us in our effort to build public trust and confidence. These relationships or partnerships must be carefully nurtured in order for community policing to become established and succeed in any troubled community.

When identifying and recruiting community representatives care must be given to ensure all parties and interests are represented. Some groups are intimidated or even coerced into having no voice, and it is important to be inclusive of all members of the community. Organizers for community outreach have to be energetic and well prepared. The programs must be loaded with community interaction aimed at building strong community interest and support. The momentum begins at this point and is supplemented with public education programs and meetings designed to maintain the excitement. The community training should first be separate from police and government training, but later merged in an effort to build a strong community-based team. Trust cannot be developed if isolated from each other.

During all community-building sessions, training, and meetings security is very important. Participants may be targeted by the criminal element that is now threatened by the formation of community policing. They also may be subjected to harassment and intimidations by the more dominant members or because of political affiliations. If they do not feel secure they will not return and value will be lost. On the same line of thinking, caution is important any time action is taken based on information gleaned from a public meeting. If people start getting arrested immediately after a meeting fear will heighten and cooperation dissipate.

A very important part of the process requires the outreach workers to be active and careful listeners. Often more is said by the unstated word than the spoken. And of course an open mind is essential throughout the process and always. This lesson needs to be learned and reinforced. These meetings will take time and effort to educate the representatives in the consensus building process. Community trainers are helpful who specialize in mobilizing citizens and providing them with team-building skills and rules that lead to successful, productive consensus building endeavors. People are not born knowing how to build consensus, and when having been at opposition for a long period the development of these skills is greatly assisted by outside community organizers and professional groups void of any local affiliation. Their only purpose is to help teach skills, empower citizens to engage, and serve as neutral facilitators in the consensus-building process.

The goal is not to relive multiple past incidents; however, it is often necessary to revisit some existing baggage in order to move forward. There must be recognition and respect for the lingering emotions, but then they need to commit to moving past them in the interest of building a new environment. End products would include a vision of what the ideal police and public interaction would look like, what services are desired and presently not fulfilled in the community, and what steps they are comfortable with for the achievement of positive, community, and police relations.

Ideally these meetings will produce general support for the concept of community policing, the need for community policing, and services to be provided to the community. Obviously, the citizens would also benefit from some educational and informational meetings with police and government representatives who will explain what community policing can be and how it might work. Then they will know some boundaries as they design their own vision. The location of the meetings is important so as not to appear oppressive, threatening, or dictating. Utilizing community centers, schools, churches, sporting facilities, and similar local public settings will facilitate the sense of being community driven and nonthreatening.

Keep in mind that the public education programs are an excellent place for police officials and local leaders to take a visible and active leadership role. Interacting with the local leaders in a change process is energizing and extremely satisfying to the participants. This builds and perpetuates the building of public trust and confidence. A goal is to create a true partnership working together toward improved quality of life and problem solving. The police do not and should not be the lead entity once the partner relationship has been established and is working. Keep in mind that policing of society is actually the responsibility of society, with the police merely being the paid staff to assist. As Sir Robert Peel stated, "The police are the public and the public are the police; the police being only members of the public who are paid to give full time attention to duties which are incumbent on every citizen in the interests of community welfare and existence."

One point to prepare for is the time factor involved. The public needs to understand that the proposed and promised change will take time. Care must be given to keep them engaged and also give updates. Otherwise they will become disenchanted and start to become skeptical of the government commitment to really make a difference. A process that appears stalled can actually result in riots and the creation of a major barrier to future collaboration between the government and the public. It becomes just one more broken promise.

This is a great opportunity for a real showing of good faith by the police and government. The higher-ranking police officials could share insight into the citizens' own personal rights and expectations during encounters with the police, as well as what the legal role of the police should include. Many citizens have never been educated about their rights or the limits of police authority.

Community outreach is so important and must be ongoing. Public trust depends on this outreach. The various stakeholders need to grasp the concepts of problem solving and consensus building. It begins with no one making judgments and listening with an open mind. One person's problem may not be the same as another's, but may be suggestive of other issues needing attention. The most common and easy-to-understand problem-solving tool is the SARA model. This involves engaging in a proactive and systematic investigation of identified problems. The review needs to be rigorous if it is going to be valid. And it is intended to develop clarity of the problems and assess appropriate responses. SARA stands for scanning, analysis, response, and assessment. In the scanning phase the goal is to identify and prioritize problems. The reported problem may be different from the actual problem, and the process will clarify the real problem and the associated problems. All need to be addressed.

Analysis involves researching all that is known about the problem. The gathering of all the facts is essential to a proper, effective solution. The response step is where solutions are developed aimed at creating a real solution or reduction of the problem. Caution throughout the process is important to prevent developing a great solution that has nothing to do with the actual problem. Finally, assessment involves follow-up evaluations to ensure the solution is on target. If not, what modifications would be appropriate or do we need to start over? This is an ongoing process and does not stop with the implementation of the first solution.

The problem-solving model provides a continuous process that is applicable to all community policing efforts. Use it to identify and clarify a problem, develop solutions, apply them, and then assess their effectiveness. This is exactly what should be done regarding the development of the community policing program tailored to a particular community. Constant monitoring is accomplished through careful listening and community interaction. Periodic meetings with the community will facilitate the gathering of information. It is not necessary to bluntly ask if there are any problems, as this may generate the creation of an artificial problem because the audience wants to satisfy you with an answer. If there are actual problems in the community, they will naturally reveal themselves, and we must be listening and sensitive enough to recognize them as early as possible. Holding town hall meetings is a great tool for community interaction. During these meetings the police and government can discuss the status of programs and potential new programs, and hear what type of assistance the citizens want.

The regular meetings tie nicely into the aftercare process or what we might call the "cleaning and altering of that suit"! More formal methods of assessing our progress and effectiveness are through professional, structure surveys. There are two models that serve this purpose well. Both the STEEP and SWOT analyses are techniques to assist the process of strategic planning. A STEEP analysis can be used in conjunction with a SWOT analysis, as they do not serve the same purpose or duplicate each process. Utilizing both gives the organization the best information for planning. They each provide valuable data and organizations rarely use both due to the cost and time involved; plus they assume redundancy. An option would be to alternate the methods in a continuing process of strategic planning.

SWOT analysis is used as a strategic tool to identify the chief objectives of an organization, and they are divided into internal and external factors describing the strengths, weaknesses, opportunities, and threat factors. The strengths and weaknesses demonstrate the internal factors and how they add or remove value of an organization, which is correctable. The opportunity and threat elements pertain to external factors that influence an organization and that the organization can utilize but has no control over. Economic, political, social, cultural, and demographic factors influence the market dynamic that creates external factors. The significance of SWOT analysis is that an organization can use external factors to reorganize internal factors, and use internal factors to expand or improve growth in an organization. An organization can use SWOT analysis to identify the areas that can be exploited, improved, developed, mitigated, or eliminated to promote efficiency and effectiveness of an organization.

A STEEP analysis is a tool to evaluate various external factors impacting a business or organization, a strategic tool that is based on the external factors, such as political, economic, social, cultural, legal, global, and technology aspects that describe environmental components. STEEP stands for social trends, technology trends, economic trends, ecological trends, and political trends. STEEP analysis is basic market research that approaches an environment issue as a whole. The degree of government intervention in the area to promote political stability, provide goods and services to the general public, and promote security and protect infrastructures of a nation is a part of the external factors that influence an organization's survival. Additionally, economic factors of inflation or deflation of economy, social and cultural, both man-made and natural aspects of environmental factors, aspects that influence the market trends, and the significance and the rates of technological change all influence an organization's well-being either directly or indirectly. Legal and international aspects are also part of the external factors that regulate and control the organizational existence and well-being.

In the justice and security arena, law enforcement utilizes both SWOT analysis and STEEP analysis to prepare, predict, and combat terrorism and crimes. SWOT allows law enforcement agencies to strengthen the law enforcement process and procedures, including the investigative techniques, appropriate training, improvement of public services, and so on, to detect and deter crimes. The STEEP analysis will enhance awareness in political climates and economic trend changes that in turn will be helpful to predict the areas that might have an increase in crime in the future. Also, analyzing the cultural migration or technological changes provides law enforcement the ability to anticipate certain types of crime that might occur in certain locations. An appropriate use of both SWOT and STEEP analysis could help law enforcement to protect the public more effectively and efficiently.

STEEP provides more outside view data that better address outside influences. SWOT tends to be an inside view and is more often conducted by internal staff. The SWOT analysis is easily adapted to internal issues and is preferred because it can be conducted by internal staff. A problem with only internal staff is that they may overlook the obvious. In Jamaica we say, "If you want to find out what smells in your house you must invite a guest into the home." Essentially, you cannot smell your own house, but an outsider can quickly detect the objectionable odor.

Each of these environmental changes as determined by the SWOT or STEEP analysis impacts our community policing philosophy, operational activity, and organizational responses. Use caution when considering modifications. Careful evaluations are required to ensure the correct adjustments. Modifications should be based on lessons learned from history as well as the new analysis data. What happens at times is the newly proposed solution will actually return you to a previous point that had been a problem, which leads to another modification. This tends to take us in circles without forward progress. This may also indicate the original solution was not the most responsive to the needs of the community, therefore rising up again for attention.

Capturing and understanding the various perspectives and concerns from each of the three spirits provides clues for solutions and for the development of a police agency into a high-performance organization. Creating a high-performance organization will elevate the service delivery and community interaction significantly. This is also spread into the community stakeholder side of the equation. The end result will be both partners functioning at a high-performance level.

There are several individual variables that will impact how employees perceive their jobs and their own performance. The first one is their perception of their own ability to do their job. If they feel fit for the role they will perform better. If they do not feel comfortable in their job they will not produce at peak performance levels. A remedy is for the organization to place people at their level of competency and provide adequate training to equip them for the job.

Job satisfaction is also an important variable that will impact job performance. Employee surveys repeatedly find that pay and benefits are not the key to job satisfaction. But rather, the feeling of being valued as an employee and employee inclusion are more important to employees. Clearly, satisfied and happy employees tend to enjoy their jobs more, and this generates higher performance. When employees are given respect for their jobs and their contribution to the organization they perform with greater purpose. Supervisors and employees will accept responsibility for their duties more readily and strive harder to ensure positive results in a safe environment.

Smart organizations recognize the importance of working with greater diversity because their individual differences bring a positive impact to organizational effectiveness and efficiency. Again, the positive impact will transfer into the community in the form of more effective and timely delivery of police services. The community receives greater satisfaction, which then translates into an elevation of their perception as being important. The reward is given back to the police in the form of greater trust, confidence, and support.

Part of creating high-performance organizations is in the design of operations and work flow. Designing jobs for ideal or maximum productivity in criminal justice organizations is imperative, as well-designed jobs facilitate high performance, high-quality work, and continuous improvement while also allowing for job satisfaction. This is a process of job analysis much like problem solving. Recognizing the relationship between job design and job performance is important. This analysis identifies how to modify tasks for enhanced productivity. Employing the concepts of teamwork and high-performance teams in criminal justice organizations has a major impact on performance. This applies equally within the police, within the community, and throughout the partnerships of police and community. As a group of employees or a collection of citizens become a team, the members begin to help one another accomplish goals. Performance and outputs are improved when they all work together toward a common end result.

Definitions and types of teams vary from organization to organization. Some have found it more beneficial to specialize. They may develop a team that only does problem solving. They might be called the research and development team. Then you would have specialized implementation teams, much like we see in the operations unit of a police department. This is where the service product actually hits the road.

When designing an effective work team, in either the police agency or the community, we find it most advantageous to have a cross-representation of people. Some call this greater diversity, but it includes members from various skill levels, cultures, religions, work groups, races, ethnicity, political persuasion, and different ranks. Each member will bring something unique to the team, which broadens the performance potential. In order to ensure high performance from a diverse group of team members we need to carefully build the team. Careful selection without discrimination of team members will help assemble the cross section of skills, talent, and other differences so important to the team diversity. Clarity of roles and goals is essential. They must incorporate rules of equality, inclusion, norms, and process to serve as a guide to performance. Cohesiveness, however, may not be a sole indicator of performance. Some groups are extremely cohesive yet from an organizational perspective dysfunctional because they cannot work with other teams. They may stray from organizational norms while creating their own team identity and norms. Management and supervisors need to monitor and mentor the process of team selection and development to guide them toward matching organizational goals.

As we develop teams and guide them in their roles we also need to provide managers and supervisors with similar assistance. Distinguishing the roles a manager must fulfill in order to be an effective member and leader of a team in a criminal justice organization is critical to developing a high-performance organization.

Identifying new roles for leaders is essential to meeting today's challenges in our constantly changing environments. The shift toward community policing is one of the changing environments, and it will cause a ripple effect into other environments. Managers must recognize their new role as a change agent and embrace it completely. They have become a catalyst for change in the community, which includes the new roles of coach and mentor, both internally and externally. Of course, this requires new skills, and just like our employees, we must provide them with the tools to do their new jobs. Education and training are mandatory.

Our leaders need to learn how to build consensus and develop effective teams. They need a more global view in order to learn from others elsewhere and share with a larger audience. Of course they must be more culturally sensitivity than ever before. And the technological changes and enhancements will require extensive training and exposure. Plus, we will need to equip them with the technology tools, giving them access to the new systems. If they cannot understand computer-generated reports, Facebook, blogs, data mining, and twittering, they will fail in the community and not be able to monitor their subordinate personnel. Organizational effectiveness may be enhanced if we properly evaluate our change and innovation processes. Changes associated with our shift to community policing have required innovation, problem-solving, and change strategies. They all need to be focused on increasing our service delivery to the public, or what is referred to as increasing our organizational effectiveness in the community. This is where we look at our model for scanning, analyzing, responding, and assessing. In this process we look at our organizational changes to ascertain if we received the anticipated results. Keep in mind that individual or organizational resistance may have caused failures or additional problems, not a bad development plan. As we previously discussed, the resistance may be reduced by education, training, and mentoring intended to reduce the fear of the unknown. Creating a new comfort zone will replace the previous comfort zone for the employee.

The organizational culture acts as a foundation for high-performance criminal justice organizations. Therefore, another change is necessary in our quest for a high-performance organization. The culture of an organization is wherein the goals and work traditions are created, maintained, and supported. Even with members from multiple cultures or backgrounds an organization will develop its own organizational culture. Failure of this natural process will result in dysfunction for the entity. This will transcend into the community where no change will happen as promised. A winning culture is one that incorporates flexibility, creativity, and innovation.

Antiterrorism is of course a real problem for some of us, and it is clear that community policing may be a significant part of the answer. For the new reality of terrorism it is imperative that police administrators provide a wide range of training that is designed to make both the police and public more aware and engaged in public safety. Traditionally officers have not looked for evidence of terrorist activities and would not have recognized it right under their noses. After all, who would have thought it possible? Risk assessment must become a second nature action of police officers. Each public encounter needs to be sized up as a potential risk and assessed quickly. Partnering with the entire community is a key element in securing our homes from all threats. Remember to learn from history.

Community policing provides the framework for professional policing that fosters problem solving and public trust. With the shift to community policing and the accompanied new public trust and confidence comes greater interaction between the police and the citizens. The openness of operations, coupled with community-based problem solving, has contributed to significant crime reduction and will enhance our vigilance in the area of potential terrorism. This is where antiterrorism is supported because the officers and citizens really know their neighborhoods. If anyone stands out because of behavior, misconduct, or any reason calling attention to themselves the police should become aware.

Even though community policing is having a positive impact in most communities, enhancements are constantly being attempted, mostly in the form of applying technology. This police executive is a firm proponent of using technology as a force multiplier. But caution must be the watchword of the day to guard against a repeat of history, like we saw when we moved away from the traditional beat cop because we applied technology such as cars, radios, and air conditioning. Technological advancements have skyrocketed over the past decade and have propelled many businesses into boom or bust futures. This is also true for the criminal justice system. Millions of dollars have been spent on computer systems and programs designed to improve overall performance of the criminal justice system. But too many of these endeavors fail. There are a multitude of reasons for this unfortunate phenomenon, yet we continue to see costly repetitious efforts with small gains.

As responsible administrators in the criminal justice system we must ethically examine why we experience setback after setback in our quest to technologically advance. It is irresponsible to continue. We must again learn from history, as stated previously. Before embarking on our new technoventure there must be an assessment of our last trip into cyberspace to identify what we did right and what we did wrong and that which we accomplished via blind luck.

Every police executive has encountered his or her fair share of techno-opportunities. Those are the opportunities to spend big bucks on uncertain products being pushed on ill-prepared, nonsuspecting, technologically challenged police executives. It is imperative that during all adventures into the computerization of the police world that we be fiscally responsible and resource conscious. We will all experience what would best be described as well-intended failures and unanticipated successes. However, being fiscally irresponsible will destroy public trust.

Technology has become a great asset in our community policing efforts, but technology is commonly viewed as a curse and a cure. There are precautions and guidelines available to minimize problems with efforts to embrace and utilize technology. Doing research and common sense are keys to success. Take your time and do it right. Be prepared for the process of acquiring new technology. In most governments we have a process that oversees expenditures and technology systems, but this does not mean they do the work for your agency. The police executive is forced to handle the innovations. Thus, the wrong person ends up responsible. We generally assign the project to someone on our staff that is clearly out of his or her realm despite his or her best intentions and efforts. Government entities either receive approval for well-funded research and project management or they don't. Often the procurement, selection, and purchase are handled by someone outside the police department who knows procurement by the numbers, but knows absolutely nothing about police work and how this acquisition applies to performance mandates and the needs of community policing.

So how do we reduce our risk while embarking on a new technoventure? Careful planning, collaboration, research, tough questioning, and, of course, blind luck are absolutely required. Probably the first tough question to be honestly answered is whether this proposed purchase is a "need to have" or "nice to have" item? We struggle with this one in our home and personal lives all the time. Using the same process for problem-solving projects, the professional criminal justice leaders must do their homework. This includes a need assessment, an explanation of expected or intended outcomes that are measurable, a planned sequencing of installation and implementation, and an assessment of the impact of this project on other elements of our operation or that of other criminal justice stakeholders.

Since there is usually a lot riding on the success or failure of technological acquisitions we should look carefully at some lessons learned from the above-recommended assessment. Your community policing program may be damaged or improved by the application of technology. This directly impacts public trust and confidence. The first step is a needs assessment. Be able to justify, not rationalize, the purchase. How will it enable or empower your department to deliver quality services to the citizens? What are the anticipated positive results for community policing?

Step two: What will this program allow us to do that we cannot do already and why is it important? It has to be value-added. If the new technology takes police personnel away from community policing duties, then we may fail in our implementation of community policing. The successful manager will detail intended or required outcomes, as well as marginal outcomes. Then these outcomes are written into the specifications for the bid process or request for proposal stage. If the outcomes are vague at this point, the actual results will be unacceptable. The finalized outcomes must then stand up to the scrutiny of comparison to what the organization is currently capable of producing. A multi-million-dollar investment should be able to produce significant enhancements or it may not be the appropriate time for this project.

Technological enhancements for the criminal justice system are imperative to meet the challenges of today and into the future. Planning them carefully and completely will help ensure sustained success. They can be extremely rewarding and organizationally satisfying when done correctly, but devastating if mistakes are made along the way. Ethics require you to do the homework and ask the tough questions.

The above process may be moot if you already have reasonable technology or helpful for the organization just starting. But a point to note is the same problem-solving process is utilized for all our challenges. The next challenge is: What technology can we add that is directly supportive of our community policing program? Basically, information technology through any media has the potential to enhance community interaction. Information is gold for the community and the police. But remember, technology can be a curse and a cure. Information important to community policing includes citizen input, geographic focus, prevention emphasis, partnerships, problem solving, incident records, crime reporting, and management accountability. All of these databases need to be searchable, accessible, secure, and properly managed.

Recognizing community policing may create a fear or distrust in some citizens; we must make certain that our technology is secure. Unauthorized access and use will destroy public trust and set the police-community relationships backwards without hope of salvaging the initiative. This is a risk we cannot afford. On the other hand, it is essential that the public be able to gain some access to the "safe" information on the system. They have a right to know about criminal activity in their community and also need to have a means to interact with the police. This should be encouraged and we need to be able to receive information by multiple means and sources.

Today police executives are faced with many technologies and managing them is critical. While we want inflows and outputs, we have to secure what goes out on the public domain. We also cannot afford to have police officers so consumed with keeping their blogs, Facebook, and twitters updated that they neglect their responsibilities. And twittering and texting while driving a police vehicle are dangerous because of the distraction. Agencies must address the issues associated with technology and the use and access to information. Rules of confidentiality and protocol are required, and accountability is mandatory. Inappropriate communication will seriously damage public trust. Consideration of the degree of technology applications will also mandate appropriate maintenance. If we develop a website we must keep it updated. If we utilize e-mail and encourage the public to contact us then we need to read and respond in a timely manner. The same goes for any of the other technological media.

As we see progress and energetic growth in our community policing initiative the police executive may recognize that the next step or natural progression of community policing is the creation of community government. Expanding from community policing to community government requires the same processes, but involves an expanded number of services and commitment from the government. So building on the success of the community policing program the government will have a degree of comfort and the public will be less skeptical or resistant to the expansion.

In a similar manner the government will work within their offices and with the community stakeholders and establish community located extension offices. They would probably need to be at a reduced scale and with limited hours of operation, but convenient to the needs of the public. There is no reason community government cannot enhance their service delivery of utilities like water, electric, roads, courts, voter registration, records, and taxes. The police executive responsible for developing and implementing community policing would be the obvious catalyst and mentor for this type of expansion of government services. This would be a worthwhile endeavor for the police commissioner, especially in light of the fact that the majority of the police calls for service are a direct or indirect result of a problem with other government service. The public knows that if they have a road problem and protest, the police will respond and the problem will be addressed. Through the expansion into community government the public would truly be organized as a community partner with experience in consensus building and problem solving. This would be a win-win situation for all. Community policing is a fragile alliance that needs constant care and feeding. You gain community trust one citizen, one police officer, and one encounter at a time. That's how you build that trust.

2 The Impact of Emotional Intelligence on Community Policing in Democratic Nigeria

Agenda Setting for National Development

A. OYESOJI AREMU

Introduction

With a population of over 150 million in Nigeria, the need for an effective, lawful, and people-oriented police organization cannot be overemphasized. In Nigeria, the development of the police force was the brainchild of the British colonial masters. During the British colonial expansion in Nigeria, the need to prevent squabbles between the native chiefs and the imperial merchants was among the reasons for the formation of the police force. Consequently, the police grew up as a paramilitary force bearing arms from its inception. Through this measure, the British colonial masters used the native police to harass, intimidate, and oppress those who opposed the British colonial expansion. This colonial legacy continues, and to date, the police still carry the militaristic bandwagon effect of colonialism in its relationship with the public. There exist negative apprehension, distrust, and disgust on the part of the public and their relationship to the police. Affirming this, Aremu (2002) notes that no good relationship exists between the public and the police. In the same vein, Alemika and Chukwuma (2000) report that the police-citizen relationship in Nigeria is characterized by deep suspicion and violence. Tamuno (1970) alludes to this by tracing this long-held public-police disdain to the seed of bitterness that was sown during the British colonial rule in Nigeria.

In spite of these, the police in Nigeria remain the constitutionally empowered agency charged with the responsibility of internal peace and security of the country. The mission of the police constitutionally is to ensure safety of life and properties; prevent, detect, and investigate crime; and maintain public order. These objectives could be the harbinger for political stability laying down a new path. Even though Nigeria just returned to democracy in 1999 after almost two decades of military rule, during which the police were further militarized, a change is possible. Democracy has further overstretched the police personnel by creating more demands to follow the rule of law and lessen the use of force. The capabilities of the police to effectively deal with a vast population with only about 365,000 personnel in the entire nation suggest the enormity of the challenge.

This responsibility goes with enormous powers. In Nigeria, the exercise of these powers by the police has always put the officers and the public on a collision course. Against this backdrop, Aremu (2009) contends that a social gulf exists between the Nigerian police and the public it is expected to serve and protect. Supporting this view, Oladele (2010) avers that effective policing in Nigeria is often handicapped by the huge gulf in precepts and practices in the engagement of the community in policing at the grassroots. In essence, it is imperative to redress this imbalance by actively engaging the community in the accountability of grassroots policing. A strong, effective police force is *sine qua non* to the sustainability of good governance, rule of law, and the economic growth and development of a country.

The Nigerian police are evidently experiencing some fundamental systemic crises. In part it is due to the instability in its hierarchy, but also in the act of confidence building arising from the force's lack of transparency, absence of checks and balances, and poor training of the personnel. For example, between 1999 and the present, the echelon of police in Nigeria has been manned by six inspectors general of police (M.A.K. Smith, 1999–2001; T.A. Balogun, 2001–2005; S.G. Ehindero, 2005–2007; Mike Okiro, 2007–2009; Ogbona Onovo, 2009–2010; and Hafiz Ringim, 2010–present). While each police chief initiated policies for a safer society in Nigeria, there was little continuity in their implementation. The instability in the office of inspector general inducted disaffection and disloyalty among the officers and rank and file. Generally, policing in Nigeria has a checkered history of unacceptability with the public. This is as a result of some unprofessional conduct among officers and men of the police. Writing on this, Alemika (1988) avers that the Nigeria Police epitomize exploitation, oppression, and gross injustices. Corroborating this, Etham (2007) stresses that since the return to civil democratic rule in 1999, Nigeria has witnessed relative deterioration of its internal security. The growing erosion of public confidence in the police raises several pertinent questions, such as: Is the state of relative insecurity in Nigeria the result of lack of adequate social, psychological, and emotional competence that could enable Nigerian police officers to be proactive other than reactive? Or is it due to a deficit in the Nigeria Police and policing strategies? And are these strategies relevant in the 21st century in view of the increasing global attention on policing? What policing strategies could help nip in the bud the increasing criminal activities profile in the country occasioned by polity?

On this premise, therefore, it is imperative not only that the Nigeria Police revisit its policing strategies, but also that efforts be made by all, including police researchers, to clinically expound better policing strategy that is in tandem with global initiative on policing. This chapter argues that community-oriented policing would be an appropriate answer to many of the above-mentioned problems.

Community Policing

The idea of community-oriented policing in Nigeria was initiated by the former president of the country, Chief Olusegun Obasanjo, after his official visit to Houston in the United Kingdom. According to Aremu (2009), this presidential awareness led to the beginning of community-oriented policing in Enugu State in February 2004. This presidential initiative introduced community-oriented policing in 18 out of 37 state police commands (including Abuja federal commands). And from these 18 state police commands, community-oriented policing exists in 129 out of 1,579 police stations in Nigeria. This statistical evidence informs the presence of community policing in only 8.17% of police stations. Clearly, the continued social gulf between the police and the public is real rather than imagined. Aremu (2009) remarks that this perhaps accounts for the constant police-public face-off. Worldwide in police agencies, community policing has emerged as an innovative law enforcement response in dealing with and preventing crime. Although it is not well rooted in the Nigeria Police, the philosophy enjoys prominence in policing policies in Nigeria. In the Nigeria Police nine-way test, community policing features prominently with a department under the leadership of an assistant commissioner of police at the headquarters saddled with its operation.

Community policing is thought to have gained momentum for a variety of reasons, not the least of which was the general community dissatisfaction with traditional law enforcement practices and the demand for greater police accountability for increasing crime rates. Community policing recognizes that community members can work together with law enforcement agencies and play an active role in reducing local crime (Segrave & Ratcliffe, 2004). Community policing is therefore based on the premise of collective responsibility for effective involvement by all members in the society. The philosophy hinges on the premise that traditional policing not only is monopolistic and not in tune with security challenges in the 21st century, but also has become obsolete and not even in tandem with original principles of policing as expounded by Robert Peel. Bayley (1988) corroborates this by asserting that community policing allows law enforcement to get back to the principles upon which it was founded.

Community policing is proactive and revolves around the principle of proactive policing through community participation and problem solving in crime prevention (Wasserman & Moore, 1988). Cordner (1998) posits that there are essentially four facets of community policing: the philosophical, where the community's role is fundamental and the police's role is expanded from traditional policing duties; the strategic, where ideas from community policing are developed into strategies for practice; the tactical, which focuses on the implementation of the strategies developed; and the organizational, where the support offered at an organizational level should be encouraged to promote community policing. Based on this context, Aremu (2009) avers that it is logical to suggest that to have an excellent community policing relationship, the police need to be constantly aware of the attitude they express while in contact with the public, and this could be achieved through the effective utilization of emotional intelligence skill. Through emotional intelligence competence therefore, the Nigeria Police could enhance positive factors, such as:

- Integrity: Avoidance of corruption and abuse of power for personal gain.
- Fairness: Treating people equally or equitably regardless of gender, race, and status.
- Civility: Treating people with respect.
- Responsiveness: Giving people what they want, showing care and concern for their problems.
- Police presence: Being available and accessible to provide police services responsively and proactively.
- Appropriate use of force: Using force only where necessary to accomplish legitimate goals.
- Competence: Having the knowledge and skills necessary to do police work.

Through these measures, Segrave and Ratcliffe (2004) contend that the police could:

- Mobilize and empower communities to identify and respond to security issues
- Improve police and public interpersonal relationship
- Increase positive attitudes toward police
- Reduce negative resentment toward the police
- Decrease police-citizen conflict
- Reduce crime rates
- Promote a dynamic flow of information between the police and the community

Emotional Intelligence

In its simplest form emotional intelligence (EI) is an individual's ability to deal effectively with emotions confronting him or her and significant others. However, some definitions of emotional intelligence depend on the model of EI and method of assessment that is used. Specifically, emotional intelligence is typically assessed in one of two ways: ability-based testing or self-report surveys. Ability-based assessments define emotional intelligence as the ability to monitor one's own and others' emotions, to discriminate among them, and to use the information to guide one's thinking and action (Salovey & Mayer, 1990). This definition highlights four aspects of EI, which include an individual's capacity to:

- Recognize his or her own and others' emotions
- Generate and use emotions in problem solving
- Understand emotions and how emotions may change
- Manage his or her own and others' emotions

Ability-based assessments measure how well an individual performs tasks using emotion and solves emotional problems. Self-report assessments of emotional intelligence, on the other hand, define EI as noncognitive (emotional and social) competencies that assist a person to cope with daily environmental demands. Accordingly, self-report assessments measure an individual's subjective assessment of his or her own emotional competencies to cope with environmental demands. Either way, EI is essentially a behavioral approach through which an individual is expected to be proactive in personal relationships.

Consequently, EI has been touted as being responsible for over 85% of outstanding performance in the workplace (Bennis, 2001). While such estimates have been criticized as being somewhat overzealous, a large body of research now exists that highlights the importance of EI for organizations. For example, Goleman (1998) contend that EI competencies are twice as important as pure (traditional) intelligence of managers. Murray (1998), while stressing the importance of emotional intelligence in the workplace, notes that not only do bosses and corporate leaders need a high dose of EI, but all people-oriented jobs like police demand it. This is because unlike the traditional intelligence (IQ), which is relatively fixed, EI can be built, learned, and fostered. This assumption implies that the police could be made to learn skills of EI. Aremu (2006a) submits that the Nigeria Police as presently constituted calls for a major transformation, which can only be achieved through EI education. Policing as presently practiced in Nigeria requires a significant degree of EI skills. This is against the backdrop that the police job is primarily based on human contact (interpersonal skills). Giving the benefit of EI in the workplace, the capacity to accurately utilize it by an individual has the potential to provide organizations with a significant competitive advantage, of which the police agency is no exception.

Emotional Intelligence and Community Policing

The public image of law enforcement is as diverse and complex as the people served by the profession. Due to the nature, visibility, and impact of law enforcement services upon society, this occupation is highly scrutinized regarding its tough demands on personnel and leadership to meet increasing public expectations (Turner, 2009). Crime statistics stress the necessity and importance for every law enforcement organization to learn how to recognize and cultivate resources (Gaston, 1997). Furthermore, in an effort to counter crime while ensuring safe and healthy communities, law enforcement officers must contend with diverse populations who are willing to challenge authority and decisions. As a result of this complex and dynamic landscape, the modern law enforcement officer needs more than tactical expertise and old autocratic styles in order to succeed (Brown, 1996).

George (2000) proposes that because of the rapid and ever-changing societal landscape, law enforcement officers require more than just task competencies or technical know-how. Officers possessing a particular blend of skills, competencies, and traits are more likely to be successful. According to Fischler (1997), law enforcement officers need to develop healthy relationships and manage conflict while achieving productive goals. To achieve their goals, law enforcement officers need skills to build, maintain, and strengthen alliances and partnerships, both within and outside the police organization. This is based on the consideration that effective performance in the protective service occupation, such as in policing, is not all about the expression of physical ability, dominance, individual achievement, and masculinity, but more about behavioral competences like emotional competence. This gives credence to Aremu and Tejumola's (2008) assertion that one of the vices the police in Nigeria are accused of other than corruption is poor interpersonal relationship, which is an important index in emotional intelligence. People who know their own emotions and are good at reading others' emotions may be more effective in their jobs (Afolabi & Adesina, 2006). This also corroborates Mayer and Salovey's (1993) view of emotional intelligence as a type of social intelligence that involves the ability to monitor one's own and others' emotions, to discriminate among them, and to use the information to guide one's thinking and actions.

Salovey and Mayer (1990) were of the opinion that emotional intelligence can be categorized into five domains: self-awareness (i.e., observing oneself and recognizing one's feeling as it happens), managing emotions (i.e., handling feelings in a more appropriate way), motivating oneself (i.e., channeling one's emotions in the direction of a goal), empathy (i.e., being sensitive to others' feelings and concerns), and handling relationships (i.e., managing others' emotions). This indicates the dynamism and relevance of emotional intelligence in human endeavors (including workplace and organization). Goleman (1995) lends support to this by asserting that emotional intelligence involves the skills that help people understand themselves and their environment. The general contention of these researchers is that emotional intelligence as a construct of interest is germane to the well-being of man, his organization, and his society. This again underscores the importance of emotional intelligence in organizations like police, where personnel are in daily contact with the public.

Brian (2009) contends that people are not disturbed by things, but by the views which they take of them. Brian further asserts that one characteristic of effective officers is the ability to recognize and manage their emotions. It could be stressed that individuals with higher levels of emotional intelligence, relative to others, could be able to perceive and manage their emotions, have more positive social interactions, and engage in fewer problem behaviors, including aggressive and violent acts. Additionally, EI appears to contribute to an increased recognition and respect for the feelings of others, improved cooperation, and better teamwork. It appears that officers who are able to increase their EI have a distinct advantage, both personally and professionally, in a number of important areas, including self-control, decision making, and interpersonal skills (Mayer, Salovey, & Caruso, 2004).

According to O'Neill and Cushing (1991), law enforcement faces daily challenges and stress that few other occupations undergo. Few occupations require the intensity of constant alertness, proper mood and demeanor, short-term memory, and physiological stamina that police work requires. To be an effective and efficient law enforcement officer in today's environment requires emotional intelligence and control to meet the demands faced on the streets. Today's law enforcement officer needs to be highly motivated with well-developed communication skills and able to engage leadership, other officers, and community members by managing relationships and emotionally connecting in order to balance the needs of the organization and community (Krimmel & Lindenmuth, 2001). Gilmartin (2002) discusses the importance of work-life balance and the consistent emotional rollercoaster ride that is associated with the life and work of a law enforcement officer. According to Gilmartin, the goal is to help law enforcement officers address the ever-present and constant internal assaults that an officer has to deal with on a career-long basis.

Based upon the above arguments, to determine what emotional intelligence looks like in the law enforcement culture, a review of the Emotional

Quotient Inventory (EQ-I), designed by Bar-On (2002), will be reviewed. EQ-I provides a quantitative assessment of emotional intelligence. To facilitate a conceptual and practical understanding of the EQ-I, an overview of the five composite scales and their respective subscales is necessary. The five composite scales are comprised of emotional competencies that have been grouped together based on both logical homogeneous and statistical clustering. The scales include:

- Intrapersonal, which includes the subscales of emotional self-awareness, assertiveness, self-regard, self-actualization, and independence
- Interpersonal, which includes the subscales of empathy, interpersonal relationship, and social responsibility
- Adaptability, which includes the subscales of problem solving, reality testing, and flexibility
- Stress management, which includes the subscales of stress tolerance and impulse control
- General mood, which includes the subscales of happiness and optimism

So what would a police officer with low or high emotional intelligence look like? If police officers have low self-regard they would be unsure of themselves, lack self-respect and self-esteem, and would not garner the respect necessary to be an effective officer. Additionally, low self-regard may be displayed by a lack of confidence and poor physical appearances, all of which are trouble indicators associated with most police officers. The goal of establishing high self-regard in a law enforcement environment would be to increase self-assurance, self-esteem, and confidence, which should be one of the primary aims of every law enforcement academy. The implementation of the EQ-I provides a quantifiable index of one's self-regard permitting a benchmark for which development and change can be monitored. Acceptance of oneself and the development of inner strength will be the result of increasing self-regard, as well as producing fulfillment with self and the law enforcement profession.

This is in agreement with Hein's (2005) assertion that emotional facilitation of thought means the ability to incorporate feelings, and the potential of feelings, to guide the individual. According to Hein (2005), emotional understanding means the ability to solve emotional problems, and the ability to understand the value of emotions for survival. And lastly, Hein contends that emotional management means the ability to take responsibility for one's emotions and happiness, the ability to turn negative emotions into positive learning and growing opportunities, and the ability to help others identify and benefit from their emotions. The foregoing assumptions could perfectly fit into the policing job, most especially in Nigeria, where police are rated low by the public mainly as a result of corruption, violence, nepotism, greed, aggression, oppression, and extra judicial killings (Aremu, 2004, 2005).

Two important similarities therefore exist between emotional intelligence and policing. First, the policing job is essentially and primarily based on human contact. And for a rewarding contact, there must be a proper understanding by the person making the contact. Aremu and Adeyoju (1998) are of the opinion that Nigerian police would fare better in interpersonal relationships if their college and academy curricula were reorganized to include psychobehavioral and management courses. According to them, this would make the police more humane when on duty. As good as the submissions of Aremu and Adeyoju (1998) were, they practically did not mention the exact courses. Thus, it stands to reason that emotional intelligence, as a program in police training, would address some identified problems of Nigerian police. Second, police need to properly value themselves by having high self-concept. Nigerian police are not only undervalued, but also reticent of the goodwill of the public. This could affect their self-presentation as police officers. Aremu (2005) theorizes that the police job involves a dyadic relationship between the police and the policed (the public). He stresses that the police job is always situated within the context of human society. This is indirectly the philosophy of community policing.

Based on the above contention, it is presumed that a number of emotional intelligence competencies would be of importance to community policing. These are:

Emotional self-awareness: This implies recognizing feelings as they happen. Goleman (1995) submits that it is the keystone of emotional intelligence. A police officer with low emotional self-awareness may have a hard time acknowledging and verbalizing his emotions and thus find it difficult to recognize how his emotions could affect his interpersonal interactions, decision making, and overall functioning. Too often, officers with low emotional self-awareness could assume too much seriousness while on duty and could therefore have self-induced stress. This could prove to be counterproductive in policing, especially in Nigeria, where community policing is not yet firmly rooted. This situation could cause an officer to verbally or physically overreact, resulting in embarrassment to himself or herself and the police agency. Law enforcement officers strong in emotional self-awareness are able to withstand and adequately deal with what Gilmartin (2002) refers to as emotional survival. In sum, community policing is all about understanding the public and establishing community trust. A community-oriented officer would therefore be proactive.

Assertiveness: Most law enforcement personnel are taught to understand the importance of assertiveness and the significance of taking charge in critical situations. Strength in assertiveness includes the ability of officers to express themselves easily, yet retain the ability to defend themselves, protect citizens, stand their ground, and enforce justice in a forthright but nonabusive manner. Stressing this, Ehindero (1986) posits that in Nigeria, the expression of poor assertive skill by police officers in the art of policing often causes friction between the police and the public. Corroborating this, Aremu (2006b) contends that police recruits and cadets need to be holistically trained for competing challenges they would face while on the field. This becomes expedient in view of the multidynamic nature of their expected responsibilities in a society that is not static and which equally expects a lot from them, other than being assertive in policing.

Self-actualization: Important to a successful career in law enforcement, as well as community policing, is self-actualization; this is the ability to realize one's potential capabilities and establish a road map with a sense of purpose. Mittelman (1995) observes that a self-actualized person is nondefensive, open to experience, spontaneous, problem-oriented, and largely autonomous.

Empathy: Empathy is the ability to be aware of, understand, and appreciate the feelings of others. Police officers high in empathy could have the ability to emotionally read other people and pick up on social cues, which could allow them to care and show concern for others. This competency is important in enabling officers to make and build personal and emotional relationships. Police officers lacking in empathy often fail to understand the feelings of others and have difficulties in relating to and with others, resulting in the misinterpretation of social cues and surprise reactions from others. In congruence, Nwolise (2004) avers that in Nigeria, the inability of police officers to display empathy in the cause of policing has led to a deep-seated dislike of the police by the public and a public perception of the police as an instrument of oppression, rather than an agent of the law and protector of the citizenry. Nwolise further contends that the public feels no sense of obligation to cooperate with the police. This could affect police performance adversely.

Social responsibility: One cannot underestimate the importance of social responsibility to the law enforcement profession. It is social responsibility that is at the core of an officer's mission and purpose and provides guidance and direction with an internal compass. Social responsibility is what makes a law enforcement officer a cooperative, contributing, and constructive member of the profession. This competency allows officers to act responsibly within and outside the profession, having a social consciousness and a concern for others. This is to a large extent lacking among members of the Nigeria Police. In support, Aremu and Adeyoju (2003) contend that the display of good sense of social responsibility is germane to the institutional rejuvenation of the Nigeria Police, which would be the pride of all. They aver that to realize this, senior personnel should be above board, humane, transparent, and show exemplary leadership qualities to young officers. Therefore, selecting officers high in the emotional intelligence competency of social responsibility is the key to successful and effective community policing.

Interpersonal relationships: Interpersonal relationships are a fulcrum to the success of community-oriented policing. The police and the community need to relate very well to have good neighborhood policing. The police would have to be essentially skilled in interpersonal relationships to ensure proactive policing, which is essential to the success of community policing. Intimacy, giving and receiving affection, and feeling at ease in social relations are some of the benefits of interpersonal relationships. These are also germane for effective principles of community policing. Ehindero (1986) contends that positive interpersonal relationships are desirable to facilitating a pragmatic police. That is, public trust, one of the essentials of community policing principles, is hinged on interpersonal relationships.

Optimism: Important to a police officer's emotional survival is the element of optimism and what Collins (2001) refers to as confronting the facts. Realistic optimism is the ability to look at the brighter side of life while maintaining a positive attitude even in face of adversity. Key to relating with others in the office and the community is keeping a hopeful approach to life and maintaining a positive approach to daily living. Police officers with high optimism are able to create and sustain positive change through concentrating on their circle of influence, as opposed to worrying about the concerns of the world. Pessimism, fear, and uncertainty are the results of low optimism. This could result in wasted time and energy with self-induced stress.

Emotional Intelligence and Community Policing: Implications on National Development

The Nigeria Police is a specialized force that provides security to all. With 1,129 police divisions, 1,579 police stations, 2,165 police posts, and 1,591 village police posts, Nigeria can be said to be underpoliced with her 150 million people and 923,678 km^2. This brings a great challenge to Nigeria, which is the largest democracy in Africa. This challenge of democracy and its attendant effects has always overstretched the personnel of the police force. This, more often than not, has implications on national development. National security is tied to social, political, economic, and cultural growth of any country.

Since independence, Nigeria has witnessed crises caused mainly by political, social, and religious factors. In recent times crises in some parts of the country like Jos in Plateau State and South Region have caused further image problems. The frequent occurrence of violence in some parts of the country, in which the police have not been able to quell, is a pointer to the need for urgent transformation and repositioning of the Nigerian police. Similarly, the Abuja bomb blast of October 1, 2010, in which 12 people died, and the June bomb blast at the police headquarters, also in Abuja, which left 8 people dead, are serious security challenges that undermined policing integrity. The twin policy innovations in this regard are the integration of emotional intelligence and community-oriented policing. It is therefore expedient that the police adopt a paradigm shift from the old traditional method of policing to a modern and dynamic approach of public partnership collaboration and policing using emotional intelligence principles.

Onovo (2009), giving credence to this position, asserts that in a developing democracy, the police force plays a creative role that no other agency of government is so critically able to assume. A central issue in policing in a newly democratized society is the relationship between the citizens and the police service. The role of management and leadership in the service is critical in ensuring an effective transition and transformation of the police service from the military era to the democratic dispensation. However, lack of physical and financial resources, adequate manpower, and skills for policing of crime can hamper the creation of a safe and secure environment for citizens who are desperate for peace. Police agencies will have to compete with other national departments for the allocation of resources from governments, which will be trying to address other pressing national issues on a mass scale. The meager budgetary allocations to the service for essential materials in the face of mounting problems have constituted a clog on the wheels of the police to perform effectively. Role modeling, shadowing, mentoring, creative problem solving, and inspirational leadership are key components for efficient and effective overseeing and creating a solid foundation for a policing agency poised to serve the community. Characteristics such as patience, vision, diplomacy, and discipline are all valuable in leading a police institution undergoing change.

Examining this context further, Maryam (2010) states that right from the return of civil rule in 1999, Nigeria democracy has been insecure, affected by electoral malpractices and mysterious deaths of political office holders. Insecurity in the Niger Delta and recently in Plateau State has created problems for which the police have no answer. The Niger Delta, Aba, and Onitsha have been seriously affected, and stories on kidnapping are also not overblown because even at the local level, there is similar media coverage. Security problems seem to be deepening as the days go by. This development has affected not only the citizens personally but also the development of the country, as most industries and organizations are and have relocated to Ghana and other neighboring West African countries.

Therefore, the major challenge is how to sustain and maintain democracy and development in the face of growing security threats. This is a matter of national importance that should be of concern to all stakeholders in the Nigerian state and one that requires comprehensive and committed contributions of all groups and interests that make up Nigeria. It is pertinent to consider security issues and problems that are affected or capable of affecting the attitude, confidence, and cooperation of all groups and segments that make up the Nigerian federation. It is also necessary to explore the gaps and grey areas in the police–community relationship that are responsible for various problems of mistrust and noncooperativeness and crises and how these gaps can be addressed. Some of the major security problems currently confronting the nation have been identified, to include political and electioneering conflicts, socioeconomic agitations, ethnic/religious crises, ethnic militias, boundary disputes, cultism, and so on. These problems individually and collectively constitute threats to the peace, security, and development of the country. Nigeria needs to see how effective utilization of emotional intelligence skills by the police and other law enforcement agencies can be deliberately construed as a positive response to these problems.

Law enforcement officers are a unique and diverse group of people who experience a wide variety of emotions since they face different and unusual challenges. Due to the nature, visibility, and important impact of law enforcement services upon society, the occupation is highly scrutinized regarding its tough demands to meet public expectations. Because of these demands and expectations, there is a need to know if emotional intelligence can be used for identifying competencies in law enforcement officers Thus, knowledge of emotional intelligence competencies is important to law enforcement and public safety officers because research has demonstrated that management of one's emotions and behavior depends upon self-awareness and positive moods that tend to heighten perceptions and affect future success and self-efficacy (Forgas, Bower, Krantz, & Moylan, 1990; Kavanagh & Bower, 1985). Kelly and Barsade's (2001). Research indicates that sharing of emotions enhances team building, and that people who model appropriate emotions during times of ambiguity can increase group solidarity, which is extremely important to law enforcement where ambiguity is faced on a daily basis.

To better serve and protect the public, law enforcement officers must learn to monitor their own and other's feelings and emotions and to use this knowledge to guide their thinking and action. Today's law enforcement officer needs to be able to motivate people and communicate effectively with coworkers and community members by managing relationships and connecting emotionally in order to balance the needs of the law enforcement agency and the community (Krimmel & Lindenmuth, 2001). This demonstrates the importance of emotional intelligence in facilitating community-based policing, which is a pragmatic and dynamic measure of modern-day policing that not only promotes security and peace, but advances development and also puts in practice the management principle of collective responsibility and management by objective.

Conclusion

The Nigeria Police seem to be in dire need of reform and enhancing emotional intelligence is the only solution. In order to overcome and outgrow the problem of security in Nigeria it is important that political players and institutions embrace the principles of true democracy and allow open, free, and fair competition that are essential in the process of aggregation of national opinion and development choices. Also, there is need to rethink and improve on policy and institutional means of dealing with security concerns arising in the country. Equally, enough funds need to be provided to guarantee a good welfare package and to facilitate effective training of Nigeria Police personnel in all ramifications to adapt to and meet policing challenges of the 21st century.

Recommendation

- The police should be structured to reflect the principles of community policing.
- The police should be educated in the science of community policing so as to understand the psychology and sociology of the community.
- The Nigeria Police should be more professionalized, primarily by making its recruitment policies much more competitive, technical, scientific, and psychological.
- The Nigeria Police personnel should be given better conditions of service, exposure to modern training techniques and facilities, and motivation for improved productivity and commitment.

References

Afolabi, A.O., & Adesina, A.A. (2006). Influence of job frustration, narcissism and demographic variables on attitudes towards professional ethical behaviour among Nigerian police officers. *African Journal for the Psychological Study of Social Issues*, *9*(1), 37–45.

Alemika, E.E.O. (1988). Policing and perceptions of police in Nigeria. *Police Studies*, *11*(4), 161–176.

Alemika, E.E.O., & Chukwuma, I.C. (2000). *Police-community violence in Nigeria.* Lagos, Nigeria: Centre for Law Enforcement Education and National Human Rights Commission.

Aremu, A.O., & Adeyoju, C.A. (1998). Enhancing job satisfaction of the Nigeria Police. *Nigerian Journal of Applied Psychology, 4*(1), 44–48.

Aremu, A.O. (2002). The impact of tribe, education and gender on Nigerian police psychological reaction to public attitude. *Ife Journal of Psychology, 4*(1), 105–113.

Aremu, A.O. (2005). A confluence of credentialing, career experience, self-efficacy, emotional intelligence and motivation on the career commitment of young police officers in Ibadan. *Policing: An International Journal of Police Strategies and Management, 28*(4), 609–618.

Aremu, A.O. (2006a). *Impact of some demographic variables on job satisfaction of women police in Ibadan,* Nigeria. Unpublished manuscript.

Aremu, A.O. (2006b). *The Nigeria Police and zero corruption tolerance: The function of emotional intelligence.* Paper delivered at the 13th Annual Conference of International, Sarimsakli, Turkey, May 26–30.

Aremu, A.O. (2009). *Understanding Nigerian police: Lessons from psychological research.* Ibadan: Spectrum Books.

Aremu, A.O., & Adeyoju, CA. (1998). Improving the police officers interpersonal relationships through social skills training. *Nigerian Journal of Clinical and Counselling Psychology, 4*(1): 18–23.

Aremu, A.O., & Adeyoju, C.A. (2003). Job commitment, job satisfaction and gender as predictors of mentoring in the Nigeria Police. *Policing: An International Journal of Police Strategies and Management, 26*(3), 377–385.

Aremu, A.O., & Tejumola, O. (2008). Assessment of emotional intelligence among Nigerian police. *Journal of Social Sciences, 16*(3), 221–226.

Bar-On, R. (2002). How important is it to educate people to be emotionally and socially intelligent and can it be done? Perspectives in Education, 21(4), 3–13.

Bayley, D.H. (1988). Measuring overall performance, In L.T. Hoover (Ed.), *Quantifying Quality in Policing,* Washington, DC: Police Executive Research Forum, 37–54.

Bennis, W. (2011). On becoming a leader, San Francisco: Jossey Bass.

Brian, D. (2009). *Emotional intelligence: Practical advice for law enforcement officers.* New York: Bantam Books.

Brown, W.J. (1996). Organization assessment: Determining the state of a police organization. *Journal of Police Science and Administration, 14*(4), 267–284.

Collins, J.C. (2001). *Good to great.* New York: Harper Collins Publishers.

Cordner, G. (1998). Community policing: Elements and effects. In Alpert & Piquero (Eds.), *Community policing: Contemporary readings* (pp. 43–61). Long Grove, IL: Waveland Press.

Etham, B.M. (2007). *Democracy, internal security and the challenges of policing in Nigeria.* Retrieved March, 24, 2010, from http//www.nigeriapolice.com (unpublished).

Fischler, G.L. (1997). Psychological examination of peace officer applicants: Theory and practice. *Minnesota Police Chief, 17,* 35–37.

Forgas, H.S., Bower, G.H., Krantz, S.E., & Moylan, S.J. (1990). Praise or blame? Affective influences on attributions for achievement. *Journal of Personality and Social Psychology, 59,* 809–819.

Gaston, A. (1997). Recognizing potential law enforcement executives *Corrections Today, 59*(3), 106–109.

George, J. (2000). Emotions and leadership: The role of emotional intelligence. *Human Relations, 53*(8), 1027–1055.

Gilmartin, K.M. (2002). *Emotional survival for law enforcement: A guide for officers and their families.* Tucson, AZ: E-S Press.

Goleman, D. (1995). *Emotional intelligence.* New York: Bantam Books.

Goleman, D. (1998). *Working with emotional intelligence.* New York: Bantam Books.

Hein, S. (2005). *Introduction to emotional intelligence.* Retrieved August 30, 2004, from http://eqi.org/history.htm

Mayer, J.D., Salovey, P., & Caruso, D.R. (2004). Emotional intelligence: Theory, findings, and implications. *Psychological Inquiry*, 15(3), 197–215.

Kavanagh, D.J., & Bower, G.H. (1985). Mood and self-efficacy: Impact of joy and sadness on perceived capabilities. *Cognitive Therapy and Research, 9*, 507–525.

Kelly, J., & Barsade, S. (2001). Moods and emotions in small groups and work teams. *Organizational Behavior and Human Decision Processes, 86*, 99–130.

Krimmel, J.T., & Lindenmuth, P. (2001). Police chief performance and leadership styles. *Police Quarterly, 4*(4), 469–483.

Maryam, G. (2010). *Security and national development.* New York: Free Press.

Mayer, J.D., & Salovey, P. (1993). The intelligence of emotional intelligence. *Intelligence, 17*, 433–442.

Mittelman, W. (1995). Openness: A final reply to Tobacyk. *Journal of Humanistic Psychology, 35*(1), 102–107.

Murray, H.A. (1998). *Explorations in personality.* New York: Oxford University Press.

Nwolise, O.B.C. (2004). *The Nigeria Police in peace keeping under the United Nations.* Ibadan: Spectrum Books.

Oladele, O.O. (2010). *An agenda for effective policing in Nigeria.* Unpublished manuscript.

O'Neill, J.L., & Cushing, C.A. (1991). The impact of shift work on police officers. *Police Executive Research Forum, 19*(3), 23–39.

Onovo, O. (2009). *Nigeria Police: Challenges and constraints* (Annual Police Report). Abuja, Nigeria.

Salovey, P., & Mayer, J.D. (1990). Emotional intelligence. *Imagination, Cognition, and Personality, 9*, 185–211.

Segrave, M., & Ratcliffe, J. (2004). *Community policing: A descriptive overview.* New York: Praeger.

Tamuno, T.N. (1970). *Police in modern Nigeria.* Ibadan: University of Ibadan Press.

Turner, T.W. (2009). Using emotional intelligence to improve officer well being. *International Journal of Emergency Mental Health, 11*(2), 30–40.

Wasserman, R., & Moore, M.H. (1988). Values in policing, Perspectives on policing, No. 8, National Institute of Justice and Harvard University, Washington, DC.

Police e Mardumi
Indigenous District-Level Civilian Policing in Afghanistan

3

DOEL MUKERJEE
MUSHTAQ RAHIM

Introduction: Country Situation

The Afghanistan National Police is the primary civilian police organization in Afghanistan, which was established in 1960. However, during and after the Soviet occupation, the police was militarized as it not only faced challenges to maintain public order, but also was the first line of control for internal insurgency. After the departure of the Soviets until 2002, the policing system was further weakened due to internal and external insurgency where several police personnel found themselves jobless and were compelled to take up other occupations while the "virtue versus vice police"* governed. This disintegrated the civilian police and created a vacuum when the democratic government was established. In 2003 the Afghan National Police was established by a presidential decree, and since 2003 the police organization has undergone a reforms process in its rank and file, pay structures, training, and so forth.

Since the Afghan Interim Authority first took office in 2002, the United Nations Development Program (UNDP) has played an important role in enabling the Ministry of Interior (MOI) to begin the process of rebuilding the civilian police by working jointly with all stakeholders. Donor resources covered the salaries of police in Kabul for the first six months of 2002 through the UNDP-managed Afghanistan Interim Authority Fund (AIAF). In May 2002, at the request of the government and United Nations Assistance Mission in Afghanistan (UNAMA), UNDP established the Law and Order Trust Fund for Afghanistan (LOTFA) to enable the police to return to operations throughout the country. The LOTFA is administered by

* Murray, T. Police-Building in Afghanistan: A Case Study of Civil Security Reform. *International Peacekeeping*, 14:1, 110. Edited and condensed by Simon de Saint-Claire, 2007.

UNDP and nationally managed through the MOI. According to the terms of reference (ToRs) for LOTFA (signed in May 2002), the fund was designed to cover "all reasonable costs associated with the start-up and operational needs of the police force." Subsequent phases of LOTFA have been developed around this component, with appropriate modifications based on situational changes. This phase of development of the police is the phase for reconstruction, which started with 50,000 to 70,000 police, consisting of some professional police trained before the civil war and a vast number of untrained and illiterate soldiers from various regimes. They lacked discipline, formal policies, procedures, facilities, equipment, uniforms, and public trust. There was also ethnic imbalance, and most of the provincial and local police commanders owed allegiances to local military commanders, and central control was virtually nonexistent. Some of the provincial police commanders were ex-warlords continuing their existence in a legitimate form. Several officers who were forced to take up premature retirement due to the civil war have rejoined, and there are also reports that there are warlords and militias who have been legitimized and accommodated in the police, making the basic structure of the civilian police organization almost defunct.*

The public opinion of the police is at an all-time low, as the Human Rights Watch Report 2009 states: "Outside the conflict areas, organized crime and warlords terrorize Afghans with impunity. Kidnapping of Afghans for ransom is common, but the police seem largely incapable or unwilling to tackle it." Coupled with this is the communities' view that the pro-government forces enjoy impunity even when accused of killing or disappearing civilians.† At present there is little confidence in the police, as the communities prefer to sort out their problems through traditional justice institutions, making the formal justice process redundant in its present form. The police are viewed as an organ of the government or even, in some areas, a particular power group rather than a solution provider of the state for the people.

During this early phase of reconstruction, the German police was involved in reconstruction of the National Police Academy, which was completely destroyed, like all other institutions. SIGAR's (2010) review identified deficiencies in Afghan security forces, including logistics, personnel attrition, corruption, drug abuse, and illiteracy. Subsequently the International Security Assistance Forces (ISAF) and North Atlantic Treaty Organization (NATO) have undertaken a wide literacy program for the police and tactical training with the provincial reconstruction teams (PRTs). The military involvement has often been criticized, and this also sometimes has been attributed to the continuation of the militarized police system. Informed

* Wilder, A., "Cops or Robbers? The Struggle to Reform the Afghan Police," AREU, July 2007, xi.

† UNAMA, "Protection of Civilians in Armed Conflict," Annual Report, 2010.

sources have identified almost 285* international police mentors located within the Ministry of Interior who are mostly military advisors. At present the MOI and ISAF have built the police from 109,000 in early 2010 to 122,000 in October 2010 and 134,000 in late 2011.

Since the Bonn Agreement (2001) and further as articulated in the Afghanistan National Development Strategy (ANDS), threats to national and personal security remain major impediments to growth and poverty reduction, and therefore the overall development of the country. As a part of Afghanistan's National Security Policy (NaSP) the government's goal with the direct support of the international community is to establish a legitimate monopoly on the Afghan National Police (ANP) and the Afghan National Army (ANA) that provides a secure environment for the rights of the Afghan people to be fulfilled, embracing the freedom of movement for people, commodities and ideas, and social and economic development. As a part of the commitment the Ministry of Interior (MOI) and ANP aim to meet the governance and security needs of the country through the development of a professional, competent, well-trained, human rights-respecting, ethnically balanced police force that over the years will become fiscally sustainable; and the emplacement of good governance processes that ensure best practice from the national to district levels in government. It was envisaged that among the prime policies it would be important to (1) enhance legal and governance structures at provincial and district levels, and (2) educate the public about the tasks and purpose of the ANP and the rights of the citizens to protect human rights and gender equality, increasing the trust of the Afghan people in the police's ability to guarantee people's access to justice and the rights of citizens with regard to the police.

In early years the MOI, with the support of the international community, drafted the National Police Strategy (NPS) and the National Police Plan (NPP) for five years. It was clearly identified that in the next five years the people of Afghanistan would get services from their police as honest, accountable, brave, impartial, and striving to create a secure and lawful society. The long-term vision is that the ANP uphold the constitution of Afghanistan and enforce the prevailing laws of the country to protect the rights of all people of Afghanistan. The ANP will perform their duties in a professional, nondiscriminatory, accountable, and trustworthy manner. These are in consonance with the basic values of the international conventions and the commitment of the Bonn Agreement. Further, NPP 1389 has clearly demarcated that the police will move away from its militarized role and primarily be responsible for law enforcement. They will work with the people to actively combat crime (including terrorism, organized crimes, and illegal armed activity) and

* In November 2010, 39–44.

disorder; prevent the cultivation, production, and smuggling of narcotics; and fight corruption. The police will ensure and extend the sovereignty of the state and protect its borders. Under the priorities spelled out in the national interest, the MOI has set the period SY* 1389–1394 (2010–2015) to gain the confidence of the public; protect Afghan national interests; eliminate corruption; improve police capabilities, including leadership, command, control, communication, training, equipment, and weapons, to counter the specific threats in Afghanistan; reform and grow the ANP *tashkil*† to improve quality and quantity of the services provided by the police; improve morale and quality of life for police personnel; and implement intelligence-led policing. Therefore the country strategy envisions a professional, disciplined, and reinvigorated police force that is responsible and loyal to the MOI, widely visible to and respected by the public, and capable of protecting human rights, as well as fighting insurgency and drug trafficking.

From Community Policing to Democratic Policing?

The MOI was aware of the growing gap between the numbers in the police and the quality of police services received by the people. The MOI, in early 2009, requested UNDP to undertake a study and prepare a strategy paper on how community and police engagements could be undertaken in the Afghan context.‡ The strategy was discussed with multiple stakeholders before an acceptable strategy was arrived at that would be applicable in the *Afghan context*. During the consultation process with various actors such as parliamentarians, NGO representatives, media personalities, academicians, and police personnel at the operational level, all had concerns on the concept of community policing, as they associated it with the arming of community groups for the maintenance of local security. Finally the MOI approved of the strategy as Police e Mardumi (Dari) or Da Toleni Police (Pashto).

The fact that large numbers of people were concerned about arming of community groups came from the fact that there was a parallel process that was taking place in the country around the same time when UNDP was preparing its strategy on Police e Mardumi, as the MOI and international forces promoted a security strategy called Afghan Public Protection Force (APPF) based on the Arbakai tribal forces in Paktia province. It is believed that in Paktia, neither the Taliban nor foreign forces have a presence, where there are just 30 police officers for the entire area, and it is left to the Arbakai to

* Afghan Lunar Year (SY).

† Police strength from tooth to tail.

‡ UNDP, "Prospects of Community Policing in Afghanistan," March 2009.

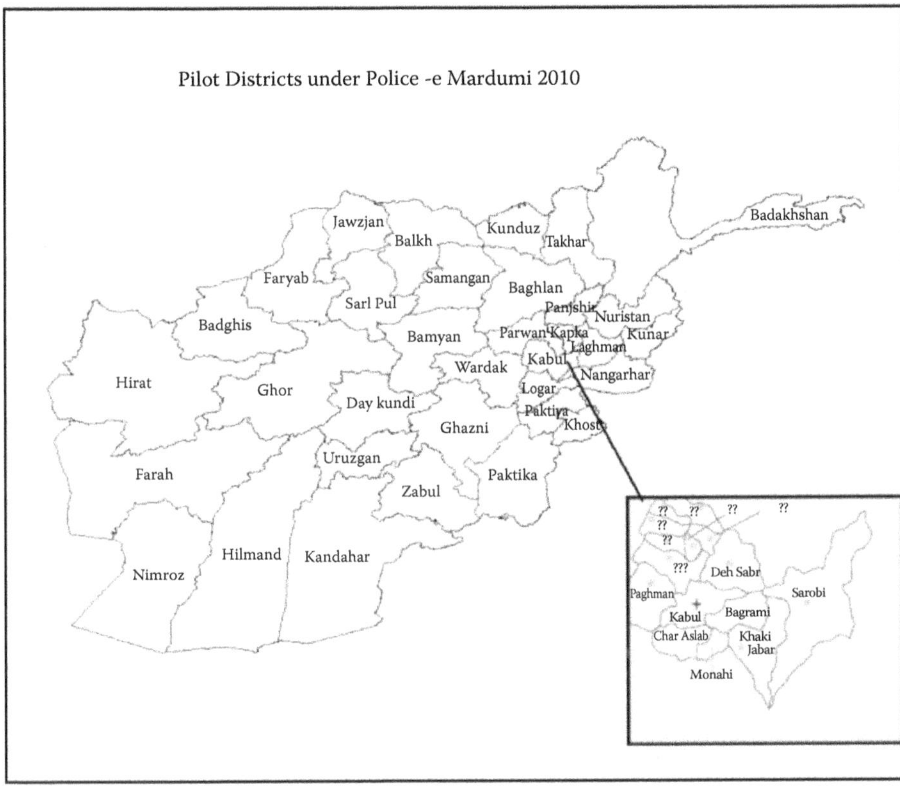

Figure 3.1 UNDP Police e Mardumi project area.

defend the local population. This volunteer force is part of a traditional code of conduct and honor called Pashtunwali. The area is stable and there is a good relationship between the people and the government (Figure 3.1). The APPF was initiated on a pilot basis in two districts in Maidan Wardak province. All recruits were between 25 and 45 years old, physically fit, free of drug use, without a criminal record, and actually from the district they were recruited to serve in. The overall objective of this plan was not to place overt tribal or ethnic dimensions on the selection process. All recruits were subjected to a background check. Each recruit received three weeks of training, including classes on values, ethics, police law, use of force, human rights, and first aid. Each recruit was equipped with one assault rifle, ammunition, and a uniform. Each unit was issued white Ford Ranger pickup trucks marked "APPF," plus communication gear. The U.S. military funded vehicles, communications, and clothing. The weapons were provided by the Afghan Ministry of Interior and the recruits were paid $100 monthly, rising to a maximum of $250 for an APPF captain. This idea was further consolidated as the Afghanistan local police (ALP) initiative in mid-2010 with little public support. It is believed that this process has not been evaluated as yet, and a lot of emphasis is currently being placed on developing oversight and reporting mechanisms.*

With this backdrop, in September 2009 Police e Mardumi, recognized as democratic policing by the international community, was launched. The democratic policing project follows the four key principles expressed by the doyen of community policing, Dr. David Bayley, as building a police agency that is *accountable to the law, protects human rights*, and promotes *civilian and intragovernmental oversight* and *responsiveness to the needs of the public*, which are promoted through engagement with the civil society, police, local governance councils, local community leaders, and the public.

Under the vision, benchmarks, and priorities set up by the MOI, democratic policing endorses all of them and specifically focuses on the Afghan civilian police to bridge the gap between police, the ordinary people, and the governance institutions, creating an opportunity for the people to not only access the first rung of the criminal justice system, but also build a course to bring people into the fold of the justice system. It provides space for people to articulate their aspirations to maintain the human security in their jurisdictions with state agencies. Therefore democratic policing engages in processes, which establishes the rule of law, ensures due process, and upholds human rights of people, which together uphold human security at the local level.

Based on the concept paper "Prospects on Community Policing in Afghanistan" (Mukerjee, 2009), in September 2009 a pilot was launched across eight northern provinces in Kabul: Guldara, Shakardara, Qarabagh, Istalif, Kalakaan, Mirbachkoot, Deh Sabz, and Police District 17 of Kabul City (Figure 3.1). A multipronged approach was initiated with a vision to develop a deeper engagement to promote public confidence in the police.

Approach: Pilot Intervention Across Eight Districts in Kabul

Strategy

As mentioned above, democratic policing undertakes a multipronged strategy (Figure 3.2) and ensures that it is contextualized to the local requirements of Afghanistan. The following broad strategies were used.

Legal Framework

From the early phase of the project, especially while preparing the concept paper on approaches to community policing, a detailed analysis was undertaken of the existing legal documents that govern the police, such as the constitution of Afghanistan, Police Act 2009, the criminal procedure code, penal code,

* UNAMA, "Protection of Civilians in Armed Conflict," Annual Report, 2010.

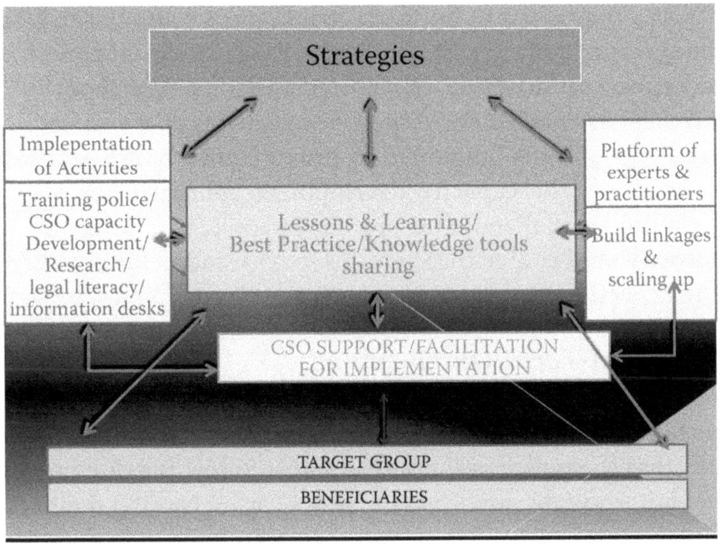

Figure 3.2 Processes identified under democratic policing.

National Police Plan, National Police Strategy 1389, ANP Vision Document 1388, and so on. Therefore the entire context of Police e Mardumi was placed within the legal framework. Since the framework does not articulate people's participation, it was placed as one of the primary results that the project could achieve through demand from stakeholders and a bottom-up approach.

Human Rights-Based Approach

During discussion with various stakeholders through the entire pilot phase, it was perceived that there is an overwhelming need to bring police reforms into the engagements. This is also considering that much of the discourse in the security sector is not Afghan led. Therefore it is imperative to initiate a program with both the duty bearers (in this case police, government, and state institutions) and the claim holders (ordinary people, civil society members, etc.) so that they can articulate their thinking, identify with systems, and build them. Among the claim holders it is important to focus on the vulnerable, that is, women, poor, and other ethnic minority groups. From this observation it was felt that community policing initiatives must be seen in the context of providing equal opportunities for skill development of the claim holders and duty bearers so that together, as equal partners, they are able to ensure service delivery and accountability.

Capacity Development as the Overarching Approach

Since capacity development is UNDP's global overarching approach to development (UNDP, 2005), for an initiative on building police community relations it was important to build an enabling environment to foster security at the district level. The focus on the capacity development approach also ensures the sustainability of the interventions. The capacity development approach has enabled the respective capacities of the various agencies, institutions, and officials mandated to provide governance and security in the area. Likewise, the capacity development approach has also empowered the poor, marginalized, and ordinary people. It is believed that all of these together would enable these groups to seek and obtain quality services beyond the expected life span of the project.

Balancing Short-Term/Quick-Impact Results With Long-Term Efforts

It is important to recognize that prior to any intervention that will support and ensure that the police and police stations follow the due process of law and deliver fair, equitable justice to the people by registering their complaints or by acting responsively, effectively, and in a humane manner with various stakeholders, a significant amount of time and resources are needed before they are fully addressed. Therefore it was recognized that the challenge of ensuring that the police upholds the rule of law will indeed have a long-term impact. However, because justice delivery and the rule of law are those services that are central to the enjoyment of all other rights and services, it is not possible to unduly delay the provision of this service. There is a serious need to balance short-term and quick-impact results with long-term strategies that will bring sustainable changes to the way in which the ordinary citizens and the marginalized people are able to access services. Therefore the Police e Mardumi intervention identified some quick-impact mechanisms such as establishment of information desks to ensure that the ordinary people in a district can approach this desk at the police station and register incidences. This strategy was also keeping in mind that there is the prevalence of the informal or traditional justice institutions, which prevent people from accessing formal justice institutions. Therefore the establishment of this desk has had a catalyzing effect on reporting of incidences, including murder and suicide, which were never reported before.

Leveraging and Strengthening Partnerships With State and CSOs

During the course of reconstruction of the police force, international police trainers and mentors were brought to Afghanistan who provided training to the ANP through interpreters. It was observed that such trainings are slow, taxing the grasping capacity of the neoliterate trainees and being completely dependent on the skills of the interpreter. While the concept was initiated it was observed and documented that there were existing civil society groups composed of mostly educated Afghans returnees who had some capacity to deliver legal training with some technical inputs. Most of the civil society members, although enthusiastic about contributing to state building, emphasized their independent existence and did not want to be in cooperation with the state. However, they wanted to support the efforts of the pilot, as they felt that this was an integral part of state building. Another observation that was made was that the international community was skeptical of the training capacity that could be provided by the civil society. However, for democracy to be realized by the citizens, it is important that citizens have engagement with the state. It is not that civil society can take the place of the state or its obligations, but civil society can take on some of the responsibilities of the state until it can completely deliver those obligations.

Ensuring Synergies With Other International Community Programs and Other Development Projects

At present there are several ongoing projects and interventions of multiple agencies on police reconstruction or preliminary stages of engaging in police reforms. Therefore it was decided that this type of intervention could not be undertaken in isolation. For maximum impact it was important to build programmatic interlinkages with other UNDP programs, such as the Subnational Governance Program working with district governors and provincial councils at the provincial level, as the Police Act 2009 places the governor and the minister of interior responsible for the police in provinces and across the country. Therefore trainings and interventions with the provincial governance actors would clarify roles and responsibilities of the police. Similarly, while undertaking training coordination is effective with those agencies, which undertake large training programs for the police and are willing to include more specialized courses by civilian trainers. Other coordination and areas of synergy are found with rule of law projects and programmatic interventions with gender as a cross-cutting thematic framework. An intervention in democratic policing therefore coordinates and works closely with all the institutions working on police reconstruction, police reforms, and training to speed up the process and get the desired results.

Mechanisms and Processes Implemented

Afghan for Afghans: Capacity Building of Community by Civil Society Organizations

Capacity development of traditional leaders and the local leaders was undertaken to initiate the process of understanding the state and its various institutions and the roles and responsibilities of the most visible mechanisms of the state, that is, the police. Training by Afghan civil society organizations and lawyers helped in creating an enabling environment and capacity for the police and public interface meetings to take place on a bimonthly basis to identify problems and local solutions. Crime and security plans were forged by the local community and the police to hold each other accountable. The civil society agencies provided the on-ground facilitation as trainers, monitors, and reporters. Also, such civil society interventions create public pressure on the police and establish a process of a *visiting* system at the police stations.

Initiatives at the Police Station

Information Desks

While initiating the plan for the implementation process (Figure 3.3) it was clear that all efforts would have to be cost-effective and low budget so that many such efforts could be replicated across the country. A low-cost project was also one of the requirements of the Ministry of Interior. It was observed that at each of the police stations there was no designated police officer to accept complaints or information from the public, visitors, or complainants. The role is centralized with all decision making at the level of the police commandant. Also, there was no specific place where a person could bring information. With the concurrence of the MOI, information desks were established with basic furniture, one computer to initiate a database system of incidences, and so on. This concept was at first discussed with the local *maliks*, *waliks*, and so forth, who were hesitant to embrace the concept, but upon involving them in detailed discussions, they agreed to participate.

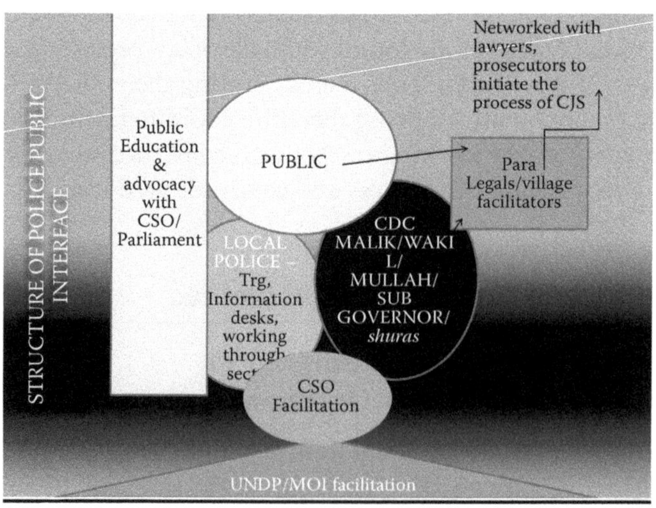

Figure 3.3 Democratic policing—initiatives at the district level.

The police personnel at the police station were trained in a short course on communication skills, psychosocial counseling, understanding legal issues (including police responsibilities, rights of vulnerable groups such as women and children), how to register an incidence, and so on.

Sector Police Approach

In an environment where there are several strategies currently being used, such as intelligence-led policing, counterinsurgency strategy (COIN), and so on, the project used a traditional method of educating the neoliterate police personnel on their jurisdiction through map reading using both topographical sheets and Google map. This was grasped enthusiastically by police personnel along with basic information on how to undertake foot and vehicle patrolling. These basic components were important for them to realize their jurisdictions but also identify potential resources. Further, although the police chief was encouraged to identify suitable staff to engage in regular duty, this was ignored by several commandants due to lack of adequate tashkil at the police stations. However, while engaged in police and public meetings and on the request of the community members, timely patrol was provided to schools and key installations such as electricity dams. Gradually during the period of one year the personnel realized the importance of the sector policing approach.

Police Training

Training of police personnel was not considered to be one of the important inputs of the Police e Mardumi project; however, it was realized that the experiential learning approach using adult education tools such as role plays, pictures, and so forth, was key for the police personnel of all ranks to be readily associated with the program. Although multiple police reconstruction and specifically police training programs have been in place since 2002 in the country, it was felt that there was value in equipping police personnel with the "softer skills" necessary for civilian policing, especially while providing services to the people. Therefore a short 14-day training module was crafted that included map reading, human rights (as per Islamic tenets), laws and legislations of the country, roles and responsibilities of the police, and rights of persons with special needs—women and children, communication skills, leadership skills, conflict resolution methods, and so forth. All these trainings were provided at the police stations to ensure the safety of the trainers and the trainees. Also, this allowed the flexibility of the police personnel to respond to local exigencies while the training was ongoing.

Crisis Response Service or Hotline

Kumar and Behrendorf (2010) suggest that creating a police hotline provides a free and anonymous avenue for citizens to report possible crimes and also complain about corruption.

At the time when the democratic policing pilot was initiated there was an existing crisis response service at the MOI developed with the support of the international community. It was assessed that there were 5,000 calls a day being received, of which 4,000 were harassment calls. Analysis and discussions undertaken with the personnel of 119 (call center) have revealed that the services are treated as:

- An emergency response hotline service for crime or incident reporting
- A complaints mechanism for the police
- An information request system

Therefore, keeping in line with the requirements of the NPP 1389 and its plans for expansion, Police e Mardumi has initiated establishing regional hubs, starting with Kandahar, and in early 2011 expansion was undertaken to other regions, such as Herat, Nangarhar, and Balkh. Also at the central 119 center a civil society-driven process of transparency is being explored to monitor complaints against police and any action taken reported to the government.

Public Education Campaign

As recorded in a baseline study initiated at the beginning of the project, police image and moral was at an all-time low coupled with the high level of attrition and 9% drug addiction in the police.* Therefore with the MOI and civil society a rigorous media campaign was initiated using a drama format to bolster the image of the police with positive stories. All the dramas and spots were played on the radio on prime time. In addition, information was provided to the public on how to use 119 (crisis response service), rights of people, and so on. The public education campaign was designed keeping the cultural context that in both rural and urban areas people listen to the radio and are receptive to dramas and music.

* CSTC, Survey report, June 2010; CSTC, Personnel asset inventory report, September 2010.

What Worked and What Didn't

After 14 months of on-ground operations an internal assessment by UNDP experts and a joint stakeholder review were undertaken where some critical areas were identified as what worked in the Afghan context, in spite of current competitive police reconstruction, training strategies, and counterinsurgency programs (UNDP, 2010). Project stakeholder review and field visits by MOI and UNDP have uncovered that the pilot districts have faced unprecedented upsurge of reporting of roadside bombs, intruders in the area, theft cases, and so on. The following are some indications as to what worked and what didn't for Police e Mardumi:

- **Pilot project tested acceptability of concept and scope for localization.** The biggest advantage that Police e Mardumi had was that it started the efforts small, constantly verifying with the stakeholders the acceptability of the program in keeping with the Islamic traditions. It ensured that each training program had a religious teacher, which greatly helped to gain the confidence of the local people, especially the community leaders. Also, that the trainings and discussions were completely driven by local needs ensured complete credibility of the project. That there was demand from districts that did not fall within the pilot area, such as Farza and Khakejabber districts, was itself a confirmation that it was acceptable to the local population. It was rewarding to see that the ordinary people wanted to participate in the police public forums, as they knew that these were locally driven without any political dimensions or external mandates.
- **Recognition of the traditional justice institutions and engaging with them proactively to support the formal justice institutions.** Currently there is little or no information available to the police, as there is a robust traditional justice system existent that does not allow incidences to be reported outside its jurisdiction. This includes legal disputes such as land disputes and criminal offenses such as murder and suicide that go unreported. At present, there is little confidence in the police as the communities prefer to sort out their problems through traditional mechanisms. Therefore Police e Mardumi initiated the whole process by building an enabling environment prior to implementation of its project components, which included several rounds of discussions with the traditional leaders, such as maliks and waliks, and local governance institutions, such as district governors and the district development assembly members and some community development council members of the villages. Once their endorsement was taken, which included that

Table 3.1 Incidence Reporting Increased After Police e Mardumi Was Implemented

Results of Bimonthly Meetings and Police Trainings				
District	Incidences Reported in January–December 2009 Prior to Project Implementation	Incidences Registered at Information Desks at Police Stations		
		From	To	
Shakardara	31	May 16, 2010	September 6, 2010	70
Qarabagh	18	June 17, 2010	September 7, 2010	173
Mirbachakot	9	May 16, 2010	September 6, 2010	1,606
Kalakan	3	May 27, 2010	September 6, 2010	1,200
Guldara	3	June 17, 2010	September 6, 2010	406
Estalif	7	June 20, 2010	September 7, 2010	100
Deh Sabz	32	June 29, 2010	September 7, 2010	80
17th Police Station	88	June 23, 2010	September 14, 2010	

Source: UNDP Afghanistan (2010) based on research by the Afghan Civil Society Forum (ACSF), unpublished.

trainers would be sent to the police stations and districts, all the various components of the projects were activated.

Also it was noted that at the early phase of the project crime reporting was low. However, once the *shuras*,* maliks, and waliks were in agreement with the process that was being undertaken, including the police and public interaction, incidence reporting went up, as seen in Table 3.1. Also, with the police trainings it was evident that the police personnel were eager to execute their duties.

Afghan for Afghans: Trainers for Police Training

Across international agencies to date, international trainers (mostly military, some contracting agencies with ex-military personnel, and some civilian police who are very few in number) provide training to police personnel. The trainers operate with interpreters. Under the pilot project local civilian trainers were provided orientation and sent to the field. These trainers were not only acceptable but became immensely popular with the trainees. An evaluation sheet was used at training (Table 3.2), which showed positive trends in grasping information. Most of the trainees had undergone a six-week training program prior to this training. Only 10% of the trainees had not received any prior training.

* Traditional community leaders.

Table 3.2 Evaluation of Training Program

No.	Question	Response			
		Before Training		After Training	
		Positive %	Negative %	Positive %	Negative %
1	What are rights of citizens?	35	65	60	40
2	What is government? What are the institutions under the government?	56	44	70	30
3	Is the ANP a part of the governance structure of Afghanistan?	76	24	92	8
4	Do you know about the constitution of the country?	51	49	68	32
5	What are basic principles of protection of children's and women's rights?	32	68	71	29
6	How can civil society support the government or the society?	27	73	68	32
7	What are good communication skills?	46	54	78	22
8	What is strategic plan of MOI from 1389 to 1393?	30	70	66	34

Source: UNDP Afghanistan (2010) based on research by ACSF, unpublished.

Low-Cost Engagement: A Process for Sustainability

While initiating the project, the senior leadership of the Ministry of Interior emphasized sustainability and low-cost solutions. Therefore the project was initiated keeping in mind that the thrust areas would have to be most critical, affecting the day-to-day functions of the police and their engagements with the people.

Information Desks

Therefore, as mentioned earlier, information desks were established and training on basic communication skills, psychosocial counseling, how to register a complaint, and so forth, was provided to the personnel. Further, legal literacy was provided for the community leaders on governance, justice issues, roles and responsibilities of the police, how to engage with the information desks at the police station, and so on, which entailed payment of stipends to law graduates and organizing a training program that included the cost for refreshments for the trainees. In other words, most of these meetings and trainings are not more than the cost of a "cup of tea" for the participants, making participants feel special with the quality of training, and this also is a sustainable process.

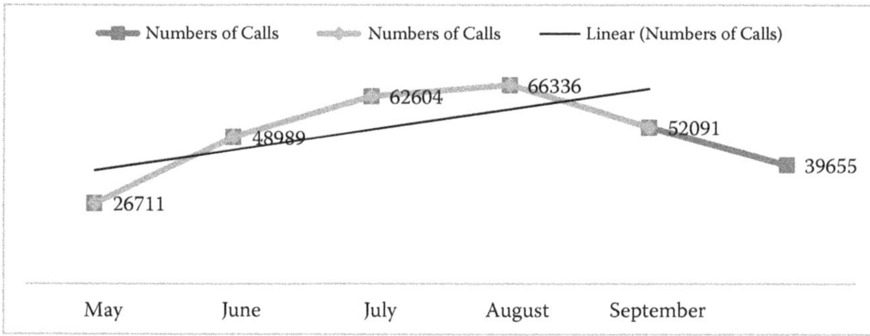

Figure 3.4 Impact of public education campaign on four radio channels, June–October 2010. *Source:* UNDP Afghanistan (2010) based on research by Ganderray, unpublished.

Accountability Mechanisms: Crisis Response Center

Another crucial point of contact for citizens and police is at the time a citizen requests for immediate response from the police. It is evident that effective reform of Afghan Police requires a model grounded in democratic principles of transparency, accountability, and protection of human rights (Kumar and Behrendorf, 2010). Earlier mentioned was the existing crisis response center (or 119 center) at the MOI since 2007. Police e Mardumi provided training to the 119 operators and has taken up the work of establishing regional hubs. Currently a regional hub is being established at Kandahar for the regional south. Further media campaigns have been undertaken to advertise how the 119 or 100* number can be used to get a response from the police.

Figure 3.4 shows the impact of the public education campaign that has being undertaken since June 2010. However, in a single day, out of the 5,000 odd calls almost 80% of them are harassment calls to the operators. Therefore AWCC, the telephone company, had used filters on some of these numbers, making it possible to reduce some of the calls (in September and October). Currently assessment is ongoing, undertaking disaggregated data to analyze the quality of calls.

- **Gender dimension.** In a society equal treatment and access to institutions are important for men and women. Therefore separate legal literacy classes were organized at the district level for women. Out

* As per the Ministry of Communication, GoIRA, the number 100 can be used as an emergency number. The 119 was started with the idea of running an emergency response telephone like 911 in the United States. This was read in the Persian script from left to right and therefore became 119 in Afghanistan.

of the eight districts, only in two districts women proactively joined in the bimonthly meetings. Interestingly, women-related issues were raised for the first time in several districts at an open forum at the bimonthly meetings. Issues such as the *Baad system* or exchange of women to settle disputes, child marriage, and so forth, were raised. Gender trainings are a core component of the police trainings and community leader trainings. However, for women to be able to fully participate in police public meetings will still take time. Currently, crime and security plans that have been developed jointly by the police, the community members, and the local governance institutions also have gender components, such as ensuring the safety of girls' schools as achievements, recognized by the districts.

- **Civil society in the security sector.** While democratic policing strategy was being planned several international community members had shown skepticism* of civil society participating in police or security sector work. However, Police e Mardumi believed that this would be a quick process to provide capacity to the people and police (as mentioned in the "Afghan for Afghans" section). Further, Police e Mardumi promotes that in democratic space, civil society has an important oversight role to play. It helps closed institutions to open and accountability mechanisms to be established. Therefore the role of civil society (CSO), especially in the Afghanistan context, is important to build the democracy, participate in governance, and initiate the dialogue on accountability. By participating and knowing the police and the security sector they can provide informed opinions more effectively. At present the international community, especially the military, expects civil society organizations to play key roles in the final *build stage* to win over Afghans to counterinsurgency. Yet many CSOs resist coordination in a mission and strategy that are different from their own visions. The CSOs seek greater policy dialogue during the planning process.† Under Police e Mardumi civil society has been able to contribute effectively in terms of both implementation and dialogue with the ministry.

Area-Based Package Program

As mentioned earlier, while introducing the democratic policing concept, it was certain that this would not be an isolated intervention; rather, synergies

* In September 2009.

† Schirch, L., "The Civil Society Military Relationship in Afghanistan," USIP, September 2010.

would have to be built with the justice and human rights program, the capacity of which builds the prosecutors and the judiciary, making all actors of the justice system a part of the process for change. Further, since the subnational governance policy identifies the roles and responsibilities between the subgovernor and the district police chief, training programs are organized for the provincial councils and district development assembly members. Therefore the democratic policing project is not seen as an isolated intervention, but rather a component for the overall area-based programming for the development of security of a district.

What Didn't Work

- **Lack of developing a common understanding of democratic policing within the international community and therefore the necessity of a coordination body.** In the entire reconstruction process there are multiple agencies with multiple mandates and strategies to mitigate the ongoing conflict. Although the police within the NPP and NPS is seen in the role of a civilian police body, in reality the ANP are also the first line of fighting force for the ongoing insurgency. Therefore even though the 14 months of intervention on ground has had modest successes, the international community has not completely embraced the concept. Arming of community groups and raising local groups to maintain their own security with the help of their personal weapons is also being touted as community policing, which is not completely acceptable to the Afghan people. Therefore it is debatable whether a military approach should prevail to fight insurgency or whether the softer development-oriented project components are successful in full-blown insurgency situations. These differing mandates of international community have deterred Police e Mardumi from being upscaled rapidly. Therefore there is need within the MOI to institutionalize this concept, especially since it conforms to the NPP and NPS crafted by the government.
- **Will it work—similar processes in high-security areas?** As mentioned above, how to conduct counterinsurgency is the critical question on the minds of the Afghan and the international community. It is certain from the Police e Mardumi experience that the concept works in safe and swing (medium-threat) areas. But it is certain that this is not the strategy to be used for high-security areas. The strategies, processes, and objectives would change. Therefore, specifically for the high-threat areas, by instituting crisis response centers like in Kandahar, the first public-police contact is essential. If the police are able to rise to the requests of the people in times of crisis, they will win the hearts of the people and

thereby public confidence will be established. Further, the public will realize the values of state institutions and provide information that is critical to fight insurgency. At present the quality of information is often weak, making recovery of weapons and information of roadside bombs difficult to detect. However, with enhanced response of the police, this component of public support can be overcome.

- **Sector policing.** Currently there are high levels of attrition in the police due to poor pay and hardship in insurgency areas. Therefore, due to lack of adequate police personnel at the district level, police commandants have resisted sector policing and deployment of dedicated personnel to specific areas within their jurisdictions. However, discussion with the community members on certain occasions, such as protection of the water dam from illegal quarrying in Shakardara district, or the case of Kalakaan in undertaking regular patrolling, has resulted in attempts in taking on sector policing.

Analysis and Key Lessons Learned for Future Expansion

Some of the key lessons and learning from the pilot intervention are:

- The consultation process improves relationships between the ANP and local community, as expressed by both groups and as seen from results of enhanced knowledge.
- Local community leadership is able to comment on human security as they are developing with the police a local-level security and crime reduction plan. This is particularly relevant because in several areas the police and the community have confided that the local people take care of almost 50% of the local security.
- Civil society organizations have competence and acceptance with government and police to undertake training in some specialized areas that are better than those provided by police or military instructors.
- Traditional leaders are open to the idea of providing legal knowledge to women in the community, thereby breaking traditional notions. However, these trainings are to be undertaken in a secure environment.
- Research studies complement implementation processes. This component effectively defined results and provided the impetus to the police reform discussion.
- Community volunteerism for maintenance of peace and security is possible in the current situation. The community leaders readily accept responsibility. However, any kind of payment to the attendees

of such meetings may result in misbalance of community leadership and supremacy.

- Community leaders, operational-level police personnel, and civil society groups have emphasized that they do not require any weapons to maintain security within the community, and instead have emphasized that maintenance of peace will be their responsibility. This point has been reiterated by the civil society at several meetings and also by the Internal Affairs Committee at the Wolesi Jirga and the Meshrano Jirga (Upper and Lower House of Parliament).
- Counterinsurgency operations with community outreach programs and civil society coordination are not necessarily identified as community policing, as the processes do not empower the citizens or the average police person, nor do they promote decentralized processes or accountability mechanisms. These programs may complement the overall civilian policing and police-community coordination strategies.
- Establishment of accountability mechanisms in the police system is key to gaining public confidence that promotes recognition of state institutions.
- One standard formula for implementation of Police e Mardumi is available for low- and medium-threat areas. Distinct operations are required for high-risk areas.

Conclusion

As Afghanistan is heading toward transition *inteqal*, where there is an urgent need to stabilize the districts to prevent any fresh wave of insurgency, it is firmly believed in some quarters that for normalcy to return and to establish governance there is a need to draw the police from its present militarized approach to take on civilian policing responsibilities to maintain law and order and provide services to the community to maintain overall security. Further, as articulated earlier, one of the mechanisms for speeding up this process is to engage local facilitators who have the skills to build capacity and bring together community and governance institutions. However, the civil society must also be engaged in the decision-making process while drawing up plans and strategies, as is quite clear from the recent civil society engagements in the security sector.

Further, to expand the concept of democratization in the security sector there is a need to engage ordinary people so that they are able to demand better services from the police and report incidences and establish contact with the state and state institutions. Therefore, to ensure that there is involvement of the people, large-scale public awareness campaigns are important through radio, television, SMS (mobile phones), and alternate media. This in turn will build a demand for services, and the demand from below will provide the bottom-up approach, which is currently missing in all security sector policies in the country. Currently in Afghanistan there has been some development projects that are small yet well coordinated by the government that have found acceptability, sustainability, and have a huge impact on the people. Similarly, it is believed that to initiate the process of civilian policing it will be of great value to institutionalize the philosophy in the Ministry of Interior through a Police e Mardumi secretariat, which can coordinate the work of multiple units and agencies, including donors. Further, the concept needs to be deeply entrenched into the trainings of new recruits at the National Police Academy and regional training centers so that there is a whole generation of police personnel who can conform to the concept as they work with the communities they serve. These processes can quickly bring the Afghan police from its reconstruction phase to the police reform phase.

In Afghanistan people-oriented policing requires coordination with programs such as justice reforms, subnational governance, institution building, rural rehabilitation and development, and disarmament to bring maximum impact. However, whether community-oriented policing should be undertaken prior to or after implementation of such programs is debatable. Further, the question arises whether Police e Mardumi can be juxtaposed with the COIN strategy, or should it wait for the COIN strategy to win before the state building mechanisms are put in place? This is also a debate within the military and the civilian development quarters.

In conclusion, it can be said that although, as stated by some critiques, Police e Mardumi is only a grassroots intervention, from the various results received in terms of enhanced information flow between the police and the people, through a series of coordinated activities in each district, a philosophy was introduced that was nonexistent before within the ministry, within the international community, and within civil society. At present there are two recently launched projects by bilateral agencies under the same process of democratic policing with similar pilot strategies. Police e Mardumi was initiated to trigger a ripple effect in informed quarters so that many more agencies recognize the concept and move the police from its present militarization to community-oriented accountable and transparent policing systems. The pilot was implemented with constant advocacy with the international community, civil society, and government agencies, providing information as to what processes were involved, how partnerships evolved and developed, and so forth, therefore making it possible for the philosophy to be acceptable. It is certain that there is much work to be undertaken on the policy side, especially since there is an urgent requirement to build civilian policing and allocate resources for district stabilization. Yet the question as to how fast this model can be upscaled and ensure sustainable processes across large jurisdictions is something that requires greater coordination by government, civil society, and the international community.

References

Kumar, S., & Behrendorf, B. (2010). *Policing best practices in conflict post conflict countries.* UNDP Afghanistan, 18.

Mukerjee, D. (2009, March). *Prospects on community policing in Afghanistan.* UNDP Afghanistan (unpublished).

Murray, T. Police-building in Afghanistan: A case study of civil security reform, Tonita. *International Peacekeeping, 14*(1), 108–126 , 2007. Edited and condensed by Simon de Saint-Claire.

SIGAR. (2010, June 29). *Actions needed to improve the reliability of Afghan security force assessments.*

UNDP. (2005). *Programming for access to justice for all: A practitioner's guide to human rights based approach.*

UNDP. (2010, February). *Afghanistan baseline study of 8 northern districts of Kabul province.*

United Nations Assistance Mission in Afghanistan (UNAMA). (2010). *Protection of civilians in armed conflict.* Annual Report 2010.

Wilder, A. (2007, July). *Cops or robbers? The struggle to reform the Afghan police.* Afghanistan Research and Evaluation Unit (AREU), xi.

The National Challenge on Increase in Crime

Comprehensive Initiatives on Crime Reduction in Japan

4

TAISUKE KANAYAMA

Introduction

In the late 1990s, following the burst of the bubble economy, Japan was struck by the financial crisis of 1997, which is comparable to the current grovel financial crisis, and Japan's economy mired in long recession. During the same period, Japan faced a sharp increase in crime; the number of recorded penal code crime reached a new postwar high for seven consecutive years until 2002. Facing the rise of crime, the Japanese government kicked off a comprehensive crime reduction campaign, including a national action plan for crime reduction, in 2003, which was named the Action Plan to Create a Crime-Resistant Society (APCCS).

During the five-year term of the plan, the crime rate fell by 33% in comparison to the rate in 2002; this represented a decrease of more than 1 million recorded penal code crimes. After 2002, the Japanese economy began to recover. In this chapter we have briefly summarized the results of the Japanese government's comprehensive measures for crime reduction and discussed both national and local police initiatives that help promote these measures.

Trends in the Economy and Crime in Japan

Economic Situation

The economic bubble that began in late 1986 and lasted until early 1991 was the third longest period of economic expansion in Japan since the end of the Second World War. At the early stages of this period, it was not considered a bubble. During the last phase of this boom, however, the mania for speculation resulted in skyrocketing land and stock prices and the term *bubble* began to be used widely in the 1990s.

A few years after the bubble burst, the growth rate of the Japanese economy declined precipitously. Then in 1997, as the economy was headed for recovery, a financial crisis struck the country, with major banks, security firms, and finance companies filing for bankruptcy primarily due to the slump in land and stock prices. Another factor contributing to the country's troubles was the Asian currency crisis that began in Thailand and spread to other Asian countries, such as Korea, Malaysia, Taiwan, and Hong Kong. As a result, there was a widespread credit crunch and the annual total debts resulting in bankruptcies reached a record high in 2000 and were estimated to be approximately 2.3 trillion yen. The recession lasted until 2002, and this period later came to be known as the lost decade.

Trends in Crime

As described by Bayley (1976), during the period from the 1960s to early 1990s, the crime rate in Japan remained stable and at a low level, with the number of recorded penal code crimes being in the proximity of 1.5 million cases per year. In 1991, however, this situation changed, with the number of recorded penal code crimes rising above 1.7 million for the first time, and then climbing above 2 million in 1998. The financial crisis was followed by another increase in crime, with penal code crimes peaking at approximately 2.85 million in 2002, which was the highest number ever recorded. Overall, the increase in the crime rate during the five-year period between 1998 and 2002 was a startling 40.3%. The latter figure is especially sobering when it is compared with the 5.5% rate of increase observed during the five years that immediately preceded this period (Figure 4.1).

The National Initiative: Action Plan to Create a Crime-Resistant Society

Ministerial Committee

While taking various countermeasures to combat the increase in crime, the National Police Agency (NPA) of Japan was also conducting a national governmental consensus on crime reduction. During this same period, the public's sense of fear regarding the increase in crime had reached lawmakers. This led legislators in the majority Liberal Democratic Party to create a party policy addressing crime reduction entitled "The Urgent Motion on Public

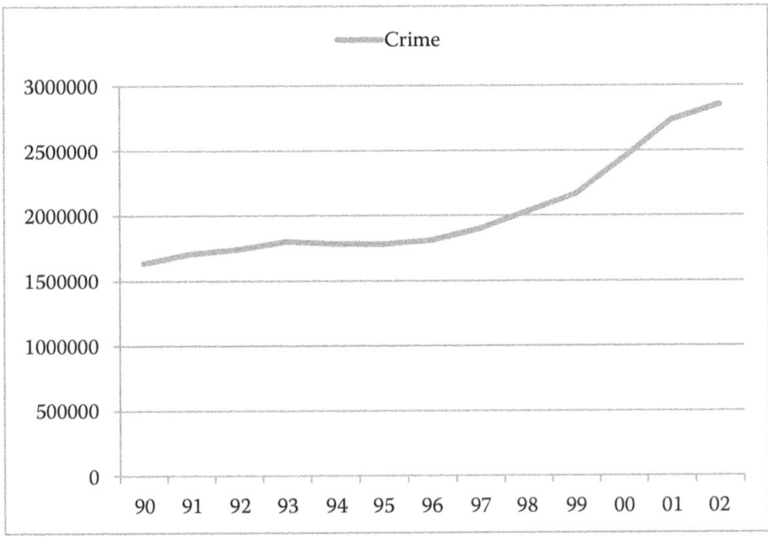

Figure 4.1 The number of recorded penal code crimes in Japan (1990–2002).

Safety." In addition, the major opposition party, the Democratic Party, also incorporated a crime reduction policy in its "The Manifesto 2003."

In response to these moves, the Japanese cabinet initiated the Ministerial Committee Against Crime in September 2003. This meeting included ministers from all branches of government and was chaired by the prime minister. In December 2003, this committee adopted the Action Plan to Create a Crime-Resistant Society (APCCS), whose final aim was stated in the preamble of APCCS as "revival of the safest country in the world, Japan."

The APCCS emphasized three main points. The first point emphasized promoting initiatives to encourage the public to participate in crime prevention. The second point endorsed the development of a social environment that is crime resistant. The third point stressed the need to overcome bureaucratic sectionalism in the course of the promotion of measures aimed at fighting crime.

In accordance with these three points, the APCCS required participating authorities to take action on 148 individual measures to implement this plan. These included activities such as support for anticrime volunteers, strengthening of police activities at *kobans*,[1] promotion of crime prevention through environmental design, an increase in the number of license plate recognition cameras, promotion of juvenile education in communities, enforcement of immigration laws, and a reduction in the number of illegal residents. After the adoption of the APCCS, the ministerial committee also created two more programs: Program to Promote Safe Community Building and Program to Protect Children From Crime.

Outlines of APCCS

Based on the points outlined in the APCCS, most ministries then worked to plan 148 individual measures, which were divided into five major categories.

1. Prevention of crime that threatens the daily lives of citizens
2. Community involvement in the prevention of juvenile crime
3. Implementation of measures to protect against transnational menace
4. Protection of the economy and society from organized crime
5. Development of fundamentals for public safety

Prevention of Crime That Threatens the Daily Lives of Citizens

The first category contains three subcategories: restoration of social bonds and building safe communities (19 measures), distribution of products and systems effective for crime prevention (15 measures), and protection of crime victims (8 measures).

The major actions taken in the first subcategory involved support for voluntary crime prevention activities conducted by community members, development of private security entities, and promotion of crime-resistant designs for roads, parks, and parking lots.

Additional steps were taken to strengthen koban-based activities that bring the police into contact with the community (e.g., community policing, problem-oriented policing, etc.). Action taken in this category also included promotion of the type of crime-resistant product design and environment that is based on the situational crime prevention theory (Clarke, 1992).

These actions brought significant results. The number of volunteer crime prevention groups active in Japan increased from 3,056 in 2003 to 40,538 in 2008. In addition, the number of people participating in these programs was 2.34 million in 2007, compared with only 0.18 million in 2003 (Figure 4.2).

The number of private security guards increased from 436,810 in 2002 to 512,331 in 2008. Furthermore, the number of private houses or business facilities equipped with security alarm systems increased from 1,164,542 in 2002 to 2,115,380 in 2008, an increase of about 1 million over the course of six years (Figure 4.3).

The major actions taken in the second subcategory include preventive measures to reduce the number of vehicle-related crimes, such as the distribution of car immobilizers and enhanced vehicle locks, strict controls on vehicle registration, and measures that help in the identification and arrest of persons involved in vehicular crimes, such as the installation of automated license plate recognition cameras. These actions have borne significant results. Vehicle-related theft has decreased dramatically (Figure 4.4).

The third subcategory included measures that stressed the protection of women and children from domestic violence. Therefore, the police and

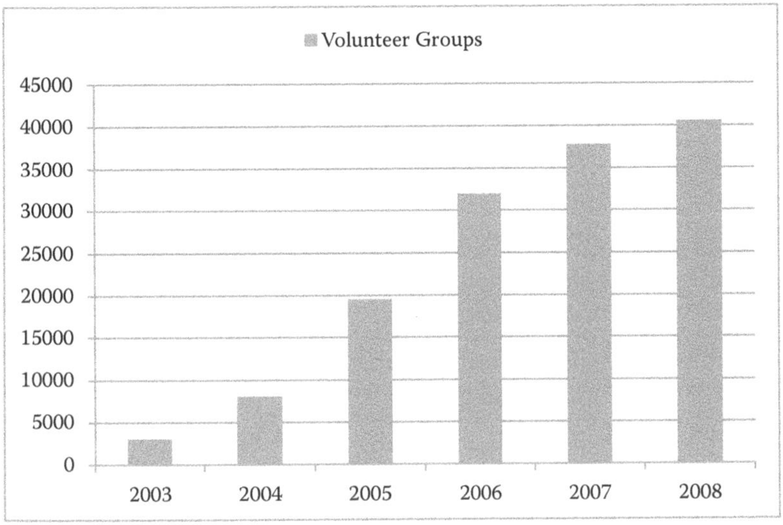

Figure 4.2 The number of volunteer groups involved in crime prevention (2003–2008). (From NPA.)

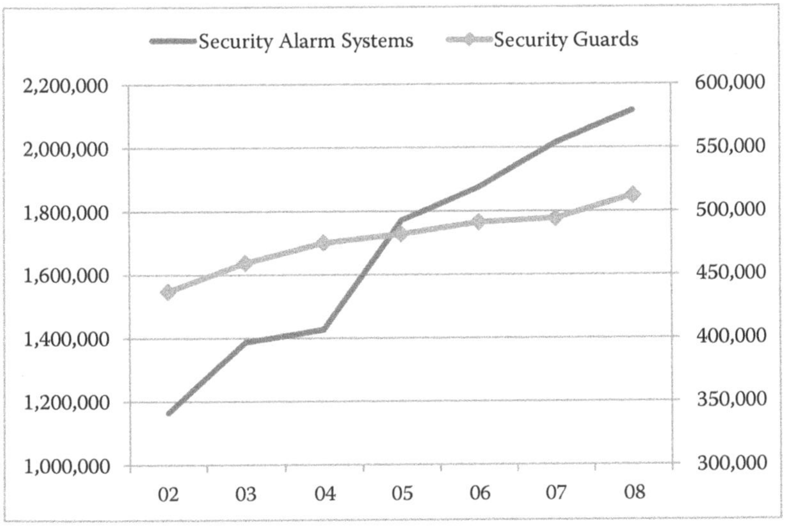

Figure 4.3 The number of private security guards and alarm systems. (From NPA.)

related agencies enhanced mutual cooperation and protective activities, including the arrest of persons for spousal battery or child abuse (Figure 4.5).

Community Involvement in the Prevention of Juvenile Crime

The second category is divided into three subcategories: stricter enforcement in juvenile crime (6 measures), community involvement in helping to

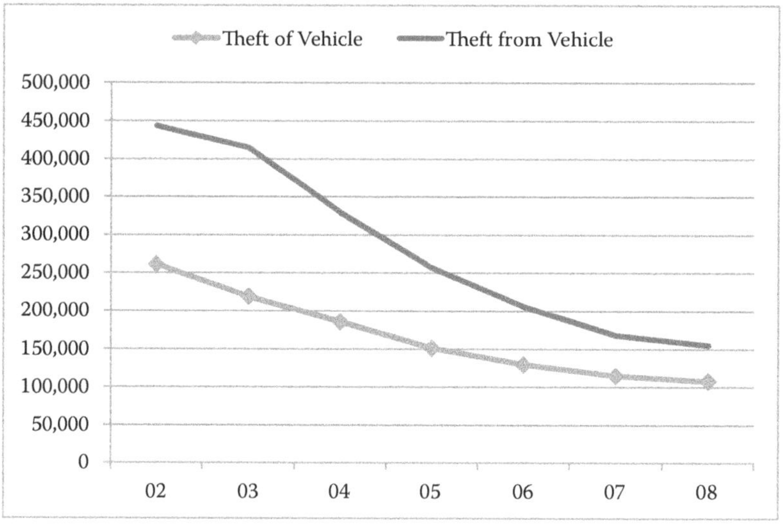

Figure 4.4 Vehicle-related theft. (From NPA.)

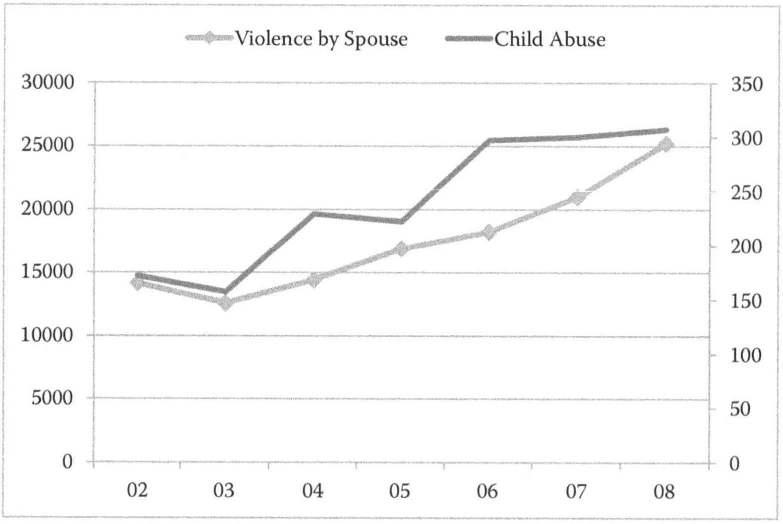

Figure 4.5 Domestic violence (spousal battery and child abuse). (From NPA.)

prevent juvenile delinquency (14 measures), and multiorganizational support for juveniles (2 measures). These actions also bore significant results. For example, there was a more than a 30% decrease in the number of arrests involving juvenile criminals.

Strict and Appropriate Enforcement of Laws Aimed at Juvenile Criminals The major steps taken in the first subcategory entail strict and appropriate enforcement of laws aimed at juvenile criminals and

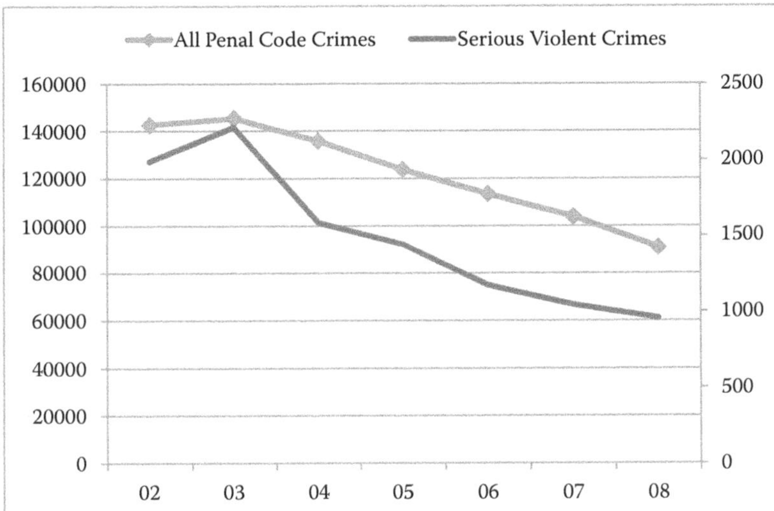

Figure 4.6 Penal code crimes and serious/violent juvenile crimes. Serious/violent crimes include murder, robbery, rape, and arson. (From NPA.)

reinforcement of treatment systems involved in helping troubled youths. As Figure 4.6 shows, the number of serious crimes committed by juveniles decreased by 50% between 2003 and 2008, while the total number of juvenile crimes decreased by 36.8% in the same period.

Community Involvement in the Prevention of Juvenile Delinquency The major action taken in the second subcategory is the expansion of guidelines involving misconduct such as loitering late at night, running away from home, and underage drinking and smoking. After this approach was adopted, the number of guidance cases involving juvenile misconduct by the police increased, while the number of juveniles arrested for criminal activity decreased (Figure 4.7). We believe the enhancement of police activity that deals with juvenile misconduct has prevented the escalation of juvenile misconduct into more serious crimes.

The major action in the third subcategory is multiorganizational intervention in cases involving juvenile delinquency. This multiorganizational body is called the Juvenile Support Team, which is composed of representatives from the police, schools, probation offices, municipalities, and community volunteer groups.

Implementation of Measures to Protect Against Transnational Menace

The third category contains four subcategories: reinforcement of border controls (9 measures), prevention of illegal entry and overstaying of visas (18 measures), strengthening the investigation of crimes committed by foreign

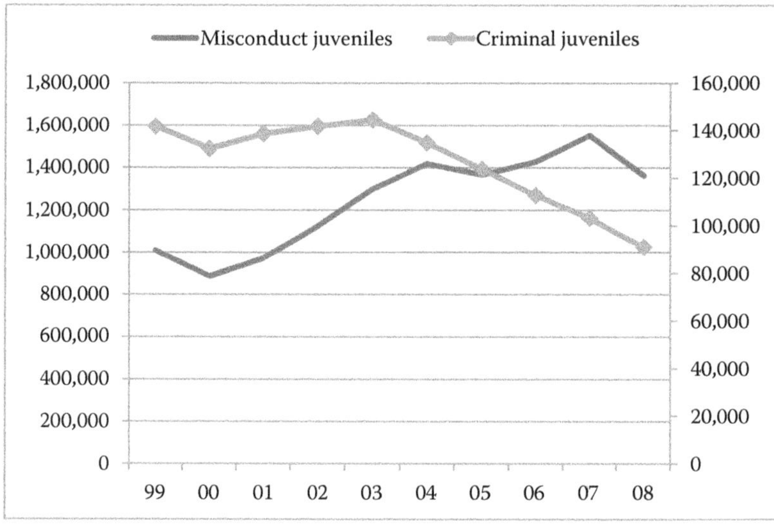

Figure 4.7 The number of penal code criminal and misconduct cases involving juveniles (1999–2008). (From NPA.)

nationals (2 measures), and enhancement of cooperation with foreign authorities (6 measures).

The outcomes of these actions are as follows. The number of illegal residents decreased from 219,000 in 2004 to 113,000 in 2008, and in addition, the number of arrested foreign visitors decreased from 21,842 in 2004 to 13,880 in 2008 (Figure 4.8).

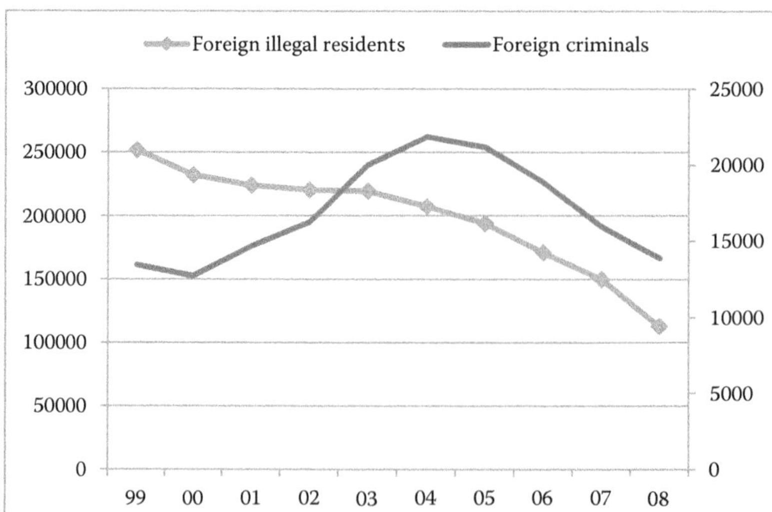

Figure 4.8 The number of illegal foreign residents and foreign nationals arrested or charged with crimes[2] (1999–2008). (From NPA.)

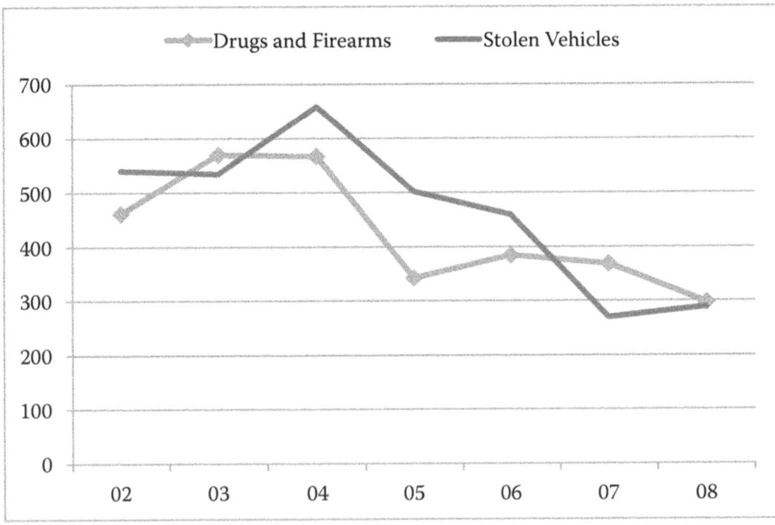

Figure 4.9 Drugs, firearms, and stolen vehicles seized by customs. (From Ministry of Finance.)

Reinforcement of Border Controls The major action taken in the first subcategory has been a crackdown on contraband and stolen vehicle trade at the borders. This has been done through the enhancement of cooperation among law enforcement authorities such as the police, the customs agency, and the maritime safety agency (Figure 4.9).

Strengthening the Investigation of Crimes Committed by Foreign Nationals As can be observed in Figure 4.10, the percentage of foreign nationals involved in criminal activity such as robbery and burglary is rather high. The percentage of foreign nationals in all arrestees charged in penal code crimes is about 2.0%, and this number has remained relatively stable. On the other hand, the percentage of foreign nationals among all arrestees charged in cases involving robbery or burglary is quite a bit higher. Therefore, the police have shifted resources to address the problem of crime committed by foreign nationals.

Enhancement of Cooperation With Foreign Authorities The third subcategory focuses on enhancement of cooperation with foreign law enforcement authorities through the conclusion of the Mutual Legal Assistance Treaty (MLAT). Coordination with authorities in mainland China has been especially strengthened.

Protection of the Economy and Society From Organized Crime

The actions taken in the fourth category are divided into four subcategories: taking action against organized crime groups including *boryokudan*[3] (10 measures), building a society that is free from both illegal drugs and firearms

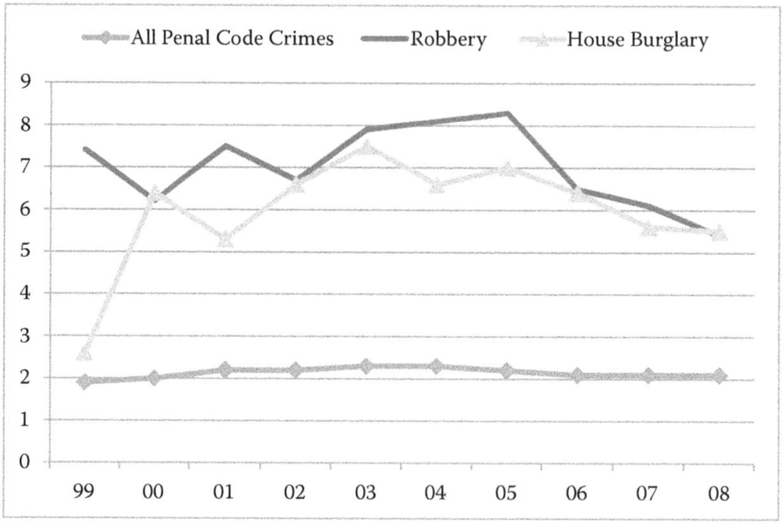

Figure 4.10 Percentage of foreign nationals among arrestees in Japan. (From NPA.)

(11 measures), taking action against crimes that threaten daily life and business (8 measures), and putting into practice initiatives designed to fight cyber crimes (6 measures).

Countermeasures Against Organized Criminal Groups Including Boryokudan The first subcategory involves measures that prevent the funding of organized criminal groups. These include the exclusion of entities with links to organized crime from the market and the strengthening of money laundering investigations. Both activities have borne results, as indicated below in Figures 4.11 and 4.12.

Building a Society That Is Free From Both Illegal Drugs and Firearms The actions taken in this subcategory emphasize both law enforcement activity and a national campaign against guns and illicit drugs. As Figures 4.13 and 4.14 show, shooting incidents have declined, but illicit drugs still represent a serious problem.

Measures to Protect the Citizenry From Crimes That Threaten Livelihoods and Businesses This subcategory includes measures aimed at preventing crimes that threaten livelihoods and business, such as corporate fraud, loan sharking, and organized pirating of brand name goods. While the number of penal code crimes is decreasing overall, the above types of criminal activity are increasing, as shown in Figure 4.15.

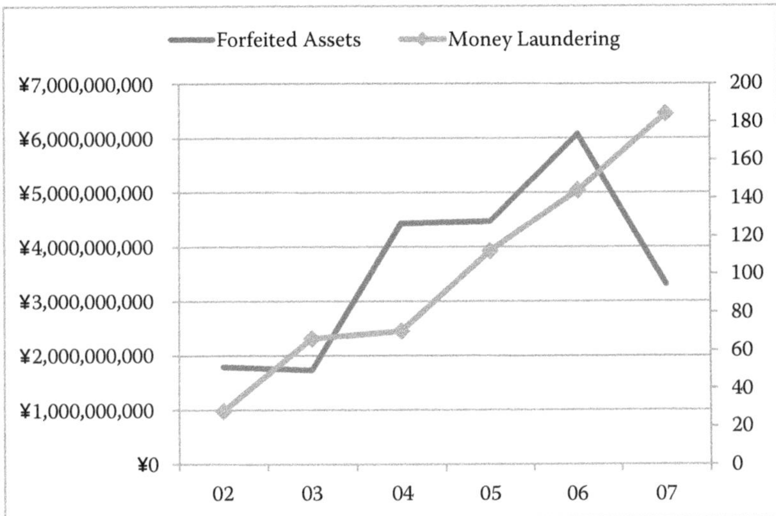

Figure 4.11 Amount of forfeited assets and money laundering cases. (From NPA.)

Measures to Protect Against Cyber Crime As computer networks have rapidly expanded, so has the number of cyber crimes (Figure 4.15). This subcategory's major initiatives are a campaign to warn computer users about various modus operandi used by cyber criminals and the reinforcement of network systems security.

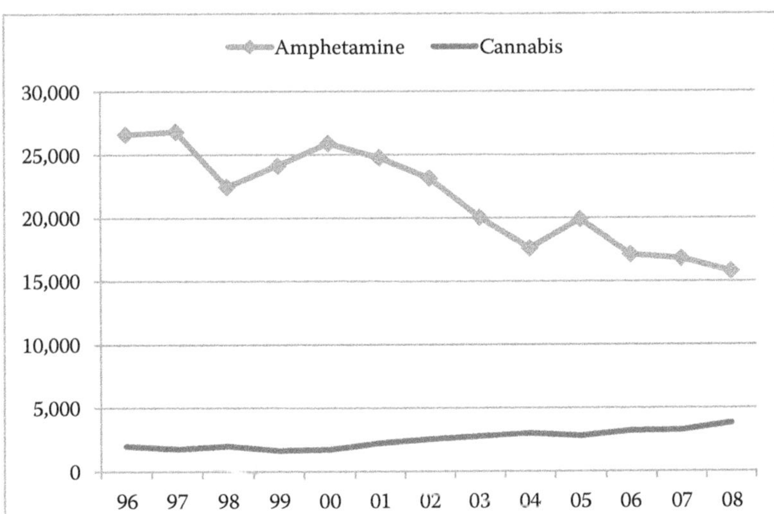

Figure 4.12 Major illicit drug cases. (From NPA.)

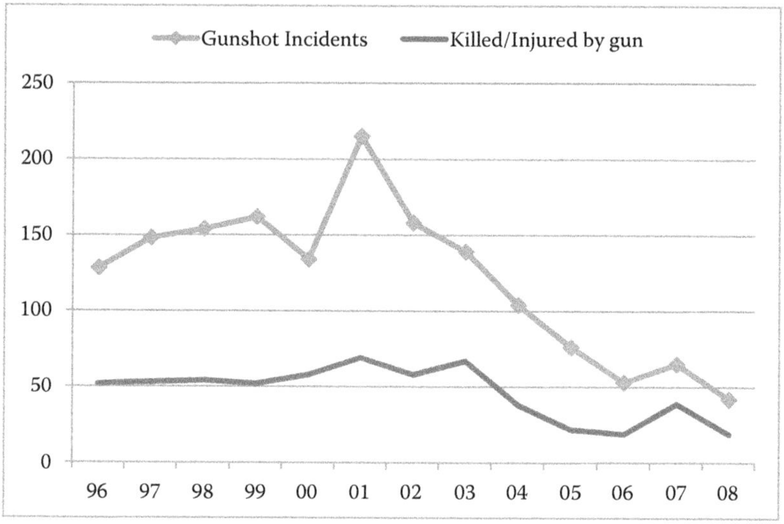

Figure 4.13 Shooting incidents. (From NPA.)

Development of Fundamentals for Public Safety

The major steps taken in the fifth category include various measures aimed at increasing public safety. They include an increase in the number of law enforcement officers, the introduction of new border control systems, such as a biological identification system, and an expansion of prisons.

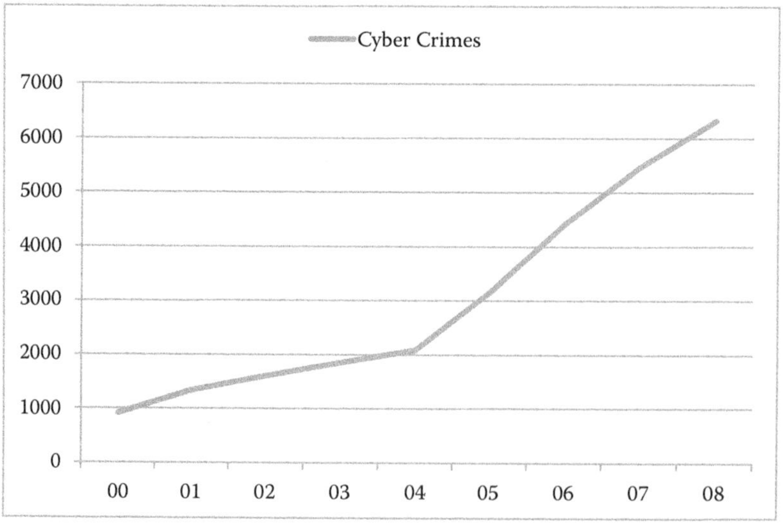

Figure 4.14 Number of cyber crimes. (From NPA.)

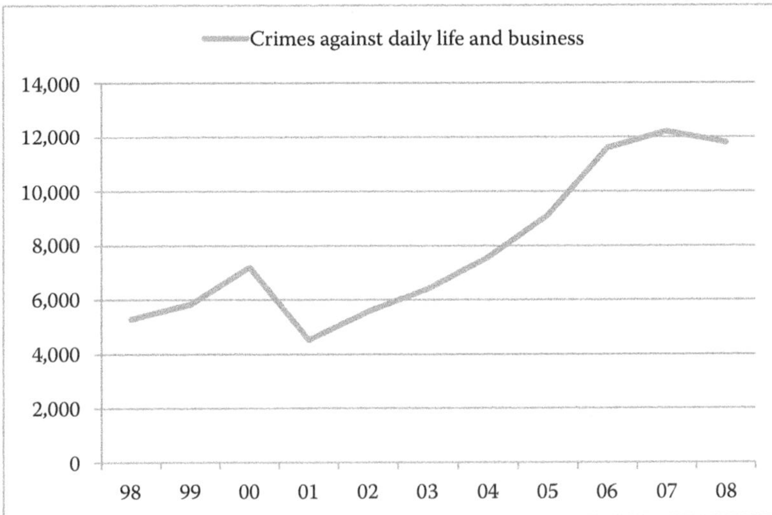

Figure 4.15 Crimes such as corporate fraud, loan sharking, and pirating of brand goods. (From NPA.)

APCCS Supplemental Programs

National Program to Promote Safe Community Building

Overview The Japanese government created the program to promote safe community building nationwide as a program supplemental to the APCCS, which was adopted at the ministerial committee on June 28, 2005. The program contains three major elements: promoting a national campaign for building safe communities, securing safety in these communities for children and residents, and the rebuilding of sound and attractive urban centers, such as downtowns and entertainment districts.

Safe Community Building Day The ministerial committee decided to designate October 11 as Safe Community Building Day. Currently, the government holds various events on this day, including a ceremony in which a member of the public is selected as having made an excellent contribution to building safe communities and is honored with an award from the prime minister.

Assistance to Volunteer Groups Involved in Community Safety There are five major factors that help support volunteer groups involved in community safety: information, training, enhancing partnerships, financial support, and equipment. First, with respect to information, the Japanese police, mainly through police stations and kobans, have long provided public information on suspected criminal activity. This information is distributed through such items as bulletins and community papers in order to promote community-based crime prevention activities. In addition, the police currently provide information to the public through websites and text messages. Members of the community can view geographic information systems (GIS), which show sites where crimes have occurred on maps. If members of the public subscribe to a text information service provided by the police on their cell phones, they can be notified immediately of general information regarding crimes, accidents, or police alerts.

Second, with respect to training, the police, in conjunction with local governments, provide training that includes advice on creating maps, leadership training, driving safety skills, and a vast array of additional activities that address crime prevention by the general public. The police supported training for 15,433 volunteer groups in 2008.

Third, partnerships between volunteer groups and the police are promoted in various combined activities. In 2008, these activities included patrols and seminars.

Fourth, with regard to financial support, the NPA has taken a lead in establishing a financial support system for volunteer groups aimed at crime prevention. The police and local governments provide subsidies for office supplies, flashlights, caps, armbands, insurance, etc. The amount of support and the type of support given to these volunteer groups depend on the area in which they are located.

And fifth, equipment is available for NGO use, as the police and local governments lend these organizations cars and office space for their activities.

Blue Warning Lights on Volunteer Patrol Cars In 2006, the NPA and the Ministry of Land, Infrastructure and Transport established a system in which volunteer patrol cars are allowed to use flashing blue lights. Volunteers wanted to use blue lights in a manner similar to police lights for their patrol cars. In Japan, emergency vehicles such as police cars and fire engines use flashing red lights.

As of December 2004, there were 120 volunteer patrol cars with blue warning lights. The number increased sharply after that, and it reached 26,622 at the end of 2008, which is indeed more than 200 times the number in 2004.

National Program to Protect Children From Crime

Overview Along with the increase in the crime rate, the number of child victims has also unfortunately increased. In 2005, a series of cases that involved the murder of children[4] shocked the people of Japan. Some of these victims were children kidnapped on the way home from the school.

Gravely concerned about the situation, people established volunteer groups nationwide to set up safety patrols for school children, and the national and local governments also took various measures aimed at protecting children from crime. The subject of children's safety was touched upon in the national program to promote safe community building and was then expanded into the National Program to Protect Children from Crime (NPPCC), which was created by the interministerial committee for child safety and endorsed at the Ministerial Committee Against Crime on December 20, 2005.

The NPPCC focuses on school zone safety through comprehensive measures such as the establishment of a multiagency committee for school safety, safety patrols and other volunteers, and practical education about safety issues for school children. These measures were seen as especially important because most public elementary schools are located within walking distance of students' homes, and therefore most Japanese children walk to school.

Volunteers and Public Employees for School Safety The Ministry of Education created a school guard project comprised of volunteers who act as safety monitors for children on the way to and from school. Many community organizations, such as the PTA and the Senior Club, participate in the school guard project. About 205,000 volunteers have completed the school guard training course.

Schools and the police have special staff positions for school safety, namely, school guard leaders, who are employed by an educational committee, and school supporters, who work part-time at local police stations. At the end of 2008, there were 2,880 school guard leaders, and some municipalities inform these volunteers of the times when children are returning home from school through a public radio broadcast system.

110 House for Children The police have been promoting the 110 house for children project. A 110 house is a volunteer's residence or a shop that displays a sign reading "110 house for children" and is available as a place where children can seek help in the case of an emergency. For example, if a child feels that a suspicious person is pursuing him or her, this child can enter a 110 house and ask the residents for assistance. 110 is the emergency number in Japan, and it is similar to the number 911 in the United States in that it is an easily recognizable symbol. By the end of 2004, about 1.9 million houses had registered as 110 houses for children.

Safety Education for Children Teachers, school guard leaders, and police officers are all involved in providing safety education to children. One of the most effective elements of this education is the safety map program. In this program children draw maps that outline their neighborhood and their commute to and from school. This allows children to check areas that could be dangerous and learn to avoid potential threats. Participants in this program who are knowledgeable about the community give children instructions on how to draw the maps.

Legislations and Guidelines for Crime Reduction

For the implementation of APPCS, necessary legislation and guidelines have been established. Major legislation and guidelines are as follows.

Local Ordinance for Safe Community Building

The first local ordinances for safe community building (LOSCBs) were enacted in Osaka prefecture in 2002. Osaka is the second largest city in Japan, and the rapid worsening of the crime situation pushed citizens and local assembly members into action. The goals of LOSCBs are to prevent crimes and rebuild community ties. LOSCBs include long-term, comprehensive plans for crime prevention and clarify the responsibilities of actors, including local government, the police, the private sector, and local residents. They support and promote crime prevention activities by these groups. LOSCBs have been introduced gradually throughout Japan, and of the 47 prefectures in the country, 44 have enacted these types of ordinances as of February 2009.

Similar ordinances have been established in other municipalities, such as cities and towns. These municipalities actively support activities by residents to prevent crime and participate in safe community building.

Safe Community Building Guidelines for Public Facilities

Following the rapid increase in street crime and burglaries, the Cabinet Secretariat, the Ministry of Education, Culture, Sports, Science and Technology, the Ministry of Land, Infrastructure and Transport, and the NPA established the Interministerial Conference for Building of Crime-Resistant Towns (ICBCT). Previous to this, the NPA had coordinated an effort called CPTED with the concerned ministries, and this effort evolved into a conference on the worsening crime situation. In 2003, the conference formed guidelines for local administrations, schools, the police, and residents aimed at the development of safe public facilities, including parks, public lavatories, streets, and parking areas.

The guidelines are summarized below:

1. Keeping public areas open to observation by installing bright streetlights and creating open sight lines in public spaces

2. Making sidewalks, streets, and parking areas less open to criminal activity
3. Enhancing the sense of community among local residents by encouraging volunteer activities such as cleaning up parks and public spaces

Lock-Picking Tools Prohibition Law

A sharp increase in the rate of burglaries was accompanied by a new modus operandi, namely, lock-picking. Lock-picking is a way to open locks with various thin tools such as a long needle, and it is much quieter than other ways of breaking and entering, such as a smashing a window or prying a door with a crowbar.

To prevent burglars from using lock-picking equipment, the Japanese government created the Lock-Picking Tools Prohibition Law in 2003. This law prohibits the possession and carrying of tools designed for picking and tampering with locks. Additionally, it includes regulations on selling and supplying these materials and carries penalties for anyone who does so with criminal intent.

Certification System for Crime-Proof Locks and Related Materials

The Lock-Picking Tools Prohibition Law also includes a measure that promotes crime-proof locks by authorizing information sharing between the NPA and lock makers concerning crime prevention, and by obliging makers to show the ability of their products to prevent break-ins.

Analyses of home and office burglaries revealed that the main ways of breaking and entering residences and offices were to break locks or parts of entrance doors and windows—or to use unlocked doors or windows. Therefore, it is critically important to improve locks on doors and windows, as well as those on windows themselves, in order to prevent these types of burglaries.

The NPA led an effort to establish a conference of related organizations, both public and private, to begin an evaluation system for locks from the standpoint of crime prevention. If a lock is able to withstand a burglar's efforts to pick it or break it for more than five minutes, it is allowed to use the CP logo, which stands for "crime prevention." More than 140,000 CP locks were made in 2008. A complete list of CP locks can be seen on the NPA website.

Crime Prevention Standards for Convenience Stores and Supermarkets

In 2003, after a sharp increase in nighttime robberies occurring at convenience stores and supermarkets, the NPA, in conjunction with related ministries and the private sector, established standards for these stores designed to prevent such crimes. These standards recommend crime prevention measures such as requiring that more than two clerks be on duty during the night shift, recommendations and requirements for handling cash at stores, and building codes covering the structure and design of stores.

Certification System for Apartment Buildings With Crime Preventive Functions

The Japanese police and the Ministry of Land, Infrastructure and Transport set up a system to ensure that certified apartment buildings have crime-preventive functions and structures and can serve as "model crime-resistant buildings." A public service foundation is charged with the certification of model crime-resistant apartment buildings. This foundation checks applicant apartment buildings to ascertain if they conform to guidelines that stipulate the design and structure of main entrances, areas for mailboxes, elevator halls, elevators, corridors, ladders, parking lots, front and back yard areas, security cameras, and so on. The system was developed in December 2008, and since that time it has been implemented in 15 prefectures.

Conclusion

As stated so far, measures taken by departments other than law enforcement are not originally designed for crime reduction purposes, but deemed to be helpful for crime reduction by each department's earnest consideration. In order to sustain those departments' earnest involvement in crime reduction, regular follow-up meetings of the Ministerial Committee Against Crime were found to work quite effectively.

Based on the review on APCCS, including the above finding, the ministerial committee against crime revised APCCS in 2008 (Kawai, 2009). The revised APCCS maintains the three viewpoints described in the former APCCS, with reference to the remark of Frantz Von Liszt: "A good social policy is the best and most effective criminal policy." The ministerial committee focused more on the background and social conditions that lead to crime, in that it aimed to promote a wider range of, and a more continuous policy on, crime deterrence. Therefore, the description of items changed from measures taken against crime and criminals to items that were more focused on society and potential victims of crime.

As Figure 4.16 shows, a trend of decrease in crime still continues under the current economic recession led by the global financial crisis. However, some kinds of crimes increased last year, such as robbery. Therefore, steady

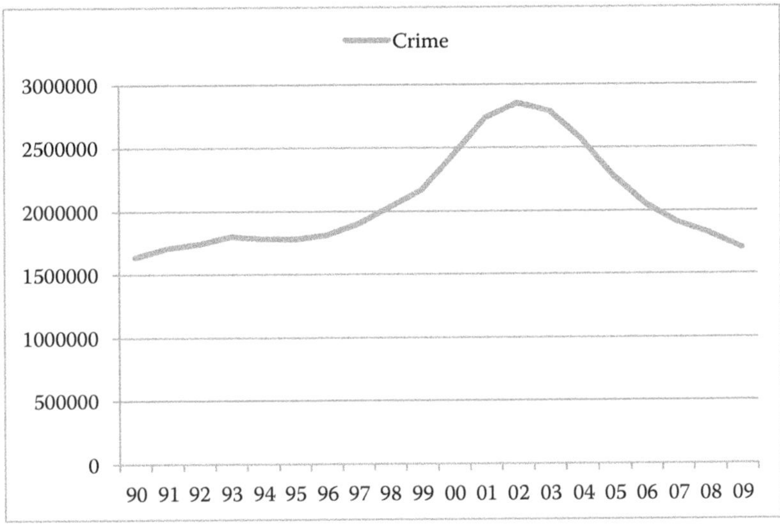

Figure 4.16 Number of reported penal code crimes. (From NPA.)

fulfillment of the revised APCCS would be indispensable for revival of the safest country in the world, Japan.

Notes

1. *Koban*, police box, is a base for community police officers.
2. Defined as foreign nationals arrested or charged by the police, not including foreigners who have permanent resident status and U.S. military personnel.
3. The general word for Japanese organized crime groups, literally translated as "violence groups."
4. At the end of 2005, three elementary school girls were killed in separate incidents. These crimes occurred in Hiroshima on November 22, in Tochigi on December 1, and in Kyoto on December 10.

References

Bayley, D.H. (1976). *Force of order: Police behavior in Japan and the United States.* Berkeley, CA: University of California Press.

Clarke, R.V. (1992). *Situational crime prevention successful case studies.* Albany, NY: Harrow and Heston.

Kawai, K. (2009). Hanzai ni tsuyoi shakai no jitsugen no tameno koudoukeikaku 2008 no suishin [The Implementation of the Action Plan for the Realization of a Society Resistant to Crime 2008]. *Security Science Review, 11.*

A Study on Mahila Dakshata/ Suraksha Samities of Maharashtra

5

MEERAN CHADHA BORWANKAR

Introduction

Crimes against women are rampant in India, yet most crimes are not reported or registered. In a patriarchal society that is still deeply rooted in traditions where women have been relegated to a secondary position for centuries, even survival has been difficult for them. In recent years, modern technology and communications have helped the country grow economically and emerge as a modern developed nation. Yet the same technology continues to be used to abort female fetuses. There is a silent consent about keeping a woman in her place and a belief that a well-educated, assertive, and aware woman "breaks a home."

> There is a sustained systemic, consistent and deliberate politics of violence against women. It is by a carefully delineated strategy that the patriarchal institutions are perpetuated by a culture of violence, which works at various levels.[*]

India, with a low sex ratio of 933 women to 1,000 men, contributes to the preponderance of males over females in the world.[†]

However, the personal and private space in the Indian society is being challenged by the formal rule of law that has not only provided equal rights to women after the independence of the country in 1947, but also promoted affirmative action in its implementation. India today has reservations for women in institutions of local self-governance, educational, and employment avenues. Both the central and state governments are committed to provide for the equality of gender and determined to enforce it at all costs.

[*] M. Khanna, "The Politics of Violence Against Women Special Focus on India," retrieved December 12, 2010, from http://www.wunrn.com.

[†] Report of Government of India, Ministry of Home Affairs, Office of the Registrar General and Census Commissioner India, retrieved December 12, 2010, from http://censusindia.gov.in.

There is thus a conflict between the status of women in society and that being assured by the law. This has led to assertive women at one end and a backlash by the traditionalists on the other. While this conflict can be seen in the urban India, the plight of women has not changed much in the rural India. Moreover, crimes against women continue unabated in both spaces.

What makes matters worse in cases of crime against women in India is that the law enforcement agency, that is, the police, is still dominated by men. The agency is reluctant to register complaints of women victims, and the society also likes to suppress these cases. Women themselves prefer to remain silent until the victimization literally drives them to the doors of a police station. Unfortunately, the police station is an unwelcoming place, where they find it most difficult to seek redress of their grievances. The police agency and the station both have traditionally bad connotation for the helpless women victims who prefer never to visit a police station in their lives ("Mi kadhi hi polisanchi payari chadale nahin"). "Whenever a woman is in trouble she hesitates to go to the police station to seek help. They are afraid of the men in uniform," admitted Director General (DG) of Police Jharkhnad G.S. Rath while talking recently about the need for police stations for women exclusively.*

Dowry, that is, the cash/gifts that a bride brings to her groom's house at the time of marriage, is a well-entrenched phenomenon that modern India has not been able to shake off. In fact, it has been reinforced with the country becoming prosperous. Though banned by law, it continues to be a major consideration for a marriage and is also a cause of serious harassment of women, leading to crime against their persons. So serious is the problem that the Indian Penal Code was amended in 1983 to account for this particular issue. Harassment by the husband and his family for dowry thus attracts special criminal provisions of the code under Section 304 B, which reads:

> (1) Where the death of a woman is caused by any burns or bodily injury or occurs otherwise than under normal circumstances within seven years of her marriage and it is shown that soon before her death she was subjected to cruelty or harassment by her husband or any relative of her husband for, or in connection with, any demand for dowry, such death shall be called "dowry death" and such husband or relative shall be deemed to have caused her death.
>
> Explanation: For the purpose of this sub-section, "dowry" shall have the same meaning as in section 2 of the Dowry Prohibition Act, 1961 (28 of 1961).

* S. Ojha, "All-Women Police Stations Without Arms and Lock-Ups," Times of India (Ranchi edition), May 23, 2011, retrieved June 26, 2011, from http://articles.timesofindia.indiatimes.com.

(2) Whoever commits dowry death shall be punished with imprisonment for a term which shall not be less than seven years but which may extend to imprisonment for life.

Despite stringent laws dowry deaths are common in urban as well as rural India and mostly not reported to police. Similarly, violence against the person in the form of the heinous crime of rape is also a grave issue. In the traditional Indian society, where virginity is still core to a marriage, families do not report this crime. The "bad name" that such reporting "begets a family" means the victim and the family suffer in silence rather than come out in the open. Thus, despite economic development and growing modernity the Indian society is clinging to old traditions where violence against women is high but rarely talked about or reported.

The National Crime Record Bureau (NCRB, 2010) has reported the following statistics about crime against women in India. (All India figures available are only until 2008.)*

2004	154,333
2005	155,553
2006	164,765
2007	185,312
2008	195,856

Specific cases under various sections of law are as follows:

Head-Wise Incidents of Crime Against Women During 2004–2008

	2004	2005	2006	2007	2008
Rape (Section 376 IPC)	18,233	18,359	19,348	20,737	21,467
Kidnapping and abduction (Sections 363–373 IPC)	15,578	15,750	17,414	20,416	22,939
Dowry death (Section 302/304 IPC)	7,026	6,787	7,618	8,093	8,172
Torture (Section 498-A IPC)	58,121	58,319	63,128	75,930	81,344
Molestation (Section 354 IPC)	34,567	34,175	36,617	38,734	40,413
Sexual harassment (Section 509 IPC)	10,001	9,984	9,966	10,950	12,214
Importation of girls (Section 366-B IPC)	89	149	67	61	67
Immoral Traffic (Prevention) Act, 1956	5,748	5,908	4,541	3,568	2,659
Indecent Representation of Women (Prohibition) Act, 1986	1,378	2,917	1,562	1,200	1,025

* Crime in India 2008, www.ncrb.nic.in.

While crime under most heads is going up, indecent representation of women and prevention of immoral trafficking of women show a decline. These days there is more tolerance to what was conceived of as indecent representation of women, as India has taken to the Western ways of dressing, and thus the definition of indecent representation itself has changed. This could be one reason for reduced registration of such criminal cases. Being a serving police officer, I have come across an enthusiastic lecturer of a Mumbai college fighting a lone battle by filing cases under this act. She was barely ever supported by anyone. Another reason could be overworked police authorities. The latter seems to be the probable reason for the decline in registration of cases for trafficking of women, which continues to be rampant in India. In fact, illegal trafficking of minor girls from the poverty-stricken areas within the country and from neighboring Nepal and Bangladesh is an issue of grave concern. Low registration of these cases needs an urgent study and intervention.

Torture of women as defined in Section 498 was instituted in the Indian Penal Code by Act 46 of 1983, Section 2. It reads as below and is widely used, mostly in urban areas of the country.

> 498A. Husband or relative of husband of a woman subjecting her to cruelty.
>
> Whoever, being the husband or the relative of the husband of a woman, subjects such woman to cruelty shall be punished with imprisonment for a term which may extend to three years and shall also be liable to fine.
>
> Explanation—For the purpose of this section, "cruelty" means—
>
> (a) Any willful conduct which is of such a nature as is likely to drive the woman to commit suicide or to cause grave injury or danger to life, limb or health (whether mental or physical) of the woman; or
> (b) Harassment of the woman where such harassment is with a view to coercing her or any person related to her to meet any unlawful demand for any property or valuable security or is on account of failure by her or any person related to her meet such demand.

The reported crime, as mentioned above, is only the tip of the iceberg; the reality is that women and their families prefer to remain silent rather than report the crime at a police station. The trust deficit about men in uniform still remains very high.

Thus there has been a strongly felt need of bringing the community, especially women, closer to the law enforcing agencies, first to understand the gravity and magnitude of crime against women, and then to redress the same. Governments at the state and central levels have been inducting more women into police departments; some even have a positive discrimination policy to reserve posts for them. Thus the state of Maharashtra has 30% posts for women in the police organization. The logic is that inducting women in uniform shall make women victims more comfortable in approaching police for redress of crime against them. Various community policing schemes have also been initiated for enlisting the cooperation of women in law enforcement. However, community policing is yet at a very nascent stage in India, with most initiatives being exercises in public relations rather than well-planned projects to collaborate with citizens. They are short-lived, ad hoc, and barely ever audited for their usefulness.

This chapter is based upon field research on the subject of community policing during 2004–2009 and study of citizen-police collaboration in three major cities (Mumbai, Pune, and Nagpur) in the state of Maharashtra.* During the research it was observed that policemen of different ranks working in the field valued citizens' participation, and the latter are keen to be actively involved in various activities of law enforcement. However, the study highlighted a few pertinent facts:

1. Police officers of the rank of subinspector/inspector studied during the research had either very inadequate or no training at all for initiating or strengthening community participation in policing.
2. Citizens studied in the sample involved students undergoing post-graduation courses in the city of Pune who, while keen to work with the police, had a very limited understanding of police working.
3. Police officers and citizens have been collaborating at different levels on an ad hoc basis, mostly through trial and error.
4. A rudimentary structure for eliciting citizens' participation thus exists, and some of these fora have been strengthened over a period of time due to their obvious usefulness having become apparent to the community as well as police officers.
5. Police as well as citizens are keen to strengthen collaboration but require funds and focused training on the subject. Lack of funds and training seriously hampers any successful partnership between citizens and the police in India.

The researcher who came across a number of good practices involving the community and law enforcement in different parts of the country decided to study one such good practice involving police and women in Maharashtra, that is, Mahila Dakshata Samities (committees for security of women). One reason for selecting this good practice has been that it is over 25 years old and well established in Maharashtra police. The Samities work quietly without much fanfare, and their acceptance by police officers is heartening.

* M.C. Borwankar, "A Study of Community Policing and Its Administration in Selected Urban Centres in Maharashtra," Pune University, 2009.

Brief History of the Committees

The Samities/committees had been constituted in the state of Maharashtra via an order* dated April 19, 1985, issued by the director general of police, Maharashtra, as "Social Security Cells" at the level of districts/commissionerates. While the superintendent/commissioner of police was to be the chairperson of the committee, "one active woman and respectable social worker" was to be selected as a member of the cell. Officers were advised to "carefully exercise their discretion and judgment in selecting the said member." The chief functions of these cells/committees as originally envisaged are as below:

- Hold monthly meetings for review of fresh cases, progress of investigation/enquiries/offences/complaints/old cases, rumors, press report etc containing offences against women, atrocities and harassment of women.
- Bring to the fore any deviations from the rules in investigation and to take steps to punish the wrong doers.
- The committees are expected to take minutes and maintain record of follow up action.

During the third legislative assembly session of 1986, the government of Maharashtra gave an assurance that one more lady social worker would be added to the district social security cells. The directorate general (DG) of police, via its circular† dated June 29, 1987, thus increased the women members to two per district, and the same was complied with by the cells of each district/commissionerate. Through DG office circular 22/1728/87, dated August 4, 1987,‡ membership was further raised to five per district. Dakshata Samities were also introduced at the Taluka level, with two women as members. Circle inspectors were to conduct the meetings of these additional Samities.

These committees are examples of community policing because they bring women into the mainstream policing environment, from which they have been excluded in the past. They are generally not aware of their legal rights or police functioning. Establishing these committees thus meant that women social workers regularly interacted with police officers. The department that is generally feared by the citizens in India has, in this instance, tried to be open to women through such committee members. Initially urban areas were catered to, as these committees were constituted in the district headquarters and well-educated women from the upper strata were inducted

* Director General of Police Maharashtra State, "Social Security Cells—Formation of," Circular 29/1728/85, April 19, 1985.

† Director General of Police Maharashtra State. "Social Security Cells—Formation of," Circular, June 29, 1987.

‡ DG Office, circular, August 4, 1987.

as committee members; however, slowly nongovernmental organizations (NGOs) working in the field of women have made inroads. During the 1980s and early 1990s Maharshtra state was rocked by a number of sex scandals. Mahila Dakshata Samities took the lead in exposing the systematic exploitation of young girls in Jalgaon, Kolhapur, and Parbhani. Being aware of how the law works, they pressured police to register and send the cases to court. In some cases, for example, in Jalgaon, they persuaded the reluctant victims and their families to come forward and register their cases.

In view of the positive response to the district-level committees, the director general of police issued another order, dated June 19, 1998,* constituting Mahila Dakshata Samities even at police station levels. It mandated that each police station shall have a Mahila Dakshata Samiti with the local subinspector/additional inspector being the chairman of the committee, and five local women as members. Selection of the members is by the local officer in charge of the police station, the assistant commissioner of police of the state intelligence department, and Deputy Superintendent of Police (DySP) of the Anti-Corruption Bureau. The selection criterion, as mentioned in the DG's order, is that the members should be nonpolitical and actively involved in the field of welfare of women. The selection is to be further approved by the local superintendent of police and the range Deputy Inspector General/ Inspector General (DIG/IG). The tenure of a member is two years, and the Dakshata committees of police stations are expected to meet bimonthly. The mandate has been expanded to include the cases of atrocities against women and children. The current study analyzes the effectiveness of the district-level Dakshata committees only and has not studied the police station-level committees.

Objectives of the Research

- To assess the effectiveness of Mahila Dakshata/Suraksha Committees at the district level and evaluate their overall performance
- To understand the profile of the members and their perception of their own role and that of the committees
- To understand if the local communities are making use of the Samities/forums
- To assess the involvement of police officers and whether they convene the meetings regularly and follow up on cases
- To recommend measures to enhance the performance of these Samities

* Circular DGP/Desk-42/PAW/98, June 19, 1998.

Methodology of Research

Since the researcher had identified Mahila Dakshata Samities as a good practice of the state of Maharashtra for collaboration between citizens and law enforcement, it was thus decided to study the committees of a few districts from the state. Metropolitan cities like Mumbai, Pune, and Nagpur have been deliberately excluded from the study, as women's groups are very strong in these cities and take up their causes on a regular basis. It is rural Maharashtra that the researcher wanted to concentrate on, to evaluate the effectiveness of these forums. Accordingly, a questionnaire was prepared to administer to members of these committees. After drafting, it was translated to the Marathi language, as most of the committee members, belonging to rural areas, were found to be comfortable with Marathi and not English. The questionnaire was vetted for ease of understanding by some of the local women.

The state of Maharashtra is broadly divided into Khandesh, Western Maharashtra, Marathwada, Vidharbha, and Konkan areas. The questionnaire was administered to the members of Dakshata committees of 10 districts, while Pune Rural, Sangli, and Satara districts are in Western Maharashtra, Latur and Aurangabad are in Marathwada, Nasik and Jalgaon are in Khandesh, Ratnagiri and Sindhudurg in Kokan, and Wardha in Vidharbha. This provides adequate representation to the different parts of the state. Fifty questionnaires were sent to the district police chiefs, who administered them to the Dakshata Samiti members.

Forty-six responses were received out of the 50 questionnaires circulated. Their responses have been analyzed as below.

Age Profile of the Respondents

	Frequency	Percent	Valid Percent	Cumulative Percent
30–40	15	32.6	32.6	32.6
40–50	13	28.3	28.3	60.9
Above 50	15	32.6	32.6	93.5
20–30	2	4.3	4.3	97.8
Not mentioned	1	2.2	2.2	100.0
Total	46	100.0	100.0	

The profile of the members of the committees shows that women of 30 years and above are well represented. But there is very low (2.2%) representation of the younger age group of 20–30. It needs to be looked into as the problems of this age group could be peculiar (e.g., eve teasing), and there is a possibility of these issues not being adequately represented/ voiced during the meetings of the committees. Including a younger age group in the committees may also lead to more dynamism, as there is a high possibility of their being better educated, more aware, and thus more vocal. The reasons for such low representation have not been studied during this research; this needs to be rectified and adequate representation given to young women.

Academic Profile of the Respondents

	Frequency	Percent	Valid Percent	Cumulative Percent
Undergraduate	13	28.3	28.3	28.3
Graduate	8	17.4	17.4	45.7
Postgraduate	24	52.2	52.2	97.8
Not mentioned	1	2.2	2.2	100.0
Total	46	100.0	100.0	

The study shows that a good number of the members are well educated, 52.2% being postgraduate and 17.4% being graduates. Many of them are lawyers and some are doctors too; this enables them to take up the cause of those who dare not enter a police station despite genuine issues. A high number of respondents have reported being active in the field of education for women. This bodes well for the committees, as educated members are more confident in their interaction with police. As mentioned earlier, citizens, especially women, are still fearful of the police in India. Thus, having educated women members is welcome, and useful for a healthy and confident exchange of views.

Professional Profile of the Respondent

	Frequency	Percent	Valid Percent	Cumulative Percent
Service	7	15.2	15.2	15.2
Self-employed	14	30.4	30.4	45.7
Housewife	4	8.7	8.7	54.3
Social worker	21	45.7	45.7	100.0
Total	46	100.0	100.0	

Only 8.7% of committee members are housewives, and thus not working outside their homes, while the rest are either self-employed or social workers. This too could be a factor responsible for sustaining the committees since 1985 and for their work. Being career women, most of the members interact with citizens from diverse fields. Thus, their knowledge and awareness about the state of women and their problems could be wide, thereby making the committee work relevant and more meaningful.

Duration of Membership/Tenure as Members of the Committees

	Frequency	Percent	Valid Percent	Cumulative Percent
Less than 5	15	32.6	32.6	32.6
5–10	11	23.9	23.9	56.5
10 and above	16	34.8	34.8	91.3
None	4	8.7	8.7	100.0
Total	46	100.0	100.0	

That 34.8% of the women are members of these committees for more than 10 years shows that these committees are of some use to them, and thus they continue with their membership. At the same time, for effective working of the committees, there needs to be induction of new blood and new thought. This means that there should be an upper limit to the tenure of membership. In fact, while forming the committees at the police station level, two-year tenure has been stipulated by the Office of the Director General of Police. A similar policy for district-level committees needs to be formulated.

NGOs' Participation in the Committee as Members

	Frequency	Percent	Valid Percent	Cumulative Percent
Yes	33	71.7	71.7	71.7
No	8	17.4	17.4	89.1
None	5	10.9	10.9	100.0
Total	46	100.0	100.0	

Selection for membership of these committees seems to be on the basis of social work done by candidates, as 71.7% of members are part of nongovernmental organizations (NGOs). Many are Bachat Gats, that is, self-help group members. This is a healthy trend, as such members are aware of the field realities, from the point of view of both women and law enforcement. Such NGOS are also aware of the working of government and police departments, and thus the objective of pursuing criminal cases/inquiries related to women can be well attended to. While introducing these committees at the police station level in 1998, the Office of the Director General of Maharashtra had specifically mentioned that nonpolitical NGOs should be selected. The same thought is reflected in selection of members in the district committees. They are found to be active in Bachat Gats (self-help groups) and Tanta Mukti Abhiyans (dispute resolution forums). Many respondents are spreading legal awareness by organizing camps on legal issues concerning the rights of women and children.

Political Affiliation of the Members

	Frequency	Percent	Valid Percent	Cumulative Percent
Yes	14	30.4	30.4	30.4
No	28	60.9	60.9	91.3
None	4	8.7	8.7	100.0
Total	46	100.0	100.0	

Some representation of political interests has crept in, as seen from the response that 30.4% had political affiliations. This is a reality and has to be faced. Political parties are as active in the field of women's welfare as NGOs in the state; complete denial of representation to them may not be possible. The real danger is that, slowly, they may take over these forums and relegate the cause of women to the background. However, a high 60.9% of members have reported not being affiliated to any political party.

Frequency of the Meetings

	Frequency	Percent	Valid Percent	Cumulative Percent
Quarterly	7	15.2	15.2	15.2
Once in a month	24	52.2	52.2	67.4
No specific timing	2	4.3	4.3	71.7
As per need	8	17.4	17.4	89.1
Once in a week	4	8.7	8.7	97.8
Not mentioned	1	2.2	2.2	100.0
Total	46	100.0	100.0	

Most of the district committees are regular in their meetings, with 52.2% holding monthly meetings and 8.7% meeting every week. As per the directions of the director general of Maharashtra, these meeting must be held every month. Thus the districts where the meetings are held only once a quarter (15.2%) and where no specific routine is followed need to be advised to conduct monthly meetings. Regular interaction and follow-up of criminal cases and inquiries relating to women can be best achieved if women members frequently interact with police officers and review the same. Hence the need to enforce once-a-month interaction between police officers and the committee members, as envisaged originally.

Police Participation in the Committees

		Frequency	Percent	Valid Percent	Cumulative Percent
Valid	Yes	35	76.1	76.1	76.1
	No	3	6.5	6.5	82.6
	Sometimes	7	15.2	15.2	97.8
	None	1	2.2	2.2	100.0
	Total	46	100.0	100.0	

Police officers have been regular in attending the committee meetings (76.1%) as reflected by the response of members. That about 24% of officers do not attend the meetings is a serious issue. Full and whole-hearted participation of police officers is essential. A reaffirmation of the backing of the Office of the Director General of Police and insistence on regular meetings seem in order. Some respondents mentioned that police should attach more resources in the form of manpower and vehicles for the committees. A few talked of lack of confidentiality about the sensitive issues of women on the part of police. However, need for additional funds was highlighted by many.

Whether Minutes of the Meeting Are Drawn and Taken Into Consideration

		Frequency	Percent	Valid Percent	Cumulative Percent
Valid	Yes	43	93.5	93.5	93.5
	Sometimes	3	6.5	6.5	100.0
	Total	46	100.0	100.0	

The Dakshata committees seem to be well organized, as minutes of the meetings are drawn and taken note of (93.5%). During the initial years the minutes had to be sent to the director general of police (refer to the DG office order dated April 19, 1985), and this could be a reason for the good practice. A minuscule 6.5% of the respondents have said that the minutes are sometimes drawn/considered. This nevertheless needs to be rectified.

Whether Minutes of the Meeting Are Sent to Members

		Frequency	Percent	Valid Percent	Cumulative Percent
Valid	Yes	41	89.1	89.1	89.1
	Sometimes	4	8.7	8.7	97.8
	None	1	2.2	2.2	100.0
	Total	46	100.0	100.0	

The committees are well organized, as minutes are not only drawn but also sent to their members. During the earlier study of community policing by the researcher, it was observed that one of the main reasons for the short life of community policing initiatives was lack of management skills, like drawing of minutes and following them up. In the instant case, Mahila Dakshata Samities have been regular in some basic features of management, which could be a reason for their having been successful over the last 25 years.

Further Action Taken on Identified Issues

		Frequency	Percent	Valid Percent	Cumulative Percent
Valid	Yes	39	84.8	84.8	84.8
	No	1	2.2	2.2	87.0
	Sometimes	4	8.7	8.7	95.7
	None	2	4.3	4.3	100.0
	Total	46	100.0	100.0	

A very high 84.8% of the respondents have deposed that action is taken on the minutes. This could be a reason for the high level of satisfaction of women members with the working of the Mahila Dakshata Samities at the district level. Police authorities can concentrate on further improving the same.

Relationship Between Police Officers and Committee Members

		Frequency	Percent	Valid Percent	Cumulative Percent
Valid	Yes	45	97.8	97.8	97.8
	No	1	2.2	2.2	100.0
	Total	46	100.0	100.0	

A very high level of satisfaction can be seen with 97.8% of women members happy with the treatment of committee members by the police authorities. This could also mean mutual backslapping, as 68.7% continued to be members of the committees for more than five years. However, the need for providing transportation or honorarium to members by police authorities has repeatedly emerged during the study.

Awareness About the Committee Among Local Women

		Frequency	Percent	Valid Percent	Cumulative Percent
Valid	Yes	42	91.3	91.3	91.3
	Rarely	3	6.5	6.5	97.8
	None	1	2.2	2.2	100.0
	Total	46	100.0	100.0	

Awareness about the Mahila Dakshata Samities at the district level is high at 91.3%. However, this has not been cross-checked with women citizens during the study. Some members have nevertheless asked for more publicity about the committees and their charter. It is observed that members of the committees are well known locally. Not only do the members publicize the same, as it gives them perceived status in society, but even police officers have been advised by the director general of police to display their names prominently in the police stations/offices. A few members even get visiting cards printed with the title of "Member Mahila Dakshata Samiti." That there is pride and prestige in being a member of this committee is a well-known fact. The emphasis has to be for using the same for the cause of women.

Whether Local Women Seek Help From the Committee for Their Problems

		Frequency	Percent	Valid Percent	Cumulative Percent
Valid	Yes	42	91.3	91.3	91.3
	Sometimes	4	8.7	8.7	100.0
	Total	46	100.0	100.0	

Since the awareness about the committees is high, local women seem to be taking advantage of the committees and coming to the members with their problems (91.3%). This is also corroborated by the experience of police officers who testify that women in distress frequently approach police stations with members of Dakshata committees.

Whether Committee Members Take Initiative to Discuss Various Issues With Local Women

		Frequency	Percent	Valid Percent	Cumulative Percent
Valid	Yes	37	80.4	80.4	80.4
	No	2	4.3	4.3	84.8
	Sometimes	7	15.2	15.2	100.0
	Total	46	100.0	100.0	

It is pertinent that 15.2% of the members have admitted that they occasionally take the initiative to discuss the issues with local women. Four percent have admitted to no initiative at all, while a very high 80.4% have responded that they take initiative.

Satisfaction Level of the Members With the Work of the Mahiala Dakshata Samities

		Frequency	Percent	Valid Percent	Cumulative Percent
Valid	Satisfied	33	71.7	71.7	71.7
	Dissatisfied	1	2.2	2.2	73.9
	Not fully Satisfied	12	26.1	26.1	100.0
	Total	46	100.0	100.0	

A very high percentage (26.1%) of members have said that they are not fully satisfied with the working of the committee. The research thus shows a need to study the reasons for their lack of satisfaction and for making this forum more relevant and useful for the cause of women. A small percentage (2.2%) have said that they are not satisfied at all, and that too needs to be looked into, however small the number may be.

During the study a few open-ended questions had also been introduced in the questionnaire to elicit the opinion of Dakshata Samiti members on general issues. Their replies have been studied and it has transpired that, broadly, Mahila Dakshata Samities undertake the following tasks:

- Help in registration of crime against women, especially harassment by husband/his family and dowry/return of stridhan-related issues. It is a known fact that police officers are often reluctant to register cases of domestic violence. Sometimes complainants approach the members of such committees instead of going to the police station directly. Some of the respondents have also mentioned being active in approaching police against eve teasing and parent/children disputes.
- The members of these committees; in a few cases, have joined in the investigation when required, for example, police officers have sometimes sought their help in recording sensitive statements of minors/disturbed women victims.
- A few times, committees have been observed to follow up the cases either until they are sent to the court or until their final trial. In a few instances their efforts have ensured conviction of the accused. It has emerged strongly during the study that district police take their help in sorting out women-related issues.

But many respondents have mentioned that police officers, being otherwise preoccupied, fail to serve summons to the parties in dispute in time, and the issues referred to the committee by police remain pending.

- Members of Mahila Dakshata Samities are active in organizing legal awareness camps to increase legal knowledge of women about their rights, police/court procedures, maintenance for deserted/divorced women/alimony, and so on.
- A few members of the committees are active in the field of anti-human trafficking. They have occasionally assisted police in conducting raids to rescue women/girls/children.
- A surprising finding of the study was that a large number of women approach members of Mahila Dakshata Samities about alcoholism/addiction of their spouses. They appear to be at the receiving end, and thus drawn to the committees seeking their help, possibly due to lack of alternative professional avenues such as de-addiction centers. The usefulness of committees in tackling the issue is doubtful.
- Another finding was that many women approach members for help against extramarital affairs/second marriage of their spouses.
- Members of the committees, though not trained counselors, appear to be acting in such capacity, and a few have mentioned following up the cases through home visits as well.
- A trend that has strongly emerged from the responses of the members is that they prefer compromise/settlement to registration of criminal cases. Registration is avoided by police authorities too, for various reasons, one being that in the traditional ethos of the Indian society, women are expected to suffer in silence. Most of the members of these committees also seem to echo the same thought and thus take up counseling the victim women.
- Most members have stated that while the district police support them for the purpose of meetings, no honorarium is given to them and they have to bear their travel and other expenses. They have asked for funds and also for transportation for home visits to victims when required.

Some Specific Success Stories

During the survey most respondents talked of their efforts in resolving marital discords and enabling the victims of domestic violence to get maintenance from the husbands, either through the court or through informal channels. Rural women, being unaware of their rights to maintenance, are many times thrown out of their homes by abusive husbands and their families. Being illiterate, they cannot pursue their cases in the courts. It has emerged in the study that Mahila Dakshata Samiti members have at such times helped them. Two girls of Chopda in Jalgaon who had been cheated on in the pretext of marriage were rescued and rehabilitated by a member. An old woman cheated of her pension by another was helped in Nasik district.

Compromise that seems to be vigorously pursued by these committees has also been referred to as reducing the court cases. However, they are not always successful. In a case where a member was tried for a compromise, the deserted wife of Miraj city did not agree and persisted in the court. She succeeded in getting Rs 1.7 million for herself and a bungalow worth Rs 1 million for her son.

Many members have talked of their efforts resulting in reduction in crime against women. Some have gone further in their efforts to rehabilitate victims of crime/violence by helping them in setting up small-scale industry. A respondent has mentioned enabling victims to avail of Savitri Bai Phule Yojna grants for small industry and farming in Aurangabad district. Some committee members have formed Bachat Gats (self-help groups) to make the women financially independent. A committee member started a group of 500 women in Sindhudurg and found them employment, for example, making of soaps, furniture, and enabling them to start cloth and grocery shops.

A respondent has mentioned having helped a mentally challenged girl of Sasawad, a subdivision Purandhar in Pune, after she was found raped and pregnant. The victim was admitted to Yerwada mental hospital with the help of the local council and the police station, where she subsequently delivered a baby girl. Similarly, a girl who was being physically abused by her uncle was rehabilitated by a member in Aurangabad and a case of rape registered against her uncle. Some members have also been active in stopping child marriages. Dissemination of information, especially on law and free legal aid, seems to be widely undertaken by Dakshata committees.

Many members have been working in the field of girl education. A member of Sangali Mahila Dakshata Samiti encouraged Gosawi Samaj to send their girls to schools. Some who had left education were encouraged to seek admission again. Many members seem to be working for awareness among the teenage girls, premarriage counseling, and handling parent-children disputes. Some have mentioned visiting remand homes, Mahila Asharams, and old-age homes. A few members have mentioned working for anti-human trafficking and against child labor. A respondent has mentioned having published a booklet on anti-human trafficking with 20 case studies, after working in this field in Latur.

Another point that emerged during the study and was corroborated by the firsthand experience of the researcher is that police officers frequently take the help of the members of the Samities when they have a woman victim and no women staff available in police stations. This is common in rural police stations where women police staff is not readily available. In delicate cases statements of victims are recorded in the presence of such members and the latter are cited witnesses in the court if the victim turns hostile during the trial.

Implications for the Future and for Community Policing

Considering that women in India are still most apprehensive about approaching police for help, and that the patriarchal system continues to dominate, involving women at the district level has been a good initiative in Maharashtra. Introduced 25 years ago, it has gone beyond the symbolic gesture stage and can be said to be active in bringing gender issues related to crime in focus. In fact, the study shows that the Mahila Dakshata Samities created to pursue registration and investigation of cases have been active in related fields too; for example, members have been holding camps for legal literacy, attending to the issues of extramarital affairs and alcoholism, and so forth. With direct access to senior police officers from whom the members get a fair amount of cooperation, they have received recognition in their areas, prompting them to deal with gender issues at their level as well as to take them to police authorities.

It has emerged from the study that while women in general may still not be comfortable in going to police stations, members of Mahila Dakshata Samities have a high degree of comfort level, and thus have been acting as mediators. Their further training and professional grooming can make the Samities more effective and improve their performance. The government of Maharashtra, by putting in some funds, can contribute to an existing good practice instead of reinventing the wheel.

Involving women in law enforcement has been a definite step forward for the traditional Indian society. It has given a positive signal to women and shall thus ensure their active participation in other police initiatives involving the community. Reserving 33% seats for women in government and in police has further helped in creating an atmosphere of inclusive growth. Despite the recent growth of the country, especially in the IT sector, women continue to be apprehensive about their security and fearful of approaching police; thus Mahila Dakshata Samities has been a successful practice that has lasted for 25 years and can be further strengthened to enable it to remain relevant and useful for women.

Recommendations

1. Having been constituted 25 years ago and having worked effectively and efficiently, the Mahila Dakshata Samities have proved their usefulness to the community. However, they need to be strengthened further. A detailed review of their performance is due for further action in this regard. Having constituted police station-level committees, the role of district committees can be debated, though the instant study found them to be useful and effective fora. Their success also lies in the fact that they have continued to work and establish themselves over a quarter century. However, by creating Mahila Kaksh at the police station level and Mahila Dakshata Samities at Taluka and police station levels, there seems to be some duplication as well as confusion. It needs to be sorted out.
2. To introduce fresh vigor, the Office of the Director General of Police, along with its district units, should repledge its faith in these committees by analyzing their original charter and broadening the same, for example, anti-human trafficking. In fact, the circular of 1985 that constituted these committees as social security cells is very brief, and only symbolic in providing a small forum for interaction between police and women at the district level. It needs to be revisited and the working of the committees broadened in view of the changed times. It is true that due to the constitution of police station-level committees, the burden of district Mahila Dakshata Samities has been reduced. However, being comprised of very senior police officers, these committees command more respect and influence. They are able to influence the policy makers, as opposed to police station committees, which are restricted to the local police station area.
3. Membership can also be further increased to 10 per district. While redefining the role of these committees has not been undertaken, membership has been revised twice by the director general of police during the last 25 years. It has thus gone up to five, from only one in 1985. Broadening the membership can enhance their working; however, selection of apolitical persons needs to be adhered to.
4. A small budget provision needs to be made for Mahila Dakshata Samities and members be paid travel expenses and honorarium for attending the meetings. This has been voiced very strongly by most members and is a justified need of the project.

5. The Office of the Director General of Police can enhance the managerial skills of the members and increase their efficiency by organizing training workshops for them at regular intervals. This can be budgeted for at the district level. Many respondents have themselves asked for training in tackling women-related issues.

Conclusion

Mahila Dakshata Samities are now well established in the state of Maharashtra, and citizens as well as police have come to expect their help in women-related issues. The committees have brought law enforcement agencies closer to the community. Their effective functioning is, however, dependent on the dynamism of the local members and the interest that the district police leadership takes. They suffer from certain infirmities, for example, low induction of new members, less representation to young women, and lack of funds and training. However, having lasted for more than 25 years, their broad contribution to the cause of the community, especially women, needs to be applauded. The instant study has strongly recommended budgetary provisions for Dakshata Samities for meeting some basic expenses, like travel and honorarium for the members. Enhancement of the managerial and counseling skills of the members through regular training is also suggested. Review of the committees and broadening of their charter and membership will ensure that they continue to address the special needs of women, for which they were created 25 years ago. Mahila Dakshata Samities can thus be safely concluded to be a successful example of a community-police partnership in Maharashtra, to be celebrated and talked about. They can be replicated in other states given the leadership.

Friends of Police (FOP)
A Concept for Empowerment and a Movement in Community Policing

6

PRATEEP V. PHILIP

A movement in community policing called Friends of Police (FOP) was started in 1993 in Ramanathapuram district of Tamil Nadu, India, and within a few months of its inception nearly 1,000 members of the public from all walks of life volunteered to become FOPs in Ramanathapuram district. Taking note of its value, the FOP movement was extended to the entire state in September 1994 by a government order following a cost-benefit analysis presented at a state-level conference in the presence of the entire cabinet, top bureaucracy, and police leadership. Through the years, the movement has been well received by the wider public, voluntary associations, and the police force. Currently, there are well nigh 300,000 FOP volunteers all over the state of Tamil Nadu. This is one of the largest community policing initiatives anywhere in the world, and it has helped establish better relations and cooperation between the police and the community. This chapter describes the movement in Tamil Nadu and analyzes its genesis as a community policing model.

The Rationale

From the moment human beings organized themselves into communities some sort of an agency was required to enforce agreed norms to safeguard themselves. As communities grew bigger, their self-policing capacity became weaker. So stronger means of legal control had to be resorted to. This ushered in the police with the mandate to prevent crime and maintain law and order. The police is the first and most immediate point of contact between citizens in their everyday life and the state.

Colonial India envisaged its first line of enforcement, that is, the police, as a means of controlling crime and maintenance of law and order.

Community policing's effectiveness should stem from the fact that crime detection would be improved as a result of more and better information being received from the public—a public inclined to cooperate with the police because of its approval of the manner in which the police become more involved with the community.

Unfortunately, despite the tremendous challenges, the police today in virtually every nation and state are isolated from friends and foes alike. They suffer a problem of not just a no-image or low-image situation, but a highly negative image among the public at large, in the minds of the leaders, in the media, as well as in their own ranks. The general image of the police, a legacy of earlier times, is that it is a blunt-edged instrument to perpetuate and perform the will and whims of the powers that be. Complaints of police torture and custodial violence have further accentuated the negative image.

A general atmosphere of lack of mutual trust, respect, and confidence between the law-abiding public and law-enforcing police prevails. This sometimes surfaces and erupts into open hostility between different sections of the public and the police. At the best and worst of times, this gulf between the police and the public hampers and hinders the functioning of the police in facing the growing challenges. The police also often fail to distinguish between the vast majority of law-abiding people and the comparatively smaller number of law breakers who have to be dealt with with an iron hand. The irony is that though the police exist for the safety of the public, they work in a vacuum of a lack of goodwill, lack of information and feedback, and a general lack of cooperation. The phenomenon of police isolation and public antagonism is global. Hence there is an urgent need the world over for aggressive social marketing of the police.

The man donning the khaki uniform is perceived as a corrupt, brutal person given to frequent use of violence and torture. People are ready to believe the worst when a policeman is involved in any misadventure. Every lapse is attributed to corruption. On the other hand, good work done by the police is rarely noticed and still rarely appreciated. The FOP movement can, to a large extent, correct this image of the policeman among the public, and the jaundiced eye with which the people view the police. Prejudice is born out of ignorance, and to a large extent the police are responsible for it. In this context, community policing is all about forging a cost-effective problem-solving partnership between the police and the people.

Philosophical, Ethical, Sociological, and Psychological Roots

The people give the police the power, and through the FOP the police can give back the power to the people. The word *friend* comes from the Latin word *phile*, which means "love." If you love yourself, you are interested in your self-preservation and promotion. The FOP concept is holistic in the sense it is based on the philosophy of true friendship or relationship. If you love yourself, you need to observe and adopt certain principles of conduct—you must be first and foremost a friend of principles. In the FOP multimedia training, we first focus on intrapersonal communication. What do you communicate to your deeper, intimate self? What is your self-view as opposed to your worldview? Unless intrapersonal communication is on sound grounds, interpersonal communication cannot be. Unless the policemen view their role as policemen or officers as holistic and sound, the enactment of their public duties would be flawed. In pursuit of this goal, the FOP training takes place on the paradigm of ASK, or attitude first and foremost, skills (soft) next, and knowledge or facts or information last. The feedback received about these modules from year to year in each district and city in separate feedback sessions has been excellent.

The FOP approach is a formula and a strategy of sharing power and corresponding responsibility with the people. There is an "inner policeman" in every individual with a conception of what constitutes right and wrong, just and unjust, good and bad. The popularity of the policeman in fiction, on the screen, or in fine print contrasts sharply with the image of the flesh and blood counterparts in real life. This hiatus is due to the failure to develop the inner policeman. The FOP approach is a way to develop and sublimate the inner policeman. At the same time, the honorific FOP meets the self-esteem needs of the average individual, as association with the police in this manner lends glamour and status to the average citizen who evinces some interest in public affairs.

The Friends of Police movement tends to end the social isolation imposed on the police, individually and as an organization, by the traditional, reactive, and negative model of policing. To illustrate, in India when a police jeep is sighted in a village a child will raise his or her hand in a reflexive salute with a broad grin of recognition. As the child grows older and gets, so to say, socialized, the reaction will vary between a stony stare or a catcall as the vehicle gets beyond reach.

The Solution

Such an all-pervasive, overpowering negative image of the police force has been sought to be negated and made positive by initiating a movement in community policing. The fundamental nature of this movement is to foster and crystallize the hitherto untapped sentiments of goodwill for the police that exist among the general public. It is expected that the movement will go a long way to transform the police image, open up channels of communication between the police and the public, and provide a reservoir of goodwill, feedback, intelligence, and manpower with a view to establishing peace and amity among people.

The movement aims at bringing police and the public closer and building a bridge between the police and the public, to use the pithy words of a fisherman from Ramanathapuram district. This movement seeks free flow of information between the police and the public. It aims to be helpful in creating channels for receiving the right information at the right time, and also help police in correcting its negative image. The public will come to know of the good work being done by police as well as the challenges and difficulties faced by them in day-to-day operations. On the other hand, the police will get the information on public sentiments on various issues. Individual empowerment of citizens will enable some of them to pass on timely and accurate criminal intelligence to appropriate levels in the police.

By becoming a member of the FOP one feels a sense of belonging and responsibility. Such feeling prevents one from doing certain acts himself and convincing others of the futility of such acts. It helps to promote crime awareness among the people and enable prevention of crimes. It also promotes a sense of civic responsibilities and duties of the public—a means of educating the general public. It can impart fairness, transparency, and impartiality in the working of police. It can help police in restoring lost faith of the public in police.

This is a useful, holistic, and proactive concept and a tool to transform the police image, strengthen the force, and create attitudinal changes both within the force and among the public. It is an experiment worth being tried in every nation and every district. It is a formula and method of sharing policing power and responsibility with the public in an increasingly complex and dangerous world. The movement received further fillip with the Queen's Award for Innovation in Police Training and Development 2002 coming its way out of a competition involving police departments of 55 nations of the commonwealth. It is expected that the movement will go a long way to transform the police image, open up channels of communication, and provide a reservoir of goodwill, feedback, intelligence, and manpower.

The FOP started in Ramanathapuram district is a movement that empowers ordinary citizens vis-à-vis the police. Social development comes when the best investments in social and economic policy are those that empower the individual. The FOP will help in projecting the right kind of image of the police. The public has come to know of the good work being done by them and help them. On the other hand, the police got the feel of public sentiments on various issues.

Sometimes the arguments of the man in uniform may not be satisfactory to the general public because of the existing perception. But the same thing from a fellow citizen can have the desired effect. The FOPs serve as ambassadors of goodwill connecting the police and the public.

Objectives of the FOP Movement

- To separate the friends from the foes of the police or "the chaff from the grain."
- To enable members of the public without regard to caste, creed, or status, to establish rapport with police. It is a method of people empowerment.
- To promote crime awareness among the people and enable prevention of crimes.
- To promote a sense of civic responsibilities and duties of the public as a means of educating the general public. To learn as well as to teach human values.
- To act as a force multiplier by involving the FOPs in community policing. With the existing low police-public ratio, the COP along with the FOP can deter and prevent crimes.
- To evolve a mechanism to get feedback.
- To channelize local resources at short notice to meet any eventuality.
- To make available a potential pool of manpower resources with positive attitudes to the police to meet the requirement of police.
- To increase transparency and openness in the police.
- FOP can take steps toward policing with consent instead of the present image of policing with contempt.
- To educate the members of the public about their role and responsibility in policing.
- To enable the police to prevent commission of criminal offenses.

Qualifications to Become an FOP

- Every Friend of Police shall be a citizen and a resident in the district in which he applies for membership as a volunteer.
- He or she shall not be involved in any civil or criminal case so that the prospective FOP has no axe to grind with the police.
- No educational qualification or employment is prescribed, but he or she shall be preferably literate to enable written communications.
- Age: minimum age of 18, maximum of 70.
- In short, any member of the public has to send a letter to the superintendent of police giving his or her name, age, and address pledging his or her friendship.

After verification, the FOPs are issued identity cards or armbands prominently marked FOP. An important caveat is that no FOP shall misuse the new identity. Involvement in a criminal case will lead to automatic disqualification as FOP. This in itself will act as a check on the number of persons joining the ranks of antisocial and criminal elements. Becoming an FOP gives a sense of identity and identification with the police. It helps every FOP to sublimate and realize the inner policeman in every individual that draws him or her to the police. Through the local media, the district chief of police can appeal to the members of the public, to join as FOPs. A member of the public willing to become an FOP will state in his or her application form his or her name, age, occupation, and the capacity in which he or she wishes to assist the police (crime prevention, antivice campaign, victim assistance, information, night beat, patrolling, traffic assistance, or any other related service). The target must be to enroll at least 1% of the total population in the area as FOPs. But each FOP must join voluntarily. Thereafter each FOP can introduce more to the fold, and eventually a few thousand will be enrolled in every police district, leading to a network of FOPs all over the nation and the world.

Judging from the success in the state of Tamil Nadu, India, the FOP movement bodes well for the image of the police. It provides an opportunity for the average citizen to contribute his or her might in whatever way possible. It has transformed the image of the police so much that constables report that villagers now approach them without fear, and indeed with some degree of regard. A great number of FOPs have given useful information to police leading to detection of crimes. The FOPs also accompany cops regularly on night patrol and beat duty.

COP and FOP: A Synergistic Model

The human rights issue has become a major factor in determining the course of policing of the country. In India, the National Human Rights Commission has been set up to monitor and check the human rights violations. Therefore, there is a need for rethinking the working of the police organization. In today's information age, information is power. If we have meaningful information, we can achieve our targets effectively and with minimum use of force. Here meaningful information means information that is relevant to our work. In earlier days, information was collected through covert sources. But nowadays it is difficult to collect all the relevant information through covert sources, because the present manpower is not sufficient for doing this job, as it is already overburdened and overworked. In this context, the FOP movement can be very helpful in creating channels for receiving the right information at the right time. It can also help police in correcting its negative image in the minds of the public. It can impart fairness, transparency, and impartiality in the working of police.

It can help police in restoring the lost faith of the public in police. The police must be careful while vetting the Friends of Police. They must check their past records, credentials, and antecedents before accepting them as FOPs, because one wrong deed by a black sheep can negate the good work done by many others. People are ready to share information with the police provided the police assure them protection. Until now a common man was scared to have any relationship with a policeman or with police in any form. The reason may be a fear psychosis regarding the police or the police culture of looking at every person with suspicion or their abrasive behavior with the public. The maxim for the police in today's world will read: "Cops alone can't do the job; cops along with FOP can do it" (COP = community-oriented police, FOP = Friends of Police). Community-oriented policemen assisted by the FOPs will constitute a humanistic, ethical, and people-oriented model, as opposed to the isolationist, amoral, reactionary, status quo paramilitary model that is in force in most parts of the world.

Impact Analysis of the Friends of Police Movement

A survey was undertaken in May 1996 covering all the districts and commissionerates in the state of Tamil Nadu. The objective of the survey was to discover the impact of the FOP movement from the point of few of those who joined as FOPs as well as station house officers of 222 police stations. Separate questionnaires were administered to the FOPs and subinspectors in charge of police stations. Their responses revealed their perceptions and attitudes as well as their views on the utility of the FOP concept and movement. Subsequent surveys were conducted several times over the years to evaluate the ongoing impact, and these surveys confirm and further reinforce the impact analysis given below.

An analysis of the data collected was quite revealing. One hundred sixty-seven FOPs in all parts of the state were interviewed. Nearly 40% of the FOPs were in the age group 18 to 25 years, while 30% were in the age group 25 to 30 years. Eighty-seven percent of the FOPs enrolled were in the active age group of 18 to 40 years. The younger elements of the population are more involved as the FOPs. Just over 17% of the FOPs interviewed were students, while 33% were either engaged in business or agriculture. The single largest group was engaged in business (23%). Thirteen percent of the FOPs were unemployed people, while 16% were self-employed. These statistics show that beyond earning a livelihood, people want an opportunity to serve society. With regard to educational qualification, 22% had studied up to 10th Standard, 18% had completed 10th Standard, 22% had completed intermediate, while the single largest group were graduates. They constituted 33%. Postgraduates accounted for less than 3% of the volunteers. The survey shows that more literate and educated persons are attracted enough to enroll as FOPs. Sixty-two percent of the respondents stated that they had helped at some time or other in the investigation of crime, while an overwhelming 83% stated they had helped in the maintenance of law and order.

Sixty-two percent of respondents stated that they could now understand and appreciate the difficulties in policing—acting as an FOP tends to create a sense of sympathy and empathy in the members of the public. An overwhelming 88% of respondents felt that they had acquired the sense of pride of policing. Eighty-three percent of the FOP stated that they had improved their knowledge of legal duties and obligations. Seventy-five percent of the FOPs propagated the concept of FOP in their circle. They tend to act as leaders within their environment.

Ninety-one percent of FOPs stated that they had not been misused by the police for their personal ends, while 84% stated that to their knowledge no FOP had misused his or her status. Misuse of the FOPs by police and misuse of status as the FOPs are at a minimal level.

Thirty-six percent of the FOPs covered stated that they had met the Station House Officer (SHO) on a monthly basis. Thirty-two percent of respondents stated that they had met the SHO on a weekly basis, while 19 and 12% of respondents met the SHO on a fortnightly and quarterly basis, respectively. Regular meetings with the FOPs keep them going while giving the SHO a feel of the pulse and needs of the community.

Sixty-eight percent of the respondents felt that the local press did not publish the good work done by the FOP, while 27% felt that the press did publish the good work done by them. Recognition by the press will go a long way to galvanize them into action.

Ninety-one percent of the respondents did not have any procedural difficulty in joining as an FOP. Ninety percent of the respondent FOPs stated that they got the cooperation of the constabulary in policing. Ninety-four percent felt that the subinspector effectively coordinated their work as the FOPs. Ninety-five percent of the FOPs stated that they had never got any rough treatment from any police officer/policeman. Eighty-seven percent of the FOPs felt that the interaction with police officers was satisfactory. With regard to involvement of superior officers, nearly 50% of the FOPs had met a superior officer above the SHO level, while 50% had not met a superior officer.

Thirty-one percent of respondents stated that they wished to serve the public and the police force. Twenty percent stated that they enrolled as FOPs to promote a better police-public relationship. Nineteen percent stated they joined to secure social status as FOPs. Four percent stated they joined due to peer pressure. Six percent stated they joined since they were unemployed. Another 6% stated they joined out of a sense of adventure. The service motivation is the predominant motive for individuals to be enrolled as FOPs.

Eighteen percent of respondents stated that they had gone on beats and night patrols. Eleven percent stated that they had assisted in traffic. Ten percent stated they had helped in crime prevention. Another 10% claimed they had helped in intelligence work. Nearly 9% stated they had been involved in bandobust (security) work, while another 9% stated they were involved in law and order maintenance. Some of the respondents (3.5%) stated that they were involved in prohibition work.

These statistics reveal that the FOP has played an active role in assisting the police in all spheres and areas of policing.

Twelve percent of the FOP respondents suggested that some allowance may be given to them as an incentive. Eight percent felt that a traveling pass may be given. One percent of respondents asked for some form of uniform and identity card. Seventy-six percent of respondents did not ask for any extra incentive. The opportunity for community service and social recognition seemed to serve as the primary incentive. Subsequent surveys and feedback sessions conducted in various districts showed that there is now a widespread expectation of some kind of honorarium to cover incidental expenses of volunteers.

The findings of the survey conducted through questionnaires administered to the SHO station house officers of 222 police stations (nearly one-third of the total number of police stations in the state) corroborate the perceptions of the FOPs. These surveys establish that the balance sheet of the FOP movement is on the plus side. The surveys revealed that more encouragement needed to be given to the movement from the level of the circle inspector upwards. Subdivision officers and district Superintendents of Police (SPs) have a crucial role in encouraging the SHOs and FOP to act as partners and prime movers of community policing. This will doubtless ensure a better quality of life, a better quality of policing, better police-public relations, and a better image for the police.

Training and Documentation of FOP Movement

After winning the 15,000 pound-sterling Queen's Award for Innovation in Police Training and Development in 2002, a pilot project was set up as Friends of Police Documentation and Multimedia Training Center in Chennai. The center was subsequently recognized by the state government as Asia's First Citizens Community Policing Academy and given funding to the tune of 2 million rupees per annum. The FOP center has succeeded in developing training modules that have been extended since 2003 to all cities and districts of Tamil Nadu. Every year since 2003, 200 police personnel and 200 FOPs are sensitized in five workshops conducted in every district/commissionerate in the state. Out of the 100,000 participants who had attended the training up to 2010, 50,000 were police personnel of ranks from police constable to assistant commissioners of police or deputy superintendents of police, and 50,000 FOPs from all ages, different backgrounds, and walks of life. As many as 1,300 workshops with unique training modules have been completed between 2003 and 2010. The training modules include the following subjects:

- What is community policing?
- Role of FOP—the dos and don'ts
- Equilibrium thinking to mold attitudes
- Neurolinguistic programming
- Team-building skills
- Communication skills
- Listening and body language
- Rapport-building skills
- Problem-solving skills
- Questioning skills

The trainers are members of the public. They are a pool of committed academics and corporate trainers who understand the vision of the FOP. Content of training includes multimedia presentations, role play, an FOP documentary, simulations, and games. The workshops conducted every year are evaluated by experts based on analyzing the pre- and posttraining questionnaires.

Harnessing Human Resources

Every time, when a state announces recruitment of say 3,000 to 10,000 constables, more than 10 times that number apply. This enables us to gauge the extent of idle human resources eager and willing to be employed as policemen or policewomen. Large numbers of these candidates have volunteered as the FOPs in Tamil Nadu, and a good number have been subsequently employed either as constables or subinspectors of police. It needs a fairly longer run-up than just six months or two years of training, as the case may be for constables or subinspectors, but when they volunteer as FOPs they develop their aptitude and abilities to serve as full-time police professionals. A few FOPs have even succeeded in joining as DySPs or Assistant Superintendents of Police (ASPs), and one FOP student coordinator belonging to a minority community has joined the Indian Foreign Service (IFS) and is currently serving in the UK. The FOP multimedia training as well as the leadership training they get while volunteering service is a huge asset in preparing them for their future career. As many as 200 students are enthusiastic members of the student FOP wing that has been started in leading colleges in Chennai, like Loyola College, Vivekananda College, and other institutions. If some weight is given at the time of selection for police personnel who had served as FOPs, it will further augment the movement.

The Future Prospects of the Movement

A former professor of Loyola College, Chennai, and director of the State Resource Center for Nonformal and Adult Education, functioning under the Human Resources Development (HRD) Ministry, has been visiting some of the districts of Tamil Nadu recently to study the functioning of the FOP. He has already visited five police commissionerates, namely, the districts of Ramanathapuram, Dindigul, Namakkal, Nilgiris, and the city of Coimbatore. In his report he stated that positive feedback that emanated from the police was amazing and their camaraderie with the FOP was exemplary and praiseworthy.

He has conducted five focus group discussions in each district and city, totally meeting about 1,000 police personnel and 1,000 members of the public to understand how the FOP movement has been evolving and how it could be made more efficient and better organized for the benefit of the people at large.

The Striking Features

- All the police personnel appreciated the Friends of Police and were of the opinion that they were very useful to them in discharging their duties. Of course, a couple of voices once in a while expressed that they did not have enough FOPs in their police station areas.
- The FOPs join the police in their night beats, bandobust duties during festivals, and traffic regulation, and give valuable information about crimes either committed or going to be committed. It is amazing to note that there are hundreds of instances where the FOPs have helped the police to apprehend culprits. The identities of the people who have given information have not been revealed for security reasons.

In short, the FOP has come to stay as a change agent ushering in peace and harmony. It emerged from the focus group discussions among the police and FOPs that an FOP network is a must under the supervision of the police and mentoring of experts from various fields for establishing an ideal civil society where people and all the departments of the government converge.

The Friends of Police should double as Friends of People, and it is a great opportunity to make it happen. The right moment has come and is beckoning the powers that be to rise to the occasion right now and strike when the iron is hot.

FOP-Central Association of Private Security Industry (CAPSI) Partnership

In December 2009, the representatives and leaders of an additional 5.5 million private security guards working in all parts of India under the umbrella of the private security industry have shown their enthusiasm to be empowered as Friends of Police. As part of this new initiative, 70 private security industry managers have been trained as trainers in community policing.

The training of trainers module administered to 70 private security industry managers has led to the know-how of community policing being imparted by them to 200 of their ground-level guards in Chennai.

Cycle Rally

On October 23, 2010, a four-member FOP team successfully completed its cycling expedition around India along the border covering more than 15,000 km. The mission was flagged off by Dr. Prateep Philip, IPS, founder director of the FOP, on May 10, 2010, near Chidambaram Bus Stand. The Friends of Police cycled through 25 states, spreading the message of the need for a public-police partnership and conservation of nature. In the process the four young men, namely, D. Mahendran (26), J. Anbuselvan (20), V. Vinothraj (22), and R. Rajaselvam (20), have met with various experiences, including a few instances of encounters with death. "We have realized new dimensions in life," opined Mahendran, the team leader. "There were at least three instances when we thought we were at the end of everything."*

The FOP volunteers enjoyed the hospitality of the police fraternity, touching more than 130 police stations across the nation where they were provided with a place to rest and food to eat. The youngsters who have just crossed their adolescence were significantly treated with an India that is overburdened with poverty and violence. These are the two dominant impressions they have brought back and they sincerely feel that they have a lot to do to make India a great nation. Even nature, according to them, has been writhing under pain and inflicting pain on humanity, sequentially having been mishandled by humans. But for the punctuated encouragement showered on

* Personal communications to the author.

them by the genuine loving care of the common man once in a while and the continued support of the police in all the states, they have only impressions of misery to carry home.

"We will devote our lives for making the grand ethos of FOP relevant to people all over India so that the movement matures into a way of life and makes the lives of people safe, joyful and beautiful,"* was their parting shot.

Concluding Remarks

For such a movement to be successful there are certain prerequisites. The supervisory officers should show a keen interest. A continuous effort is necessary. Just enrollment as members of the FOP would not serve the purpose of the movement. The public has to be really involved so that they feel they are part of the system. For the Friends of Police movement to be successful it is necessary that the public begin to perceive police as friends of the public or the public as friends of the police.

Every forward movement produces a counterforce of resistance and the FOP is no exception. The police are not everywhere, all the time, but people are everywhere, all the time. Hence, any ground-level intelligence can percolate from the local people. Take the case of the landing of Pakistan-based terrorists in a fishing hamlet off the coast of Mumbai: had there been FOP in that locality, they would have noticed the 10 young men with backpacks, dressed neatly in jeans and T-shirts, landing in rubber dinghys on the beach. Ground-level intelligence can emanate only from citizens on the spot where the action begins. It will give a head start or a lead to the police.

FOP is a cost-effective solution in the sense that it resolves the quantitative problem of numbers, of inadequate police personnel for a given population. It also addresses the qualitative problem of motivation and morale of the police personnel, the commitment of the citizenry to a good quality life and good quality policing, the ground support for the police, the empathy of the public with the difficulties of the police, and the flow of information, intelligence, and goodwill toward the police. The police in India, as elsewhere, face the issue of the quantitative problem of an inadequate police-public ratio given the spectrum of problems facing the country and the security forces, and the qualitative problem of insufficient motivation and training. FOP makes a contribution to resolving both questions cost-effectively.

To conclude, the FOP movement is a hearts and minds strategy that seeks to turn people not just into eyes and ears for the police in these troubled

* Personal communications to the author.

times, but into hands of friendship and partnership in addressing common challenges. There is no gainsaying the fact that it is a concept for empowerment and a movement in community policing. For one thing, the fear level among the public regarding the police has fallen drastically because of community participation in policing. The hostility toward the police has declined given the fact that the number of attacks on policemen and police stations has declined.

7

Janamaithri Suraksha Project
Community Policing Project of the Government of Kerala

B. SANDHYA

Introduction

Even though the Indian police were shaped by the British for maintaining their Raj and yet institutionalized to serve British colonial policies, in modern India the same force has transformed itself to abide by the democratic ethos of the country. Law enforcement in Indian democracy seeks to ensure public security by securing and enlisting the willing cooperation of people. Kerala police have been at the forefront in implementing a variety of community policing schemes that have provided a safe and secure environment for the residents. Kerala police subscribe to the perspective that the citizens are subject to the law, which they themselves create by means of established legislative processes. Therefore they also need to proactively participate in the process of preventing violations of enacted law. Community policing seeks the responsible participation of the citizens in crime prevention at the level of the local community. This helps in not only conserving the resources, both of the community and of the police, but also effectively fighting crimes that threaten the security of the people. Kerala experience shows that by seeking the active cooperation of the public in performance of police duties, the process of law enforcement becomes far more effective.

Social Context of Community Policing in Kerala

Kerala is the most literate state of India and has also been reported as the least corrupt state (Transparency International, 2005).* High literacy has led to an

* Transparency International. 2005. India Corruption Study 2005 — Summary Highlights, Press Release June 30.

interesting situation wherein the state has high media penetration, with 0.78 million copies of print media and 16 TV channels. This has further ensured that any new idea will be immediately under media scrutiny. Furthermore, 10% of Kerala population lives outside the country, generally in Gulf states. At least 20% of the population has visited a foreign country, and by these reasons alone it is safe to presume that the people view things in a global perspective. Kerala is also a highly politicized state with a long history of people's participation in civic affairs. Kerala was the first state in the world to freely elect a communist government in 1959. Ever since, the communist parties have been elected to office a number of times. Kerala is also a diverse state with large proportions of Muslims and Christian people. The population is multireligious, with 50% belonging to minority groups. Nevertheless, the people are highly tolerant, and in comparison to the rest of India, communal riots and conflicts have been minimal. This tolerance extends in other dimensions too. For example, in the same family you may find people working for different political parties. There are no nuclear villages, and everywhere the people live intermixed in dense congregations. Kerala is not highly industrialized and the state has no major industries. But, the service sector is well developed and tourism, with the slogan "God's own country," is a major contributor to the state's economy.

The Police in Kerala

The region of Kerala was earlier part of the Madras province and governed from the erstwhile Madras city. The region consisted of the princely states of Travancore and Cochin, as well as the Malabar region. While some form of traditional royal police system prevailed, the modern police were created in 1861, along with the reorganization of Indian police by the British rulers. The system has continued ever since, but in 1956, after India's independence, a reorganization of states was carried out and the new state of Kerala with Malayalam-speaking people was established. At present, the police are organized provincially, consisting of approximately 42,149 personnel of various ranks. The director general of police (DGP) is the senior-most officer, and most of the senior ranks are held by the members of the Indian Police Service (IPS), who control district-level police units and all the specialized branches. The Kerala police serve a population of over 31.8 million, residing in 5 cities, 53 municipal towns, and 1,452 villages spread over an area of 38,863 square kilometers, with an average population density of 819 per square kilometer. Of this, about 8.2 million people live in urban areas and 23.6 million live in rural areas. The police investigate about 175,000 crimes per year.

The lowest rank is of police constable, where traditionally a high school-level education is required for appointment. However, constables of Kerala are highly qualified, and perhaps the highest-qualified police personnel in India. This has a historical background. The *Travancore State Manual*, by T.K. Velu Pillai (1882–1950) (first published in 1940), mentioned that only literate persons were recruited in the police force. Men of high education were commonly chosen to fill places in the subordinate ranks. The document further states that "prominent persons like Mahatma Gandhi have been so much impressed with the discipline and courtesy exhibited by the generality of the force that they have thought it fit to give them high compliment by comparing them with London Police."

Community-Oriented Policing in Kerala

Against the backdrop of such a social milieu, many individual officers of Kerala had attempted and succeeded in implementing community policing programs. An institutionalized effort was made on the recommendation of the Justice K.T. Thomas Commission, appointed by the government of Kerala to suggest police reforms. The report recommended that the government should implement community policing on an experimental basis. Accordingly the government asked the police department to prepare and submit a draft scheme. The draft scheme submitted by the department in 2007 was discussed elaborately at various levels, and based on suggestions/recommendations by various persons, a final project was prepared by the police department.

The community policing scheme of the Kerala police was named Janamaithri Suraksha Paddhathi, and initially implemented on an experimental basis in three police station limits, each in the Kozhikode, Kochi, and Thiruvananthapuram districts. The project was conceived to provide security to the community as its prime objective, and the effort of the department was to achieve this with people's participation and closer liaison between the police and the general public.

The project is structured so as to facilitate closer community involvement in ensuring security and safety within communities. The project envisages to achieve the following objectives:

1. To prevent crime
2. Cooperation of the police and the public in security matters
3. To ensure mutual cooperation of members of the public in the domain of security

The project envisaged strengthening the police by seeking support of the local community. It was not a project aimed at bettering the image of the police, and it was also not a project wherein police duties were to be performed by the citizens. Rather, it was a project to professionally strengthen police and increase their accessibility to the needy public through closer interaction with and better understanding of the public. The responsibility was entrusted to the beat officers, who were instructed to ensure that all the citizens living in the area were known to the police and every citizen was acquainted with the beat officers. The project centered around beat officers who were the police constables/head constables/assistant subinspectors, specially selected and trained.

Beat Officer Duties

The scheme was designed so that for each residential area, forming one Jana Souhrida consisting of around 1000 houses within an area of 3 km there will be a beat officer. All the duties of the police relating to patrolling, process service, petition enquiry, verification, collection of public complaints, servicing of complaint boxes, etc. will be done, subject to proper supervision through such a Beat Officer. It was also stressed that within two or three months of becoming the beat officer, the concerned police personnel should personally know at least one member of each family living in his beat, all the roads and by-lanes in the area, the working habits of the local people, and their special needs on a house-to-house basis. At least three days a week, the beat officer should be available for an hour or so at a preannounced place in the beat so that anybody who wants to communicate information to the police station may meet him there. The beat officer has been provided with a Janamaithri bike specially painted, depicting the Janamaithri emblem, which makes it easier for everyone to recognize the officer.

The beat officer is also required to maintain a beat register showing the daily activities and daily transactions with respect to the beat, and such a beat register is examined by the station house officer everyday. Women police constables have also been detailed as assistant beat officers, so that problems of women could be addressed properly. As a novel incentive the women police constables have been provided with a two-wheeler. The beat officers are further required to attend the Janamaithri Suraksha Samithi meeting every month with the local community. The scheme ensures that the beat officer shall spend at least 20 hours a week actually moving about and meeting residents in his beat. A major issue has been to stress that the beat officer conducts himself in an exemplary manner. Special training courses and periodical evaluations are done for making beat officers fully competent for the task.

Janamaithri Suraksha Samithi

Janamaithri Suraksha Samithi is a local committee formed to assist the project function smoothly. It was stressed that Samithi members should have time to spare for its activities, and they shall not be involved in any criminal cases. Further, to ensure that the Samithi does not get involved in any political activity, the scheme lays down that this committee will not have any statutory powers.

The Janamaithri Suraksha Samithi is composed of corporation/municipal councilors, representatives of each active residents' association, non-governmental organizations (NGOs), local representatives, nominees of every high school head master/college principal, reputed persons of the locality, retired police personnel, and ex-service personnel. The Samithi is stipulated to have 10% senior citizens, 30% ladies, and 20% scheduled caste/scheduled tribe members to ensure that weaker sections of society are well represented in the committee. Active members of political parties are not included in the Samiti even though the membership ranges from 10 to 25 people.

This scheme has been institutionalized through police administrative arrangements by requiring that Janamaithri Suraksha Samithi has to be formed in the police station based upon the report submitted by the circle inspector, through the subdivisional police officer to the superintendent of police/commissioner of police, who ultimately sanctions the formation of Samithi.

Meetings of the Samithi

The Samithi is required to meet at least once in a month at a previously notified place, and any member of the public, residing within the local area of the police station, may also attend the meeting to give suggestions/air complaints.

No criminal cases under investigation or trial, however, can be discussed in the Samithi. Similarly, no discussion can be made of arrests or any other statutory functions of the police. The circle inspector convenes the meeting and Station House Officer (SHO) serves as the secretary of the Samithi. The subdivisional police officer also attends the meetings once every month, and the superintendent of police at least once a year. The minutes of the Samithi meetings are recorded and kept in a book, and these minutes are forwarded to the subdivisional police office on a regular basis.

Activities Under the Janamaithri Suraksha Samithi

The Janamaithri Suraksha Samithi formulates and implements, depending upon the local need, the following types of plans for betterment of policing and crime prevention in the concerned area:

- Formulation of joint police-community patrols, including night patrols to prevent thefts and street crimes in residential areas
- Identification of strangers and migrants to the area, to help the police ascertain their identity and antecedents
- Coordination with security guards of private establishments and residential colonies
- Establishment of 24-hour telephone help lines for use by citizens, especially the needy sections of society
- Formulation of plans for security measures and installation of security devices in houses, flats, shopping complexes, and so forth
- Identification of the needs of the disabled and aged population and of weaker sections living in the limits, and the devising of plans for ensuring their security
- Psychological counseling for victims of crime as well as disaster victims, suicide prevention
- Provision of accurate and timely information on faulty signal systems, street lighting arrangements, poorly maintained roads, and so forth, to the concerned authorities
- Organization and encouragement of blood donation camps, as well as eye and other organ donations, by willing donors in the local communities
- Development and implementation of plans for improved traffic regulation in the area, including coordination and management of traffic wardens
- Development of plans to give training to youth in first aid and trauma care, palliative care, blood donation, self-employment, and so forth, and to involve the youth in community-oriented projects
- Formation of Jagratha Samithis for women and for school/college students to arrange legal aid/counseling, and so on
- Organization of legal awareness classes, traffic awareness programs, blood donation camps, and so forth
- The setting up of a special program for security of taxi drivers and others involving local community road accident victims, highway Suraksha Jagratha Samithis
- Organization of volunteers to protect the environment
- Establishment of victim support cells

District Advisory Samithi

The superintendent of police and commissioner of police are required to form a Jilla Upadesaka Samithi, a committee comprising the local member of parliament, member of legislative assembly, municipal chairman/mayor, and also other representatives nominated by the superintendent of police/commissioner of police. This Samiti also has 10 to 20 numbers and is convened once in three months by the superintendent of police/commissioner of police. This committee acts in a supervisory manner and reviews the activities of the Janamaithri Suraksha Samithi and functions for the successful implementation of the community policing scheme.

Janamaithri Kendram

To popularize the concept of the Janamaithri Suraksha Project, Janamaithri Kendrams were opened in some places. These centers help people to come and learn about traffic safety, seek career guidance, and other helpful activities. Janamaithri Kendrams have begun functioning in some of the districts and in police battalion headquarters. The main objectives of the Kendram are to function as an information developing Janamaithri Yuvakendram, to provide sports and youth training facilities and counseling facilities for women, giving career planning and self-employment training, antidrug campaigns, and palliative care training, and to have a traffic education center/traffic park and other activities facilitating police-community interface to serve the community in a better manner. It is proposed to start Janamaithri Kendrams at 10 more places.

These centers also provide space to put up a notice board giving various news items, photographs, and so forth, on the Janamaithri Suraksha Project. Various posters inculcating traffic sense, civic sense, and so on among student communities are regularly displayed. Posters depicting help line numbers and awareness posters on drug abuse and crime against women are also prominently displayed. The center is developed as a community interaction place that also serves as the focal point to seek help from the public in educating the citizens about traffic accidents, quickly responding during natural calamities, and so on. These centers also bring together various voluntary groups/organizations that are working in the field of promoting peace, national integration, and communal harmony and are encouraged to associate with the center.

From the Nodal Officer's Diary

In order to describe the field activities of community policing a short case study is presented in terms of notes recorded by a police officer working at one such center.

> In 2007, I got an order from the government, giving me an additional responsibility to be the nodal officer for the community policing project of Kerala, to be conceived and implemented, as suggested by the Justice K.T. Thomas Commission. Mr. Jacob Punnoose, the then additional director general of police intelligence and chairman, Implementation Committee, asked me to prepare a project report. He specifically told me not to make it an exercise of literature review and dabbling in theoretical research papers. I was asked to develop a down-to-earth practical project to implement community-oriented policing in the area.
>
> We listed out a number of successful community policing initiatives of Kerala and various other states. Based on the models, around 17 feasible projects were prepared. Then we had discussions on the modalities, taking into consideration the demographic distribution, number of houses in urban and rural localities, and various other aspects. Finally our draft scheme was submitted to the authorities. The government was very particular about a dialogue and consultation with each and every section of the society, before finalizing what we could do. It was decided to have a state-level consultation meeting involving all political parties and representatives from each and every section of the society. The draft scheme was widely publicized, making it into a small booklet titled "Community Policing Project of Kerala (Draft) (Janamaithri Suraksha Project)."
>
> In Kerala the society is extremely skeptical about anything new. When the draft was circulated, many eyebrows were raised. However, we reiterated that it is only a draft and anybody interested has a stake in finalizing the scheme and that everybody is free and welcome to put forward his or her suggestions through email or post. The state-level consultation was held under the leadership of the home minister, opposition leader, and Justice K.T. Thomas at the government guest Thiruvananthapuram in September 2007. There was participation of all political party state-level leaders, intellectuals, sociologists, journalists, literature, planning board members, and even the NGOs. Indeed, each and every section of the society was well represented in these initial meetings. Many officers who were pioneers in community policing projects throughout the country were also invited to share their experiences.
>
> In the beginning, many apprehensions were shared in the meeting by various dignitaries. There were divided opinions and heated discussions. By the end of these sessions there was consensus that we needed a community policing project for a more secure and safe neighborhood and society. Everybody was requested to email or post his or her thoughtful written suggestions also. Those who attended the deliberations and studied the draft project were very positive during their private conversations with me and

other participating officers. However, many others, including police officers who never read the draft or studied the project, commented that we might burn fingers by trying to implement something that is necessarily bound to fail. Their arguments were that the lack of personnel, external interference, and misuse by political parties are bound to adversely affect anything so ambitious. The next responsibility was to modify the draft project based on the large number of suggestions. This was done fast and a final draft was sent to the government. The government accepted the scheme and GO (Rt) No. 3161/2007/Home Dated 23.11.2007 launched the pilot project in 20 police stations in the state.

This was followed by a state-level seminar with the participation of members of parliament, members of legislative assembly, municipal chairmen, and officers of the places pilot projects were planned. Training for the officers was arranged at the Kerala Police Academy. Preparing the draft syllabus for the training of beat officers again was a process that required a lot of diligent attention even on minutest details. It was not an easy task to train the constable/head constable to work as a responsible beat officer, who deals with all kinds of people from all sections of the society on a daily basis. A beat officer's personality has to be molded so that he can have interpersonal proficiency, communication abilities, and behavioral skills! It was a big challenge to shape the character of an ordinary head constable who has served for years in a hierarchical organization and is trained to follow the commands! Now, the requirement was to generate leadership qualities! Selection of beat officer was made a personal responsibility of the superintendent of police/commissioner of police and the standards were kept high to ensure that suitable police personnel were selected for the onerous responsibilities. The training syllabus was discussed and modified repeatedly till is could be customized to the local conditions. Committed senior police officers, psychologists, management experts, etc., were selected and discussions were held with them about the modalities of the training. Classes were arranged in batches at the police training college so as to ensure that everybody got the same training input.

The training also involved visiting and interacting with the beat officers and the Janamaithri Suraksha Samithi members in all the districts, organizing state-level meetings, and attending seminars. It was the most hectic period in my professional life, but slowly we found that skepticism was giving way to enthusiasm. People who were reluctant to share intelligence with the police started voluntarily coming forward with information. The women started requesting in some places that their beat officers should not be changed. Municipal chairmen of Payyannur, Perinthalmanna, Thodupuzha, etc., started constantly interacting, proposing project Janamaithri in their municipalities; crime cases were being solved through information gathered under the project.

Janamaithri Suraksha Project—Implementation

The Janamaithri Suraksha Project seeks to develop closer ties between the police and citizens, and create synergistic partnerships within local communities to deal effectively with antisocial activities and prevent crime. Janamaithri Suraksha Project was a product of concerted and inclusive deliberations, involving the whole cross section of society. The program was cogently drafted, providing detailed guidelines for uniform compliance across the state. Yet, it afforded sufficient scope for local adaptations, facilitating the evolution of the program with qualitative improvement as the implementation continued. Police associations too contributed their support toward the project, thus ensuring that the process of reform was from within, and not pushed down.

Following its statewide launch in March 2008, it has been adopted within the jurisdictions of 20 police stations across the state, with three each in the metropolitan areas of Kozhikode, Kochi, and Thiruvananthapuram, and one in each of the other districts. Residential areas within the jurisdictions of each Janamaithri Suraksha police station were demarcated into separate and distinct beats, and one beat officer, attached to that particular police station, was assigned to cover each beat. As part of their duties, these beat officers were required to visit all residences within their given beat areas. Often, women police constables, functioning as assistant beat officers, accompanied these beat officers, particularly during the house visits. Since the program sought to maximize contact with the local community members, these beat officers also made it a point to pay regular visits to local educational institutions such as schools and colleges that fell in their respective beat areas. In each area where the program was launched several community initiatives for enhanced security were also formulated jointly with the citizens. Regular meetings between police personnel and local residents were conducted within each beat area, as well as at the police station level. Senior police officers of each jurisdiction also took part in these community meetings.

The success of the program could be understood from the fact that at a number of places, the local ward Sabhas of municipalities (elected representatives' body) shifted their venue to the Samithi meeting/beat officers' meeting place. This cut across the political divide, and hence earned a lot of support from all segments of the society.

In Calicut city, where the basic ingredients were all in place for Janamaithri to prosper, it was implemented in Chemmangad, Panniyankara, and Kasaba police stations. While the first two were relatively small police stations, Kasaba held the pride of place among all police stations, housing the central market area as well as well-to-do residences. Chemmangad police station encompasses the backward coastal area that is home to a lot of antisocial activities. Surprisingly, Janamaithri efforts in Chemmangad yielded maximum results. From the start of the program, people had great enthusiasm. Beyond expectations, poor Muslim women in hundreds flocked to the ward-level meetings, participating meaningfully in the deliberations. Beat officers, in fact, used to complain that their preliminary house visits were often inordinately delayed because inquiries at each house usually took up to an hour. As time passed, the ward-level meetings turned out to be less about police issues and more about community problems. People wanted problems of housing, sanitation, and garbage disposal to be solved by the police too! Many sought police help to provide employment to the youth and less educated people. Eve teasing, which figured prominently in the initial meetings, was slowly brought under control with widespread cooperation of the people and education about gender issues. Crime statistics started showing a declining trend, although, admittedly, the difference was not all too perceptible. Training in palliative care in turn helped the beat officers effectively provide solace to the terminally ill in their beat areas, which earned appreciation for the police. A grand Kudumba Sangamam in the station compound, consisting of staff, their families, and all the residents of the area, was probably the highlight of the program as far as Chemmangad was concerned.

In Payyannur, Kannur district, the Janamaithri experiment was also a community celebration initiated by the citizens. Payyannur municipality embraced Janamaithri as if it were its program and the municipal chairman, G.D. Nair, took on, with admirable zeal, the successful navigation during the early stage. Today Janamaithri has become a synonym for police in Payyannur. Standards of accessibility, courtesy, competence, and professionalism have begun to be expected from the police. Besides regular beats, ward-level meetings and general/local issues are now tackled under the ambit of Janamaithri. These meetings have led to satisfactory solutions for long-standing boundary disputes, opened up clogged water channels, and even brought the people together to open a brand new bus bay. What is significant is that a general feeling of safety permeates across the Janamaithri wards in Payyannur, and importantly, people have developed confidence in the friendly neighborhood beat officer. Citizens have trust in the police officer as one to whom they could rush in times of crisis. The ruling party of Irinjalakkuda municipality is United Democratic Front, whereas in Almanna municipality it is Left Democratic Front. But both municipal chairmen are ardent advocates and supporters of the project, and the project is highly successful in both places.

In Cherthala, the project has taken the shape of a people's movement. When Janamc Suraksha Project convener Mr. Varghese, circle inspector of police, got transferred out, people requested for a cancellation of that transfer, because he had already become part and parcel of the local community through successful implementation of the project. Kochi city bagged an international recognition on implementing the project by winning an award from the International Chiefs of Policing Association (IACP) for its community policing project. In the South Asian Regional Conference of Commonwealth Human Rights Initiative held in Delhi in 2009, the Kerala model of community policing became the focal point of discussion.

Impact Study

An independent impact assessment study of this scheme was conducted by sociology students of Feroke College, Calicut. The researchers surveyed a random sample of 1,101 people in Chemmangad and Panniyar police stations. Of the sample surveyed, 85.8% knew about the project, of which 80% stated that this knowledge was acquired through direct contact. For a government program, on every count, this is a laudable achievement. Significantly, a vast majority of the people perceived police as courteous, and they gave a rating of over 4/7 to the police on its performance. Keeping in mind the general negative mindset that people had of the police, such a good rating was clearly an indicator of the success achieved by the project.

Undoubtedly, the Janamaithri experiment has clearly taken wings in the 18 months of its existence. Its primary success has been that it has transformed people's perception of what the police ought to be. By constant endeavor standards of performance were improved and rose to the expectation of the people. Interestingly, the level of responsibility displayed by the subordinate police personnel surprised everyone, including the senior leadership.

Within the organization, the project has been a revelation. Policemen and head constables, when designated as beat officers and assigned the task of proper policing in their beats, instantly rose up to the task. Besides turning into self-motivated individuals, beat officers went about their tasks with a remarkable degree of self-confidence that had so far been alien to them. Indeed, at every ward meeting, it was sheer joy to watch these beat officers hold forth eloquently on the successes and issues in their beat area. In fact, many of the beat officers are more popular in the locality than the local leaders.

An evaluation done by the police leadership also found growing support for the projects. The following are among the more interesting results reported from Janamaithri Suraksha police stations across the state of Kerala:

- In Kasaragod police station (Kasaragod district) limits, it is reported that the white jeep of the Janamaithri Suraksha program gets a warm welcome from local residents as they see it pass. Here, located as it is along the national highway (NH 17), there are usually incidents of vehicular accidents, and the local police have made it a point to respond with urgency to such incidents.

- At Payyannur (Kannur district), local residents were sufficiently motivated by the initiatives of the local police in countering instances of illicit liquor distilling and sale, so much so that entire communities have come together to eradicate it from their midst.
- In Kalpetta (Wynad district), which has a large adivasi (tribal) population, the genuine concern on the part of police regarding issues affecting tribal women has inspired community leaders to take steps to address the issue on a priority basis.
- In Kozhikode city (Kozhikode district), the police initiatives in delivering palliative care to local residents have evoked admiration of the citizens, and members of the residents' associations have come forward to work with local police in addressing community issues.
- Within the jurisdiction of Perinthalmanna police station (Malappuram district), house owners reported that immediately after the visits by the local beat officers, the tenants in some rented houses disappeared, even foregoing the advances paid to the house owners. It is surmised that at least some of these visitors to the area had criminal motives in coming there, and that the visits by the police caused them to rethink their plans.
- In Irinjalakuda (Thrissur district), the police have been successful in motivating local residents to develop a community-wide blood donor forum, as a valuable community resource. In addition, college students have been associating with the police as traffic wardens, with the encouragement of college authorities.
- At Ottapalam (Palakkad district), the police have reported success in curtailing instances of illegal sand mining, with the assistance of local communities. The program has also received a lot of positive feedback from the large number of elderly citizens resident in the area.
- In Kochi city (Ernakulam district), police have been working closely with residents' associations to make local communities safe for the citizens. Police have been making efforts to spread awareness about the utility of burglar alarms and other household security devices.
- Cherthala police station (Alappuzha district) officers report that the local citizens are highly appreciative of the beat officers and their involvement in delivery of counseling services within families, especially to members of the socially backward Kudumbi community. Here too, instances of antisocial activities such as illicit distilling and sale of liquor have come down significantly.
- In Thodupuzha (Idukki district), instances of environmental pollution caused by dumping of hotel wastes into local rivers and water bodies have been curtailed, due to the interest shown by the police personnel, and the cooperation of local community members.

- Vaikom (Kottayam district) reports that, with the cooperation of the public, police have been able to deal effectively with antisocial activities such as distillation of illicit liquor, illegal sale of pan masala, and so on.
- In Paravoor (Kollam district), incidents of chain snatching by gangs in broad daylight, as well as increasing instances of house burglaries at night, were effectively brought down, as a result of the close interaction between the police officers and the citizens. Information of the perpetrators of such crimes was instantly brought to the notice of the police officers, and immediate action by the police resulted in many arrests.
- In Adoor (Pathanamthitta district), an area where many residents are elderly and living alone in their residences, the house visits by the beat officers have been warmly welcomed. Here, it is reported that the residents often treat these police personnel as family members. These citizens have expressed a feeling of increased personal security and household safety, due to these visits to their houses by uniformed police personnel.
- In Thiruvananthapuram city, police were able to arrest a gang of antisocials, who were making use of school students to deal in drugs and other banned substances, with the assistance of school authorities as well as students.
- Volunteer groups of policemen in each of the seven battalions of the Kerala Armed Police have undergone training in palliative care, and stand ready to perform these services to the needy sections of society. In addition, sports facilities in these camps are being used to provide professional training in athletics and sports to local school and college students by the trained sportsmen in these police battalions. As a result, there has been a noticeable change in perceptions regarding the police among communities adjacent to these camps.

Conclusion

In spite of constraints due to deficiency of personnel, reports about program implementation from all over the state indicate that there has been unprecedented support of the community to this initiative of the Kerala police. On the one hand, police personnel reported an increased level of job satisfaction while carrying out their duties as part of the project, while on the other, community members have been quite forthcoming in responding positively to these efforts by the local police personnel.

The project is now seeking further improvements and envisages strengthening the police by achieving the support of the local community.

It is not a project aimed at bettering the image of the police. It is also not a project wherein the citizens perform police duties. Rather, it is a project to professionalize the police and increase their accessibility to the needy public through closer interaction and better understanding of the public. Through the beat officers, the police will know every citizen living in the area and every citizen will be acquainted with the beat officers.

8 Predatory Leadership as a Foil to Community Policing Partnerships
A West African Case Study

STEPHEN B. PERROTT

Introduction

Police reform initiatives in the developing world, especially those with a community-based, inclusive focus, face numerous obstacles and are likely to produce results falling far short of expectations (Davis, Henderson, & Merrick, 2003). Some of these roadblocks are fundamental and relatively obvious, such as the inherent problem in introducing democratically based programs where there is little history of such practices or support for change from government power brokers (see Perrott, 2012). Others are less obvious and remain "under the radar"; these more subterranean problems, however, may prove just as injurious to positive outcomes insofar as they remain untreated while their deleterious effects build cumulatively.

This review of a failed community-based policing (CBP) project focuses on one of the myriad of dysfunctional government problems observed in developing nations, especially across sub-Saharan Africa (e.g., Baker, 2010; Calderisi, 2006). The under the radar focus in this analysis is the resistance of government departments to work collaboratively or transparently with one another or with agencies outside of government (see Tapscott, 2000). As civil services in Western nations are also known for bureaucratic inefficiency and turf protection, problems reported here differ not so much in kind as in quantity.

Community-based policing in the Gambia was a development project I directed in the tiny West African nation from 2004 to 2010 (for background information see Perrott, 2012). The lead partner was Mount Saint Vincent University, located in Halifax, Nova Scotia, Canada, and the program was funded by the Canadian International Development Agency (CIDA) and administered by the Association of Universities and Colleges of Canada (AUCC). Although interdepartmental and interagency cooperation is desirable to any development initiative, it was absolutely imperative to this initiative given that partnership building is a central tenet of CBP. In this chapter I provide a number of anecdotes to demonstrate how the failure to cooperate manifested; then I identify four factors to which I believe much of the phenomenon may be attributed, and conclude by proposing a single unifying framework by which to explain all of the problems encountered.

The Partners

The primary Gambian partners were the Gambia Police Force (GPF), the project leaders, and Gambia College. Gambia College provided credibility from a postsecondary institution, the input and skills important for developing and delivering the pedagogical materials necessary to launch and maintain the street-level training, and the institutional home for a proposed certificate program in CBP. The lead government department, under which the police force functioned, was the Department of State for the Interior. Also essential, given Gambia College's role, was the Department of State for Higher Education, Research and Technology. Cooperation with two additional departments was important: the Department of State for Basic and Secondary Education (our access point to the nation's school children) and the Department of State for Justice (responsible for the judiciary and the nation's bar). In addition to a number of core Canadian partners (e.g., Halifax Regional Police, Province of Nova Scotia Restorative Justice Program), we sought additional partners as the project evolved; for example, the Youth Crime Watch of the Gambia proved to be an important partner in community and school outreach. The Nova Scotia Gambia Association (NSGA), a Gambian-based, Canadian-sponsored NGO, collaborated by sharing its infrastructure, trained staff, and other resources with the project.

Sociopolitical Context

The Gambia, a former British colony, was an exemplar of African democracy prior to the 1994 bloodless coup when current president, His Excellency Sheik Professor Alhaji Dr. Yahya A.J.J. Jammeh, seized power (see Jawara, 2009; Saine, 2008). Supposedly one of the "soldiers with a difference" (Ceesay, 2006, p. 90), then Lieutenant Jammeh, returned the country nominally to civilian rule two years after the coup and periodically showed signs that democracy might grow. Further movement toward real democracy was the optimistic premise on which I sought funding for this project, even while recognizing a larger milieu of repression, corruption, extra-legal measures to maintain control, and the president's growing eccentricity. Unfortunately, Jammeh became increasingly unpredictable and bizarre (he claims to cure HIV/AIDS with his own herbal remedy and has conducted witch hunts), narcissistic (note his title), and repressive over the six years of the project. Ratings of civil and political freedom continued to drop, and although the Gambia claims, and is nominally granted, democratic status, it is in reality a dictatorship (see analyses by Ceesay, 2006, and Saine, 2008, 2009; also see www.freedomhouse.com). I purport that this lack of democracy blocked a more optimal CBP project outcome (see Perrott, 2012); here, I more specifically take up how Gambia's culture of fear, engendered by the Jammeh government, contributed to thwarting the growth of the necessary partnerships in this project.

Like most sub-Saharan African police forces (see Baker, 2010), the GPF has earned its reputation as being inept and corrupt. If the force serves any purpose whatsoever, it is as an agent of regime protection (see Alemika, 2009). The pomp, circumstance, and groveling deference to rank, grossly exaggerated remnants from the British colonizers, stand in caricatured contrast to what is, in truth, an institution devoid of real discipline (Perrott, 2009). The reputation of the GPF, historically low in Gambian society, and the relative amount of government support provided to this institution, also historically low, have further deteriorated under Jammeh's rule in favor of the national army. Morale has been further depleted by the president's growing tendency to parachute members of his own ethnic group into high-ranking positions without regard to merit.

Lost or Never Achieved Partnerships

Department of State for Justice and the Alternative Dispute Resolution Program

A main adjunct to the central CBP thrust was the introduction of restorative justice (RJ) techniques. We situated the police as central actors in the proposed RJ protocol and envisioned officers working hand in hand with others already using community-based conciliation and restorative techniques at the village level (in bodies known as circles of elders). We sought to take pressure off a crowded, corrupt, ineffective, and adversarial court system while being more culturally consistent with traditional West African means of conflict resolution.

Early on we learned that an alternative dispute resolution (ADR) program was being introduced to the nation's judiciary and bar. Although ADR and RJ are far from synonymous, they overlap sufficiently in philosophy and practice that some level of program partnership would serve to (1) create a level of shared understanding throughout the entire justice system, and (2) allow for some pooling of scarce resources. The Gambian project lead and I worked hard to link up with our counterparts in the ADR program, receiving numerous assurances from ranking government officials that this was indeed a good idea. Belying this expressed sentiment were repeated demands for letters of introduction and for the fulfillment of various other unnecessary bureaucratic tasks. Whenever we got close to an actual meeting, the rendezvous would be postponed, usually to a time when the Canadian partners had already departed for home.

It initially seemed that we were simply encountering the excessive bureaucratic roadblocks that habitually tie up government functions in the Gambia. Ultimately, however, it became clear that, despite assurances to the contrary, power brokers from one or both of the overseeing government departments did not want this partnership to form, though we never actually learned why. Ironically, the American scholar who spearheaded the ADR initiative serendipitously learned about our project activities and accessed my contact information online just before project closure. The two of us formed an academic partnership based on our shared interests in the Gambia, agreeing that it was highly unfortunate that we had been unable to form a more practical partnership in the Gambia to advance the RJ and ADR initiatives.

Disjointed Efforts From Donor Nations

The encouraging, hospitable, even effusive, welcome that I and members of the Canadian team initially received from GPF senior brass was heartening but almost too good to be true. As it turns out, it was. It now appears that GPF managers had learned to play the "project game," whereby Western partners are encouraged to pursue and secure funding. Once funding is secured, further hospitality and enthusiasm extend only to the point that ensures the Western partner leaves various material resources that benefit the GPF or, more particularly, the senior officers personally (my experience across a dozen years of project work in this country suggests that this behavior extends across other Gambian government departments). In the case of this project, it was clear even at this point that the attention of GPF managers had shifted to the next potential partner proposing to pursue funding for another project (see section below dealing with one-off initiatives).

During the life of the project a number of other donor countries and their police forces offered various training initiatives to the GPF (see, for example, Gambia News, 2008; Mascarenhas, 2010; Sallah, 2009). Although I and my colleagues would have welcomed the opportunity to work with teams from Sweden, Great Britain, or Gibraltar, GPF managers had little interest in such collaborations. Rather, there appeared to be some effort to ensure that the various Western teams not become aware of the presence of the others. One can but speculate that bringing Western partners together was not how they saw the project game best played, perhaps because they viewed the consolidation of resources as a potential loss of immediately accessible resources. One also suspects there was concern that Western partners would come to "share notes." Such was the case when I serendipitously encountered an African Union, UN-backed team at my hotel one evening. Their mission was to select certain Gambian police officers for a deployment to Sudan. I knew nothing about the team's arrival, nor did they know of my presence or the project I was directing. A retired Royal Canadian Mounted Police officer on the team and I did share notes on this phenomenon and agreed little could be done other than acknowledge that this was the way that project "business" is conducted in the Gambia.

Faltering Partnerships With NGOs and Community Groups

Our partnership with the NSGA, a well-regarded NGO founded and directed by a retired Canadian school principal, proved invaluable over the initial three years of the project. We rented office space from it and its staff, who consulted on the project, and the NGO provided a physical presence for continuity, particularly when the other Canadians and I were not in the country.

The NSGA drama troupe was particularly important for community and school outreach, and had a significant role by dramatizing sensitive issues such as spousal abuse, police corruption, and gender equity. The value of the drama troupe was as a vehicle for presenting ideas that would otherwise cause offense coming from young people—who typically have little voice—in a nonoffensive, humorous, and most importantly, effective manner (such troupes have been similarly used in other sub-Saharan countries; e.g., Mitchell, Nakamanya, Kamali, & Whitworth, 2001). Although the GPF had no history of transparency, and police officers first observing the troupe's activities were initially apprehensive about exposing "dirty laundry," it quickly became clear that these outreach sessions (involving open periods of dialogue between police and citizens) actually enhanced the perception of the police in the public eye. It was, after all, hardly a secret that the police shook down motorists for bribes; that they would acknowledge this and other problems promoted the belief that change was possible.

Despite the positive reviews being garnered by the drama troupe, top GPF brass, who did not attend sessions, remained suspicious of the activities. Although purportedly buying into the notion of partnerships, transparency, and dialogue, they wanted nothing to do with acknowledging police misconduct and certainly did not want to cede any control to the young people in the drama troupe (despite the fact that the messages were more about reconciliation and empathy than about criticism). Increasingly, dictates flowed from Inspector General of Police Ousman Sonko (now secretary of state for the interior) that the drama troupe was not to deploy without police supervision, while he repeatedly found "more pressing" issues to justify the last-minute redeployment of officers scheduled to attend public forums. As a result, drama troupe activities were essentially immobilized by the fourth year of the project (as were, more generally, all community outreach activities).

In the first few years of the project, we worked hard to involve community members and groups in our outreach and began a process whereby citizens broadly representative of various constituencies were able to act as stakeholders whose views would be respected and acted on in partnership with the GPF. However, this inclusive, participatory approach annoyed senior GPF managers who thought involved citizens should be supporters of the ruling party. Additionally, as was the case with the drama troupe, senior officers were uncomfortable exhibiting any transparency and refused to share any decision-making power with the public.

GPF and Gambia College Breakdown

With two years left in the planned tenure of the project, growing partnership failures had resulted in CBP field activities being almost stopped, and those remaining deviating significantly from the philosophy and practice of true community policing (see Perrott, 2012). It was decided that the remaining two years of the project would be solely focused on launching the certificate program at Gambia College. GPF managers immediately saw the enhanced role of Gambia College as a threat and as evidence that I, as director, had capriciously and arbitrarily stolen the project for the college, despite documents demonstrating that this had been the plan from the outset. (The cadre of senior managers had changed many times since project inception due to President Jammeh's so-called electric broom policy; see below. The new leaders never perceived any compulsion to live up to the commitments of their predecessors nor, for that matter, to even review archival documentation.)

Against this backdrop, repeated failures of the GPF to sign a memorandum of agreement with Gambia College, more than once when the GPF pulled out of the signing ceremony at the last moment, were not entirely surprising. An agreement to have been formalized in a matter of weeks following my last trip to the Gambia in May 2009 dragged on for months until the Canadian funding agency, now growing impatient, advised that the project would be terminated if an agreement was not soon reached. I provided both institutions with a final deadline by which the memorandum had to be signed, and when this date passed I sought, and received, yet another extension from the funder. Senior GPF managers continued to attribute the failure to a lack of cooperation by Gambia College, and indeed leaders from Gambia

College, in an apparent bid to get as much as possible from the arrangement, did contribute to the breakdown of the partnership. The preponderance of blame, however, is appropriately attributed to the senior managers of the GPF and Secretary of State Ousman Sonko, who were clearly intent on finding excuses to not proceed while continuing to profess their commitment to the project. Finally, the project was terminated early in 2010, less than a year before its scheduled end.

Factors Underlying Partnership Failure

Some half century since most of sub-Saharan Africa achieved independence from colonial powers, huge quantities of foreign aid monies have been sunk into developing the subcontinent. There is considerable evidence that the situation, on balance, has actually deteriorated (Calderisi, 2006) and a plausible argument that foreign aid and celebrity "do-gooders" (including Bono of the rock band U2) actually harm Africa by feeding corruption and dependency (Moyo, 2009). Other typically cited factors for the continent's failure to develop include greedy, authoritarian leaders, poor infrastructure, and otherwise dysfunctional governance. Although it is beyond debate that these factors remain central to why "fifty years after the beginning of the independence movement, Africa's prospects are bleaker than ever before" (Meredith, 2005, p. 681), they are too generic to be helpful for policy makers interested in the failure of specific initiatives. Below, I propose four specific factors to which I attribute most of the difficulties encountered in this West African policing initiative, proffered in a more psychological framework than seen through more typical political science or sociological analyses.

The Historic One-Off Nature of Development Initiatives

Aid initiatives are often of a one-off nature—focusing on projects rather than on systemic programs—typically encompassing short time periods in which Western partners are quickly in and out of the developing nation. During the life of this project, police forces from a variety of European nations (e.g., United Kingdom, Sweden) came to the Gambia to deliver a two- or three-week training initiative while depositing certain material resources (e.g., police equipment, uniforms, computers). These in-and-out forays would inevitably result in fawning attention to the Europeans by senior GPF officers, highly favorable press coverage, and seemingly enthusiastic commitments about how the GPF would continue to expand on the "important" training received.

My observations led me to conclude that GPF managers only worked to extract whatever material goods they could from the visitors who went home with the "feel good" but erroneous belief that they had effected positive change. Whatever human capacity development that might have occurred was thrown to the Gambian sand. This scenario is, in my experience, true of many aid projects in the Gambia, where one-offs, typically in the form of workshops where participants are rewarded with coveted per diems, serve as a revenue-generating machine for the country's elite while doing little for the supposed real beneficiaries.

This six-year community policing project was therefore an anomaly for the GPF insofar as it allowed for the workshops and professed commitments to bear developmental fruit through sustained effort and follow-through. Unfortunately, this is not part of the entrenched view of aid projects in the Gambia. Much time was wasted trying to convince the principal actors that we were not there on what is pejoratively known as project tourism junkets, but rather that we intended to promote sustainable change through capacity building.

However, even were we able to sustain forward activity throughout the entire life of the project, 6.5 years is a relatively brief window in which to achieve lasting change, as the "failure to win hearts and minds" in Afghanistan and Iraq over the last decade is now proving. In the view of Canadian Senator and retired Lieutenant General Roméo Dallaire, leader of the ill-fated UNIMAR mission in Rwanda, a more realistic period for achieving sustainable change is 40 years (personal communication in a small group setting in 1995). Despite occasionally posturing to the contrary, Western donor nations remain unwilling to commit to such long-term efforts.

Men Do Not Share Well: Challenging the Patriarchy

That the best route out of sub-Saharan Africa's current predicament starts with female leadership is often heard in development circles. Indeed, the election of Liberia's Ellen Johnson Sirleaf, the first-ever female leader of an African nation, is viewed as hugely significant in this regard (Bauer, 2009). A wide swath of literature on gender-based differences worldwide suggests that women generally, and female leaders in particular, are more inclined toward the collective, and that they value teamwork and group-based outcomes more than men do. Women are therefore more culturally inclined toward partnerships than are men, a finding that holds in both the industrialized West and collectivist South (Cheung & Halpern, 2010).

Although Gambian society is collectivist overall, I repeatedly observed that Gambian men and women had very different views about partnerships and sharing. Whereas the men had a relative focus on individual achievement (albeit within a collectivist framework and a clear desire to provide for extended family), Gambian women appeared more concerned about equality within relationships and collective advancement extending outside of kinship circles. I watched, in frustration, as this dynamic played out over a year with two civilian project employees leading the community outreach team. The leader was a man who did little to advance the project (other than to lend his maleness for credibility) but did much to promote his personal position; his assistant was a young woman who, although paid much less, worked hard and effectively in the background to move the project forward. Any notion of fairness, and any consideration of merit, would have seen their positions transposed. However, it is very difficult to advance women to positions of leadership in such a patriarchal society, where men have become comfortable with the notion that although women do most of the work, they, as men, remain entitled to the fruits of those efforts (see Schroeder, 1999).

Realistic Conflict and Zero-Sum Politics

Given the real dearth of resources in the Gambia specifically, and sub-Saharan Africa more generally, it is not surprising that members of the GPF (and other Gambian partners) would see themselves in competition for the limited material resources available in this project. Tensions were inevitably automatically evoked between partners following any significant purchase, and the primary beneficiary or resource holder was identified—despite constant reinforcement that all project resources were for the benefit of all partners. So, for example, the purchase of an LCD projector to be held and maintained by Gambia College resulted in significant disgruntlement by the police even though (1) nominal control of the projector by Gambia College was clearly of the greatest benefit to the project overall, and (2) the GPF (appropriately) received more material benefits than all other partners combined. In order to be clear about the pervasiveness of the problem, Gambia College administrators showed an equal lack of concern about the greater good when it came to the disbursement of resources. For example, a computer, printer, and Internet hookup purchased for the college's female project lead quickly ended up in the possession of the higher-ranking, male principal who fulfilled a more peripheral project role.

Muzafer Sherif's realistic conflict theory (1966) allows for the competition and conflict that face groups competing for scarce resources and for the perception—accurately held or not—that there need to be winners and losers in the acquisition of resources (see Jackson, 1993; Taylor & Moghaddam, 2004). Despite entreaties and actions to disabuse partners of this erroneous notion in regard to their efforts in this project, adherence to the belief that one's gain was another's loss always smoldered just below the surface. The reality of sufficient resources to achieve all project goals was lost to a very real history of poverty and deprivation, further fueled by a sub-Saharan African zero-sum political mindset (Kirschke, 2000); the attendant distrust and tension resulting from this mindset proved highly damaging to the formation of productive partnerships.

The Social Darwinism of African Dictatorships

In a pattern identified some time ago (see Ihonvbere, 1996) President Jammeh quickly developed into an African "strongman," in part by embracing the terminology and mechanisms of democracy to subvert democracy (see also Meredith, 2005, for an extended discussion of the postindependence history of African "big men"). At the same time, any remnants of a pro-democratic opposition movement twist and turn against themselves. As Saine (2008) aptly points out, Jammeh's ascendance to and grip on power "lies in the emergence of a junior officer class, which disingenuously appropriated the language of the IMF and World Bank to promise Gambians 'real democracy,' 'human rights,' 'probity,' 'accountability,' and 'transparency in government'" (p. 469).

Most of the Gambia's current political and economic instability arises from a ruling class that has achieved power through nepotism and is otherwise simply incompetent. However, much instability is certainly purposely maintained by Jammeh as a means to keep others who might aspire to power from forming havens of psychological safety and confidence. His electric broom policies, where he incessantly promotes surprise candidates to positions of power and then just as quickly fires them (often dispatching them to the country's infamous Mile 2 prison; see PNMBAI, 2007; Sankereh, 2007), leaves even his elite fearful that they will at any moment be visited by the dreaded National Intelligence Agency (similar strategies have long been used by other big men across Sub-Saharan Africa; see Meredith, 2005). In the Gambia, there exists a nationwide atmosphere in which people self-censor their views from even close friends and family members lest an informer feed information back to the government (ironically, this atmosphere undoubtedly further fuels Jammeh's own legendary paranoia).

This social Darwinism impacted the ability to foster partnerships in two ways: (1) powerful actors in the project were fearful to reach out to others lest they be seen as being disloyal and ceding influence to those outside their "house," and (2) living in authoritarian fear diminishes any sort of vision for long-term planning that might involve the greater good in lieu of a "here and now" focus on getting *what* one can *when* one can. This pattern is, of course, hardly unique to the Gambia and President Jammeh (see, Adeleke, 1997, for a particularly astute analysis outlined within a neocolonial framework).

Predatory Leadership and a Sober Glance to the Future

The project failures reviewed here and the four underlying factors outlined in the preceding section can be explained by a predatory leadership style that is, unfortunately, the rule rather than the exception across sub-Saharan Africa. In his review of why predatory leadership dominates the subcontinent, Goldsmith (2004) points to postcolonial dynamics and cultural beliefs that have taken hold since the heady days of independence a half century ago (see also Meredith, 2005). An inevitable corollary of this leadership style is the pervasive, systemic corruption that envelopes the subcontinent. In the Gambia, as in many other African nations, secondary corruption occurs in the absence of good governance and is normative throughout society; it can be conducted largely in the absence of sanction or perceptions of shame (see Werlin, 2005).

As an example of one of Guest's (2004) so-called vampire states, attempts in this project to have senior Gambian government and police officials engage in transparent team play was tantamount to asking them "to give up the very powers that enable them to feed on their fellow citizens" (p. 49). Furthermore, the systemic cultural backdrop on which the mindset of these power brokers rests is such that they cannot perceive anything but a zero-sum game were they to sacrifice any personal gain for the common good. Rather, they are stuck in an ongoing dynamic where governance "is more a matter of seamanship and less one of navigation—that is, staying afloat rather than going somewhere" (Jackson & Rosberg, 1982, p. 18).

The failure to develop or maintain the necessary partnerships in this project is but a single symptom of predatory leadership. It is, however, a symptom that, if present, should be seen by police reformers as almost certain to thwart any proposed CBP program. As our experience shows, reformers should not be fooled by superficially professed enthusiasm for forming partnerships during the planning stages; indeed, if our experience in the Gambia is indicative, partners in developing nations will be cognizant of the need to express a commitment to collaboration (and indeed, all the democratically based commitments for which Western donors are known to press) as necessary to playing the project game.

Rather, police reformers should, from the outset, look for concrete manifestations that partnerships are truly being embraced by the actions of the targeted police institution, backed up by unambiguous documentation that demarcates the roles, responsibilities, and reasonable expectations of all partners. It is wishful thinking, if not complete folly, for reformers to believe they can overcome resistance to forming the necessary core collaborations as the project evolves. Rather, this resistance should be seen as symptomatic of a broader and fundamental set of problems that will not be overcome.

CBP is essentially a bottom-up, grassroots, inclusive, and democratically styled form of policing. When it works, it is because the rank and file has embraced the vision inherent in the philosophy. However, no amount of work and apparent success on the ground can truly transform a police force unless solid endorsement comes from the top. In this project, senior GPF managers failed to embrace CBP not only because of the greed and corruption generated within their ranks, but also because of the predatory leadership style with which President Jammeh controls the Gambia. As argued here, trouble forming healthy partnerships not only signals a weakness in one of CBP's basic pillars, but is likely symptomatic of the larger problem of predatory leadership. There is a time and place for police reform; it's important to be realistic about government's commitment to change before embarking on any change-based initiative.

References

Adeleke, T. (1997). Africa and Pan-Africanism: Betrayal of a historical cause. *Western Journal of Black Studies, 21*, 106–116.

Alemika, E.E.O. (2009). Police practice and police research in Africa. *Police Practice and Research: An International Journal, 10*, 483–502.

Baker, B. (2010). *Security in post-conflict Africa: The role of non-state policing*. Boca Raton, FL: CRC Press.

Bauer, J. (2009). Women and the 2005 election in Liberia. *Journal of Modern African Studies, 47*, 193–211.

Calderisi, R. (2006). *The trouble with Africa: Why foreign aid is not working*. New York: Palgrave MacMillan.

Ceesay, E.J. (2006). *The military and "democratisation" in the Gambia: 1994–2003*. Oxford: Trafford Publishing.

Cheung, F.M., & Halpern, D.F. (2010). Women at the top: Powerful leaders define success as work + family in a culture of gender. *American Psychologist, 65*, 182–193.

Davis, R., Henderson, N.J., & Merrick, C. (2003). Community policing: Variations on the Western model in the developing world. *Police Practice and Research: An International Journal, 4*, 285–300.

Gambia News. (2008, April 10). Gambia news: Swedish police to train Gambian police. *Gambia News*. Retrieved August 4, 2010, from http://www.gambianow.com/news/News/1064.html

Goldsmith, A.A. (2004). Predatory versus developmental rule in Africa. *Democratization, 11*, 88–110.

Guest, R. (2004). *The shackled continent: Power, corruption, and African lives*. Washington, DC: Smithsonian Books.

Ihonvbere, J.O. (1996). On the threshold of another false start? A critical evaluation of prodemocracy movements in Africa. *Journal of Asian and African Studies, 31*, 125–144.

Jackson, J.W. (1993). Realistic group conflict theory: A review and evaluation of the theoretical and empirical literature. *Psychological Record, 43*, 395–414.

Jackson, R.H., & Rosberg Jr., C.G. (1982). *Personal rule in Black Africa*. Berkeley: University of California Press.

Jawara, D.K. (2009). *Kairaba*. West Sussex: Domtom Publishing.

Kirschke, L. (2000). Informal repression, zero-sum politics and late third wave transitions. *Journal of Modern African Studies, 38*, 383–405.

Mascarenhas, A. (2010, April 28). RGP: Raising policing standards in the Gambia. *Gibraltar Chronicle*. Retrieved August 4, 2010, from http://www.chronicle.gi/headlines_details.php?id=18859

Meredith, M. (2005). *The fate of Africa: A history of fifty years of independence*. New York: Public Affairs.

Mitchell, K., Nakamanya, A., Kamali, A., & Whitworth, J.A.G. (2001). Community-based HIV/AIDS education in rural Uganda: Which channel is most effective? *Health Education Research, 16*, 411–423.

Moyo, D. (2009). *Dead aid: Why aid is not working and how there is a better way for Africa*. New York: Farrar, Straus and Giroux.

Perrott, S.B. (2009). *Vertical collectivism as an obstacle to democratic policing and restorative justice in the Gambia*. Africa Peace and Conflict Network Occasional Paper 3. Available at www.africapeace.org

Perrott, S.B. (2012). Community policing in the Gambia: A case study in democratic strategies and best intentions being turned upside down. In A. Saine, E. Ceesay, & E. Sall (Eds.), *The Gambia: Essays on contemporary issues and future direction(s); 1965–2009*. Trenton, NJ: Africa World Press (in press).

PNMBAI. (2007, October 14). Jammeh's electric broom: Who is next? Town crier is back. *Freedom Newspaper*. Retrieved May 14, 2010, from http://www.freedom-newspaper.com/Homepage/tabid/36/newsid367/2406/Default.aspx

Saine, A. (2008). The Gambia's elected autocrat poverty, peripherality, and political instability, 1994–2006: A political economy assessment. *Armed Forces and Society, 34*, 450–473.

Saine, A. (2009). *The paradox of third-wave democratization in Africa: The Gambia under AFPRC-APRC Rule, 1994-2008*. Lanham, MD: Lexington Books.

Sallah, A. (2009, January 13). Pre-deployment training for police officers underway. *Daily Observer Online*. Retrieved August 4, 2010, from http://observer.gm/africa/gambia/article/pre-deployment-training-for-police-officers-underway

Sankereh, E.G. (2007, February 21). President Jammeh sacks Cabinet Dean Susa Waffa-Ogoo. *Gambia Echo*. Retrieved May 13, 2010, from http://www.thegambiaecho.com/Homepage/tabid/36/articleType/ArticleView/articleId/316/Default.aspx

Schroeder, R.A. (1999). *Shady practices: Agroforestry and gender politics in the Gambia*. Berkeley: University of California Press.

Sherif, M. (1966). *In common predicament: Social psychology of intergroup conflict and cooperation*. Boston: Houghton-Mifflin.

Tapscott, C. (2000). Intergovernmental relations in South Africa: The challenges of co-operative government. *Public Administration and Development, 20*, 119–128.

Taylor, D.M., & Moghaddam, F.M. (2004). *Theories of intergroup relations: International social psychological perspectives* (2nd ed.). Westport, CT: Praeger.

Werlin, H.H. (2005). Corruption and foreign aid in Africa. *Orbis, 49*, 517–527.

9

Public Satisfaction With Police
Case Study From Sweden

KJELL ELEFALK

Introduction

Police activity, and public satisfaction or dissatisfaction with it, is the subject of constant public debate. The media, politicians, and broad sections of the public are critical of the police's ability to counteract petty and organized crime. There is a wide range of opinions, even within the judicial system. Sometimes investigation is regarded as most important, and sometimes visibility is highest on the wish list. The debate is sprawling largely because what constitutes good police activity is unclear. Is it the number of successful investigations per policeman? The number of speeding tickets issued? How fast police cars arrive when there is an emergency call? A low cost per violent crime investigation? Or should the police be measured in terms of the growth in the number of reported offenses? Crime clearance rates appear to be one good way of measuring a part of police work. But it is well understood that more resources for investigation would increase clearance rates. On the other hand, many people would still remain dissatisfied and the criticism of police may persist.

Is there some methodology to measure police performance? Many commentators use, and would like, concepts like the citizen's perspective and customer satisfaction. However, few succeed in practically synthesizing these theories. The police authorities in the southern part of Sweden have tried heading in this direction by measuring the sense of safety in collaboration with many of the county's municipalities and crime prevention bodies. Analyzing the results provides an accurate impression of disturbances, criminality, and other factors creating insecurity. A wide range of measures intended to increase safety have then been introduced in the municipalities over the past seven years. The working method for achieving greater safety involves greater visibility, addressing the municipality's defined problems. A low tolerance of problems and disturbances applies, and the results have been positive.

Greater safety is apparent in recent years in most municipalities in the south of Sweden, particularly cities like Malmö and Landskrona. Petty crime has also been heavily reduced in recent years. Although there are difficulties in evaluating the police impact on safety in municipalities, what is clear is that the police have conducted prioritized initiatives based on information from the public, obtaining positive results exactly where and when these initiatives are conducted. The citizen-based approach has also resulted in the public taking a less critical view of the police than previously. Much of the evidence suggests that if the police use safety measures and are able to work according to these indications, relations with the public immediately improve.

The police have also examined satisfaction with police work among parties that have reported crime. The public is satisfied with police work for housebreaking, bag snatching, and car theft. However, police handling of assault by an unknown assailant has low satisfaction. Nor has there been any improvement in reporting crime over the years. Plaintiffs' evaluation of police work on rape/attempted rape indicates that there is dissatisfaction with the legal process. However, police activity and commitment are rated fairly highly.

Satisfaction of people making emergency calls was also examined in the south of Sweden. The results indicated fairly low satisfaction, especially among the people prioritized lowest. There were also sizable local differences. In fact, the number of critics of the police in Scania could be measured in tens of thousands, possibly created by a working method that was not well thought out. The police altered its working methods by feeding back to those callers assigned low priority. The results of this new processing of emergencies in Scania caused a near-sensational improvement of emergency caller satisfaction. Local differences among the people served by the police were also reduced.

Essentially, the police are dependent on public trust and acceptance of their operations functioning smoothly. If trust increases, so does the willingness to report crime, be a witness in legal processes, and call for the police in emergencies. The resistance to serious criminality also increases, as does understanding of police work during high-activity holiday periods, and during other events. Accordingly, one important conclusion is that police effectiveness against minor disturbances and petty crime has a larger impact on serious criminality and major disturbances than appears to be the case at first glance. To all intents and purposes, customer satisfaction and fighting crime are the same thing.

Even if there are many hazards to watch for when the police work in the way the police have piloted in southern Sweden, this is one way of working that should be given increased scope within the police. Public satisfaction is one of the fundamentals for understanding what good police activity is.

Background

The four counties in southern Sweden have a population totaling some 2 million and are located close to Denmark and continental Europe. There are five major cities: Malmö (population: approximately 300,000), Helsingborg (approximately 124.000), Lund (approximately 105,000), Karlskrona (approximately 70,000), and Växjö (approximately 61,000). There are also 50 other towns and municipalities of importance as administrative and political geographical areas in this part of the country.

The Swedish police have been working since 1996 to develop new methods and reforms for the direction and management of police work and for improving the quality of their service. This work has entailed the use of a wide variety of different tools and methods, for example, the balanced scorecard, the Swedish Quality Award, citizen surveys, various techniques for entering into dialogues with citizens, staff commitment measurements, management/direction through dialogues, methods for developing learning organizations and for the setting up of operational goals in organizations with complex activities, the Swedish Quality Index, e-learning, benchmarking, Common Assessment Framework (CAF), and the council method for increased staff participation. All of this has given the authorities a great deal of experience and has helped them to develop the police service in a very interesting manner. Especially the police authorities of southern Sweden have been among the most active participants in experimenting with new evaluation methods of police performance.

Measuring safety with the aid of public surveys has now become an important part of the police's operational analysis methodologies. The process is conducted through questionnaires across all 66 municipalities, divided into 112 different geographical segments. Public surveys used for measuring the citizens' perspective are of various kinds, such as "The Emergency Callout Process in Scania—Public Satisfaction" and "When the Public Report a Crime, How Satisfied Are They With Police Work in Scania—Assessed Using the SQI Method."

Measuring the safety outlook in southern Sweden in certain police areas or parts of police areas where this study is based was initiated in the years 1998, 2000, 2001, and 2003, although a little inconsistently across the various police areas. In 2004, a decision was taken to conduct systematic safety measurements in each police area and municipality at the same time. Since then, this has occurred annually with some exceptions.

The operational police safety plans that emerged from the survey in 2007 were utilized for police work in the Scania Police Authority. This meant that the concrete reviews and analyses were always *relative*, so expressions such as "high," "high value for," and "very" were to be compared with other values obtained in Scania and the rest of Sweden, and in the same geographical regions over time. For example, "high values for unsafe late at night" need not mean that the residents in this geographical area were constantly worried about going out late at night, or that "high values for damage" meant that there was a lot of criminal damage in the area in absolute terms. However, it did imply that individual inhabitants have reported that they feel unsafe or have experienced damage. If a very high number of respondents made the same response regarding circumstances in this geographical area, then this geographical area was *relatively* worse than other places with fewer responses reporting the problem. Increased/reduced values over the year in the same geographical area were considered a clear indication that a specific problem has become worse/better. Such interpretation was applied to all safety indicators. To evaluate the progress of safety, all 33 indicators/measures were aggregated, a complex task using a new method, and accordingly, results have been interpreted with some caution.

The Police Safety Index—A New Model to Facilitate Analysis of the Problem Outlook for a Geographical Area Such as a Municipality, District, or Other Geographical Area

The operational police safety outlook in the counties of southern Sweden with its 63 municipalities use the safety survey instrument to guide the work of the police authorities. To utilize existing safety measures better within and outside the police, the use of a new analysis model has been started whose primary purpose is to support local police work. For instance, the model for the safety index, prepared specifically for the police in Scania in year 2007, is an attempt to approach a more concrete analysis tool. Preliminarily, this model would appear very useful in police operational terms, while its methodological development has only just got underway—it is still an embryonic system. The main value is expected to lie in making it easier to develop an overview, through the simplified quantitative techniques that provide means to compare performance in different ways.

The model is based exclusively on results and indicators from police safety surveys through postal questionnaires conducted in Sweden since 1997 in over 200 municipalities. Exactly the same questions are used, and the raw data are collected in a similar manner. There are 33 indicators for problems/disturbances (14 measures), exposure to petty crime (4 measures), undefined concerns about crime (5 measures), defined concern in residential areas (7 measures), and police actions in residential areas (3 measures). These are aggregated in various ways into a number of indices.

Apart from the indices of these main groups, the average values for problem levels on all 33 indicators comprise a model's aggregate index or safety index.

The model contains 7 levels, with the negative and positive extremes ranging from 6 to 0 occurring very seldomly. In practice, these levels are confidence intervals for perceived problems. Fewer respondents perceiving a problem means the problem level is downgraded.

The average of all 33 indicators from the police's largest data run of 167,961 questionnaire responses in March 2003 is the starting point for the model, the base level, and is designated level 2. The data are designed so that they can be analyzed not only to perceive differences among different areas, but also in terms of gender, age, economic status, and so forth, since these factors are also captured in the survey.

The expression "obvious problem" is used to clarify feasible priorities and perceive the effects of previous police work in the model. An *obvious problem* is defined as a clearly apparent, predominant, visible statement attracting public consciousness to a high degree. Such questions seek to bring out the common topics of conversation in the local community. This is the police's working concept, a tactical tool rather than scientifically founded truth, and one that should not be assigned exaggerated significance in absolute terms.

The levels of response are measured on the following scale:

Level 0 = Virtually nonexistent problem
Level 1 = Not an obvious problem at all
Level 2 = Not a particularly obvious problem
Level 3 = Fairly obvious problem
Level 4 = Obvious problem
Level 5 = Very obvious problem
Level 6 = Alarmingly obvious problem

Every area, town, and municipality, and also more important minor areas (110 geographical segments in southern Sweden), have been covered by this survey since 2007. The results are briefly summarized in Table 9.1.

Analysis of Results—Main Conclusions Regarding the Safety Outlook in Scania, 2000–2010

Safety in Scania has progressed positively in the last five years after having deteriorated in the period 2000–2005. Conclusions are from the five police areas in Scania (Swedish Skåne). Together with previous information, the

Table 9.1 Strategic Card—City of Malmö Retroactive Values, 2000–2006

Police Area City of Malmö	År 2000	År 2003	År 2004	År 2005	År 2006
Total Safety Index, Overall Picture	2.39	2.73	2.91	2.94	2.79
Problems by:					
Littering	3	3	3	3	3
Criminal public damages	3	3	3	3	3
Outdoor environment	3.00	3.00	3.00	3.00	3.00
Drunk people outdoors	2	3	3	3	3
Drug abuser outdoors	2	3	3	3	3
Apartments disposed by alcoholics	2	2	2	2	2
Apartments disposed by drug abusers	2	2	2	2	2
Drug abuse problems	2.00	2.50	2.50	2.50	2.50
People rows and fights outdoors	2	3	3	3	3
Accosted women	2	3	4	4	3
Youth gang rows and disturbances	3	4	4	5	4
Road traffic problems	2	3	3	3	3
Speeding cars	1	2	2	2	3
Reckless driving of moped and motorcycle riders	4	4	4	4	4
Nonobservance of traffic rules	2	2	2	2	2
Outdoor disturbances	2.29	3.00	3.14	3.29	3.14
Total problem of any kind observation rate	2	2	3	2	2
Problems/Disturbances of the Peace	2.29	2.79	2.93	2.93	2.86
Individual/household exposed to:					
Violent crimes within 12 months	2	2	2	2	2
Theft within 12 months	3	3	3	3	2
Criminal damage within 12 months	3	3	3	3	3
Total individuals exposed to crimes within 12 months	3	3	3	3	3
Exposed to Petty Crimes	2.75	2.75	2.75	2.75	2.50
Anxiety befalled to:					
Burglary dwelling	1	1	2	2	2
Burglary in attics, stores, garage	2	2	2	3	2
Burglary/inflicting damage to parked vehicle	3	3	3	3	3
Abstract anxiety of property crimes	2.00	2.00	2.33	2.67	2.33
Assaults outdoors	3	3	4	4	4

(continued)

Table 9.1 Strategic Card—City of Malmö Retroactive Values, 2000–2006 (continued)

Police Area City of Malmö	År 2000	År 2003	År 2004	År 2005	År 2006
Abstract anxiety of violent crimes against individuals	3.00	3.00	4.00	4.00	4.00
Total anxiety befalled to crimes	2	2	3	3	2
Anxiety of Crime Victimization	2.20	2.20	2.80	3.00	2.60
Concrete insecurity:					
Secure outdoors (when alone late night)	4	5	5	5	5
Unsafe outdoors (when alone late night)	3	3	3	4	3
Afraid of particular people (in own residential area)	2	2	2	2	2
Concrete feeling unsafe	3.00	3.33	3.33	3.67	3.33
Refrained from certain activities (being afraid of violence):					
Visiting restaurants, bars, or discos	2	2	3	3	3
Visiting sport events	2	2	2	2	2
Going by train or bus	2	3	3	3	3
Total people refraining from any activity	2	2	3	3	3
Concrete Unsafety	2.43	2.71	3.00	3.14	3.00
The local police acting against the problems:					
Agree the police care about the local problems	3	4	3	3	3
Disagree the police care about the local problems	1	2	2	2	2
The public is informed about local police work	4	4	4	3	3
Attitude to Police Efforts to Deal With Local Problems	2.67	3.33	3.00	2.67	2.67
Estimated Level of the Problems	2.39	2.73	2.91	2.94	2.79

main conclusion of the safety survey in the Malmö police area in 2010 is that inhabitants' perceived safety deteriorated in Malmö between 2000 and 2007, and then recovered to a level approaching that of 2000, without that historically unique situation actually being repeated (Table 9.2).

The main conclusion from aggregating various parameters regarding the situation in northwest Scania in 2007 is that inhabitants' perception of safety

Table 9.2 Safety Index per Neighborhood, City of Malmö During Years 2000–2009

Geographical Area	2009	2008	2007	2006	2005	2004	2003	2000
Police area of Malmö	2.36	2.64	2.55	2.79	2.94	2.88	2.79	2.33
			Towns					
City of Malmö	2.36	2.64	2.58	2.82	2.91	2.91	2.67	2.39
Municipality of Burlöv	2.30	2.00	2.33	2.36	2.70	2.48	2.61	1.73
			Precincts					
Södra innerstaden	3.64	3.58	4.06	3.91	3.94	4.00	3.61	3.55
Rosengård	3.03	3.18	3.21	3.21	3.30	3.67	3.27	2.48
Centrum	2.82	3.09	3.30	3.45	3.73	3.67	3.61	3.15
Fosie	2.76	3.03	2.70	3.39	3.30	2.82	2.79	2.48
Kirseberg	2.24	2.55	2.73	2.85	3.00	2.97	2.85	2.24
Oxie	2.18	2.09	2.09	2.39	2.58	2.15	2.45	2.52
Hyllie	2.12	2.30	2.09	2.18	2.36	2.21	1.88	1.73
Husie	1.94	1.91	1.88	2.18	2.58	2.55	2.48	1.97
Limhamn/Bunkeflo	1.85	1.88	1.55	1.79	2.18	1.79	1.61	1.55
Västra innerstaden	1.70	2.18	1.85	2.06	2.18	2.24	1.76	1.67

is fairly unchanged in the period considered, 2001–2009. The year 2010 is actually much better than previous years.

The main conclusion regarding inhabitants' perceived safety in central Scania in 2010 is that there has been positive progress since 2004 (apart from 2005), the first year when all central Scanian municipalities were measured.

The main conclusion of the results from northeastern Scania in 2010 is fairly similar to that of the results of the Malmö police area: first a deterioration of inhabitants' perceived safety since 2001, followed by recovery, although this was not clear until 2010.

The main conclusion of residents' information from southern Scania is that perceived safety has been fairly unchanged since 2003, although in some respects, significantly better in 2007 than previously. The period 2008–2010 is actually better than 2007 (Table 9.3).

Table 9.3 Overall Score—General Safety Index

Area	2000	2001	2003	2004	2005	2006	2007	2008	2009	2010
Northwest		2.18		2.27	2.27	2.33	2.21	2.12	1.88	1.67
Malmö	2.33		2.70	2.88	2.94	2.79	2.55	2.64	2.36	2.39
Northeast		1.67		1.94	2.06	1.85	1.73	2.00	1.76	1.79
Central				1.79	2.00	1.79	1.52	1.79	1.64	1.48
South			1.67	1.85	1.91	1.76	1.64	1.67	1.55	1.48

Results of the Safety Index in August 2007

In safety surveys since 2004, the Scania Police Authority has been divided into 5 police areas, 14 community police areas, 33 municipalities, and approximately 30 smaller geographical areas.

The year 2007 was the first time the safety index methodology had been used, while also being retroactively calculated on all reporting geographical areas from 2000. The Malmö police area has the highest problem outlook (safety index) of the five police areas in Scania. This is followed by northwest, northeast, southern, and central Scania, which have less significant differences in their indices. The municipality of Bjuv has the highest value for the overall problem outlook (safety index) of all Scania's municipalities, marginally higher than Malmö. This is followed by Landskrona and Helsingborg. Southern City Center has the highest value for problem outlook (safety index) in the county of Scania, at level 4, followed by the districts of Planteringen and Högaborg in Helsingborg. Southern City Center is also high in comparison with all greater Stockholm's municipalities. Parts of municipalities in Limhamn-Bunkeflo and Dalby had the best problem outlook (safety index) in the county for small communities.

Problems/Disturbances—Index

The Malmö police area has the highest levels for disturbances, followed by northwestern Scania. Central Scania has the low level of 1.57. The municipality of Bjuv (northwest) was the only municipality with level 3. Bromölla and the city of Malmö are just below this level. The municipalities of Ängelholm, Höganäs, Båstad, and Lund have low levels of disturbances. For smaller areas, the districts of Southern City Center and Planteringen in Helsingborg have level 4. The districts of Limhamn-Bunkeflo, Linero, and Norra Fäladen have very low values. For the outdoor environment, Bjuv has level 4. Osby, Trelleborg, Ängelholm, Båstad, Hörby, Höganäs, and Ystad have the low level of 1.00. For substance abuse problems, Bjuv and Bromölla have level 3. Vellinge does not even reach level 1. For traffic problems and other outdoor disturbances, the municipalities of Landskrona, Malmö, Bjuv, and Burlöv are up to level 3. Båstad, Simrishamn, and Lund are at low level 1 (Table 9.4).

Exposure to Crime

The Malmö police area has the highest index for exposure to crime, the only area above level 2. Southern Scania has a very low level of 1.00. The

Table 9.4 Problem Levels of Disturbance of the Peace in Scania Towns, 2004–2007

Problems/Disturbance of the Peace				Present Situation
Towns Ranking 2007	2004 Level	2005 Level	2006 Level	2007 Level
Bjuvs kommun	2.71	3.00	2.93	3.29
Bromölla kommun	2.86	3.00	2.79	2.93
Malmö kommun	3.00	2.93	2.86	2.86
Landskrona kommun	2.93	2.71	2.57	2.57
Burlövs kommun	2.71	2.93	2.43	2.57
Helsingborgs kommun	2.57	2.50	2.43	2.57
Perstorps kommun	2.71	4.07	2.93	2.50
Åstorps kommun	2.57	2.43	2.29	2.50
Tomelilla kommun	1.86	2.29	1.93	2.36
Skurups kommun	2.29	2.43	2.93	2.29
Klippans kommun	2.57	2.57	3.14	2.21
Hörby kommun	1.86	2.21	2.36	2.21
Östra Göinge kommun	2.07	2.64	2.36	2.21
Sjöbo kommun	2.50	2.71	2.29	2.14
Svedala kommun	2.14	2.14	2.07	2.07
Kävlinge kommun	1.79	2.00	2.36	2.00
Svalövs kommun	2.00	2.21	2.14	2.00
Lomma kommun	1.29	1.43	1.57	2.00
Eslövs kommun	2.21	2.36	2.50	1.93
Örkelljunga kommun	2.29	2.00	2.07	1.93
Höör kommun	1.93	1.93	2.00	1.93
Kristianstads kommun	1.71	1.93	1.86	1.93
Hässleholms kommun	1.57	2.07	1.57	1.93
Ystads kommun	1.29	1.50	1.93	1.86
Trelleborgs kommun	2.07	1.79	1.79	1.86
Staffanstorps kommun	1.93	2.14	1.79	1.79
Osby kommun	1.71	1.93	2.07	1.71
Vellinge kommun	1.64	1.79	1.86	1.71
Simrishamns kommun	2.00	1.43	1.79	1.64
Ängelholms kommun	1.50	1.57	2.00	1.50
Höganäs kommun	1.79	1.71	1.64	1.50
Båstads kommun	1.57	1.50	1.71	1.43
Lunds kommun	1.57	1.79	1.43	1.43

municipalities of Malmö and Helsingborg have the highest indices among municipalities, where Landskrona and Bjuv also have level 2. Very low criminality, below level 1, was reported in the municipalities of Höör, Sjöbo, and Båstad. The Southern City Center is the only area to reach level 4 among the smaller geographical areas, with central Malmö, Högaborg, and Rosengård

Table 9.5 Percent Respondents Exposed to Everyday Crimes, Years 2000–2009, City of Malmö

City of Malmö, Years 2009–2000	2009	2008	2007	2006	2005	2004	2003	2000
Exposed to everyday crimes, self-declaration percent	29	33	33	34	34	36	36	35
Exposed to violence, percent	4	4	4	3	4	3	4	3
Exposed to theft, percent	19	21	22	24	24	26	26	27
Exposed to criminal damage, percent	15	20	19	19	19	22		

also reaching level 3. Areas outside the built-up parts of Landskrona and Östra Göinge North and Östra Göinge South have particularly low exposure (Tables 9.5 and 9.6).

Undefined Concerns About Crime

The Malmö police area has the highest undefined general concern of the police areas in the county of Scania. However, the differences are not so notable in Scania, but around levels 1 and 2. Malmö police area and northwestern Scania are at level 2, and central, southern, and northeast are at level 1. The city of Malmo is joint second among the municipalities, with Hörby and Helsingborg after Bjuv. Undefined concerns in the city of Malmö feature a wide variation between parts of municipalities in terms of the level of general concern and very high general concern for assault and battery in some parts of municipalities.

The municipalities of Båstad, Höör, Simrishamn, Vellinge, Ystad, and Kristianstad have low general concern about crime.

The Southern City Center (concern level 4) had the highest general concern for parts of municipalities. This was followed by concern level 3 in central Malmö and Högaborg. The built-up parts of Osby and Dalby had low concern levels.

For general undefined concerns for assault and battery, the concern levels were very high throughout Malmö. For example, Malmö City Center has very high levels (Southern City Center and Center at levels 6 and 5, respectively). The municipalities of Landskrona and Bjuv are also high, at level 3. Of the districts, Högaborg was at level 5, and Planteringen at 4. The built-up parts of Osby, Åstorp, Kvidinge, Hyllinge, Dalby, Kävlinge Öster, Kävlinge Väster, Östra Göinge North, and Östra Göinge South have very low levels of concern about crime.

Table 9.6 Problem Level of Exposed to Everyday Crimes in Various Towns, 2004–2007

Exposed to Everyday Crimes				Present Situation
Towns Ranking 2007	2004 Level	2005 Level	2006 Level	2007 Level
Malmö kommun	2.75	2.75	2.75	2.50
Helsingborgs kommun	2.25	2.25	2.25	2.50
Landskrona kommun	2.25	2.25	2.50	2.00
Bjuvs kommun	1.75	2.00	2.00	2.00
Tomelilla kommun	1.75	1.75	2.00	1.75
Lunds kommun	2.00	2.00	1.75	1.75
Kävlinge kommun	1.50	1.25	0.75	1.75
Burlövs kommun	2.25	2.25	2.00	1.50
Åstorps kommun	2.25	1.75	2.00	1.50
Klippans kommun	1.75	2.25	1.75	1.50
Kristianstads kommun	1.50	2.00	1.75	1.50
Hässleholms kommun	1.75	1.00	1.75	1.50
Ängelholms kommun	2.00	1.75	1.25	1.50
Bromölla kommun	1.25	1.75	1.25	1.50
Skurups kommun	2.00	2.00	1.75	1.25
Trelleborgs kommun	1.75	1.25	1.50	1.25
Lomma kommun	1.00	1.25	1.25	1.25
Svedala kommun	1.00	1.50	1.25	1.25
Osby kommun	1.00	1.25	1.00	1.25
Perstorps kommun	1.75	2.50	2.25	1.00
Eslövs kommun	2.00	1.75	2.00	1.00
Ystads kommun	1.25	1.00	1.75	1.00
Svalövs kommun	1.00	1.75	1.25	1.00
Hörby kommun	1.75	1.00	1.25	1.00
Staffanstorps kommun	1.75	1.00	1.25	1.00
Vellinge kommun	1.00	1.50	1.25	1.00
Örkelljunga kommun	1.75	1.25	1.00	1.00
Höganäs kommun	1.50	1.00	1.00	1.00
Östra Göinge kommun	1.25	1.50	1.00	1.00
Simrishamns kommun	1.75	1.25	1.00	1.00
Höör kommun	1.25	1.75	1.75	0.75
Sjöbo kommun	1.75	1.75	1.75	0.75
Båstads kommun	1.50	1.25	1.00	0.75

Defined Danger/Concrete Unsafety

As for more defined concerns, going out alone in residential areas late at night, being fearful of particular individuals in the area, and abstaining from activities due to fear, Malmö police area has the highest average values of the county of Scania. Landskrona has the worst values, Burlöv is in second place, and Malmö third of the municipalities of Scania. However, only Landskrona in first place has the relatively high level 3. Höganäs, Svalöv, and Svedala are the safest in this respect, at 1.00. The high-level districts are Planteringen, built-up Landskrona, Högaborg, and Southern City Center. Rosengård and Fosie are also at level 3. The residents of Dalby, the surroundings of Lund, and Osby's surrounding countryside have a very defined perception of safety.

It would appear that insecurity outdoors late at night alone in residential areas is polarized in Scania. Malmö police area has level 3, while central and southern Scania have the low level 1.33. The municipalities of Landskrona, Malmö, and Burlöv have a low level 3. Vellinge does not even attain level 1, while in this respect, the municipalities of Lomma, Svedala, Kävlinge, Båstad, Höganäs, Svalöv, Trelleborg, Ystad, and Lund can only be considered very safe. The districts at a high level 4 in 2007 are Southern City Center, Planteringen, Högaborg, built-up Landskrona, Rosengård, Fosie, and Fredriksdal in Helsingborg (Table 9.7).

Police Activity—Local Problems and Police Operations

On average in 2007, the values for whether the police care about local problems in residential areas are at normal levels in a nationwide context. The number of direct criticisms of the police has reduced over time. The most negative attitudes to local police work were in northwestern Scania and southern Scania. The most positively inclined people were in the Malmö police area and central Scania. These results did not have any dramatic, or even particularly large, variations. The municipalities of Malmö, Landskrona, Eslöv, Hörby, Klippan, Båstad, Bromölla, Perstorp, Ystad, Skurup, Bjuv, Åstorp, Lund, Staffanstorp, Kristianstad, Sjöbo, and Burlöv are among those with Scania's best values. For example, the number of expressed criticisms of the local police work in Malmö is the lowest measured since 2000, and in 2007, only about 13 of the 100 respondents expressed dissatisfaction. The inhabitants of Vellinge and Simrishamn have the most critical attitude to local police work.

The district of Rosengård has the highest share of residents positive to local police work. Rosengård's values are the most positive conducted throughout Scania. For a lengthy period, Rosengård has also returned good values.

A more expressed critical attitude to local police work is apparent in the residents of the Malmö Western City Center, Östra Göinge North, and the countryside surrounding the built-up parts of Landskrona, some parts of Helsingborg, Kävlinge West, the built-up parts of Osby, other parts of the

Table 9.7 Problem Levels of Defined Danger/Concrete Unsafety in Various Towns, 2004–2007

Defined Danger/Concrete Unsafety				
Towns Ranking 2007	2004 Level	2005 Level	2006 Level	2007 Level
Landskrona kommun	2.71	3.29	3.71	3.14
Burlövs kommun	2.43	2.71	3.00	2.71
Malmö kommun	3.00	3.14	3.00	2.43
Bjuvs kommun	2.00	2.00	2.00	2.43
Tomelilla kommun	1.86	2.00	2.29	2.29
Helsingborgs kommun	2.29	2.43	2.14	2.29
Åstorps kommun	1.71	1.86	1.71	2.29
Perstorps kommun	1.71	2.86	2.00	2.14
Bromölla kommun	1.29	1.71	1.29	2.00
Hörby kommun	1.57	1.71	1.71	1.71
Trelleborgs kommun	1.71	1.57	1.57	1.71
Eslövs kommun	2.29	2.57	2.29	1.57
Hässleholms kommun	1.57	1.57	1.29	1.57
Klippans kommun	1.57	1.86	1.86	1.43
Staffanstorps kommun	2.00	2.14	1.86	1.43
Skurups kommun	1.43	2.00	1.71	1.43
Ystads kommun	1.00	1.29	1.43	1.43
Sjöbo kommun	1.71	1.71	1.43	1.43
Ängelholms kommun	1.71	1.86	1.86	1.29
Kävlinge kommun	1.43	1.57	1.43	1.29
Osby kommun	1.29	1.43	1.43	1.29
Kristianstads kommun	1.71	1.29	1.29	1.29
Östra Göinge kommun	1.43	1.43	1.29	1.29
Örkelljunga kommun	2.00	1.57	1.14	1.29
Båstads kommun	1.29	1.43	1.14	1.29
Lomma kommun	1.29	1.29	1.00	1.29
Vellinge kommun	0.71	0.86	1.00	1.29
Höör kommun	1.29	2.29	1.29	1.14
Simrishamns kommun	1.43	1.29	1.14	1.14
Lunds kommun	1.43	1.57	1.86	1.00
Höganäs kommun	1.14	1.43	1.57	1.00
Svalövs kommun	1.00	1.71	1.29	1.00
Svedala kommun	1.43	1.71	1.29	1.00

municipality of Osby, Norra Fäladen in Lund, and central Lund. However, without being particularly conspicuous, these values are negative. In most cases, this is also a matter of ignorance of police work, because the share unable to evaluate local police work is sizable, exerting a negative impact on the index (Table 9.8).

Table 9.8 Problem Levels of Police Efforts to Deal With Local Problems in Various Towns in Scania, 2004–2007

Attitude to Police Efforts to Deal With Local Problems—Index				Present Situation
Towns Ranking 2007	2004 Level	2005 Level	2006 Level	2007 Level
Simrishamns kommun	3.33	3.33	3.33	3.67
Vellinge kommun	3.33	3.00	3.33	3.67
Lomma kommun	3.33	3.33	3.67	3.33
Osby kommun	2.67	3.00	3.67	3.33
Tomelilla kommun	3.67	2.67	3.67	3.33
Svedala kommun	3.33	4.00	3.67	3.33
Helsingborgs kommun	2.67	3.33	3.33	3.33
Svalövs kommun	3.00	3.00	3.33	3.33
Höganäs kommun	3.67	3.33	3.33	3.33
Höör kommun	3.33	3.33	3.33	3.33
Hässleholms kommun	3.33	3.00	3.33	3.33
Östra Göinge kommun	2.67	3.67	3.33	3.33
Trelleborgs kommun	3.33	3.67	3.33	3.33
Ängelholms kommun	3.67	2.67	3.00	3.33
Örkelljunga kommun	3.00	3.33	2.67	3.33
Kävlinge kommun	3.00	3.33	3.33	3.00
Landskrona kommun	2.67	3.33	3.33	2.67
Eslövs kommun	3.33	3.33	3.33	2.67
Hörby kommun	3.33	3.33	3.33	2.67
Klippans kommun	2.67	2.67	3.00	2.67
Båstads kommun	2.67	3.33	3.00	2.67
Bromölla kommun	2.67	2.67	3.00	2.67
Perstorps kommun	2.67	2.00	3.00	2.67
Ystads kommun	3.33	3.33	3.00	2.67
Skurups kommun	2.00	3.33	3.00	2.67
Malmö kommun	3.00	2.67	2.67	2.67
Burlövs kommun	2.67	3.00	2.67	2.67
Bjuvs kommun	3.00	3.00	2.67	2.67
Åstorps kommun	3.00	2.67	2.67	2.67
Lunds kommun	3.00	3.00	2.67	2.67
Staffanstorps kommun	3.33	2.67	2.67	2.67
Kristianstads kommun	3.00	3.00	2.67	2.67
Sjöbo kommun	2.00	2.33	2.67	2.67

Example 9.1: The Emergency Callout Process in Scania—Public Satisfaction

In July 2007, calls were made to 2,800 people that had been connected to the police regional communications center in Malmö in May, and that had left their phone numbers coincident with either wanting something from or informing something to the police. The purpose of conducting telephone interviews on the callers was to examine how satisfied they were with the police processing of their telephone call, in terms of the case itself and from a service perspective. The Swedish quality index (SQI)—a major scientific methodology prepared to evaluate user satisfaction with a specific activity and applied in over 2,000 studies nationwide and internationally—underpinned the evaluation. The quality index is a model-based analysis system to prepare, process, and present information on quality, as perceived by actual users (operational police services). Accordingly, it is entirely based on these parties' assessments, based on personal experience and, accordingly, on actual police actions. This model also implies an ambition to produce statements on the causal link between simultaneous estimation techniques. The model can be used for comparisons over time, between police units, various geographical regions or societal groups, and also for concrete international comparisons.

Corresponding surveys had previously been conducted in Scania in 2002 and 2005. Previous surveys indicated deterioration in satisfaction in Scania between 2002 and 2005, substantial differences between different geographical areas, and relatively low satisfaction among the general public of mass cases in priority groups 3 and 4.

The survey in 2007 reports a significant improvement in public satisfaction in all the previously more problematic respects. Overall, public satisfaction in Scania increased in 2007, the quality differences between various geographical areas decreased, and a distinct improvement in caller satisfaction in priority groups 3 and 4 was achieved.

A rolling update system was introduced in the fall with monthly reporting, with the first report of October indicating that the improvements do not appear temporary, but primarily corroborate improvement in public satisfaction in Scania with police assistance from the county communications center, and that mass cases in priority groups 3 and 4 saw a stable quality improvement since 2005.

Example 9.2: When the Public Report a Crime, How Satisfied Are They with Police Work in Scania in 2007—Assessed Using the SQI Method

From the reporting perspective, the police authority in Scania examined the quality of police crime investigations in Scania generally, and by police area in 2007. Specific examinations of different types of crime were conducted, because experience indicates that the differences in quality between the types of crime are very sizable. The reporting party's perceptions and experience of actual work on individual crime reports, and continuous contact with the police, were examined using the SQI method (equal to the measurement system for the callout process). Respondents were sampled according to scientific statistic principles from the reporting register. Reports were conducted in all five police areas, with the general situation for all crime investigations measured, and two crime types (housebreaking and assault by an unknown assailant) subject to specific examination. Reporters of rape/attempted rape were questioned for the whole of Scania, and reported without division into police areas. A total of 5,571 questionnaires were sent by post in June 2007, with 3,107 completed questionnaires received. The response frequency is as high as previously in Sweden.

Summarizing Results for 2007

Plaintiff satisfaction with police work on housebreaking has always been fairly high, particularly in Scania and Stockholm. A comparison with the results for 2001 suggests sustained positive progress in Scania toward still higher satisfaction. Very good to good values were measured across all police areas in Scania. The POMS quality index in 2007 of 70 for reporters of housebreaking is the highest single value ever for police crime investigation, and is fully commensurate with the highest Swedish standards of customer satisfaction in other sectors.

The police in Scania are no exception from other police authorities on assault by unknown assailant, which all have a low quality index. In Scania in 2007, the average was 46. Plaintiff satisfaction for reported assault by unknown assailant has been a known problem throughout Sweden on investigation, ever since the SQI surveys were introduced for the Swedish police in 2000. Nor has any improvement in reporting party satisfaction occurred since the measures of plaintive satisfaction for this were last conducted in 2001–2003. The police in Scania are still unable to satisfy the reporting parties' high expectations of police work and legal process when assaults are reported.

The quality index was at level 50 for rape/attempted rape, which is not fully satisfactory. The main reason that satisfaction is not higher is that expectations are not satisfied in respect to the police/complete legal process. However, relatively good values were achieved on service quality/availability/encounter, satisfying plaintiff expectations of the police in Scania. Respondents stated low values for complaints processing on rape investigations. These complaints have a far higher element of criticism of encounters and communication than complaints on investigations of housebreaking and assault, although here too the majority of complaints by reporting parties are on case processing. However, there is a complete absence of previous reference material, and accordingly, any conclusions should be subject to considerable caution.

For the first time, the survey investigated the other (all) crime category to gain a perception of the satisfaction of petty crimes and the possibility to evaluate the more abstract concept of crime investigation. Generally, the values are good in Scania, and perhaps above expectations, considering previous investigations of various crime types in Sweden. However, a discrepancy between police areas has been discovered, necessitating more in-depth analysis, which began in September (Table 9.9).

Reporters of Rape/Attempted Rape During the Period September 3, 2005 to April 15, 2007 in the County of Skåne

Sent out: 475 questionnaires. Return: 162 answers. Total response rate: 34.1%. Relatively low response rate, and the findings should be carefully demonstrated. Complaints during the process: 23%, 37 respondents are not satisfied with the handling of the complaints, just 31 points. If you compare to house burglary, normal 47–66 points and overall average 37–60 points for handling complaints on police investigations, the value is low (Table 9.10).

Table 9.9 House Burglary—Public Satisfaction Values

Police Area	Index Satisfaction	Image	Expectations	Product Quality	Service Quality	Loyality
Malmö 2007	63	56	59	62	70	81
Emergency unit Malmö 2003	62	53	62	63	71	82
Emergency unit Malmö 2001	69	61	68	68	76	
Malmö 2001	63	56	66	61	69	
Central 2007	70	62	66	69	76	86
Central 2001	62	57	64	64	70	
Northeast 2007	62	58	65	63	69	81
Northeast 2001	61	53	66	59	67	
Northwest 2007	64	58	63	65	71	81
Northwest 2007	61	52	65	60	69	
South 2007	66	59	65	66	73	83
South 2001	59	53	66	59	67	
Stockholm 2001, earlier best value in Sweden	65	55	62	64	73	

Table 9.10 Rape/Attempted Rape—Public Satisfaction Values

County	Total Index	Image	Expectations	Product Quality	Service Quality	Value	Loyality
Skåne	50	50	60	50	61	52	58

Main Conclusions of Customer Satisfaction Studies—Crime Investigations

Differences in plaintiff satisfaction between client types are greater than expressed by previous discourse. Accordingly, any general conclusions regarding the satisfaction of crime investigation are not possible, but rather, satisfaction of the investigation of different crime types.

The broad mass of the public/plaintiffs/people needing assistance needs to be influenced in order to increase satisfaction with police investigation work significantly.

Normally, no single action is enough, but instead, notable improvements are achieved through persistent, long-term small improvements —continuously.

Plaintiffs are very satisfied with police work in Scania for various types of crime, such as housebreaking, bag snatching, and car theft.

Generally, staff willingness and personal commitment gain high values. Some values can be considered very positive, even in comparison with other organizations, institutions, and corporations, nationally and internationally.

However, reporting party satisfaction with police work needs to increase for certain crime types (such as assault by unknown assailant, rape/attempted rape), and moreover, SQI results should be a far more significant starting point for overall police operational planning than they have until now.

Until the present, the police have had relatively low values for image/perception in local communities. This is a worrying indication, and very consistent with the results of safety questionnaires in the 2000s. However, some improvement is notable in 2007.

Plaintiffs, the police, and senior management levels often have differing perceptions of good quality crime investigation.

Knowledge of the victim's perspective is very important for managing and controlling policing activities.

Crime and insecurity in recent years have been a dominant theme in southern Sweden. How it really looks like, it may seem difficult to get an idea. Most have been solved opinions and pure myth. It is much debated and controversial how safety and security should be measured. Safety here means a combination of problems with the outdoor environment, abuse, drugs, disorder, traffic, everyday crimes, concern for burglary, assault or abuse, feeling afraid alone at night, afraid of others, refraining from activities, and if the police care about the local neighborhood problems. The logic is clear. If many residents perceive a problem, the problem is widespread. If few perceive a problem, it is less. What percentage perceive a problem is also compared with the average for Sweden. In this way, priority can be made. Over a longer period, police in southern Sweden conducted safety surveys in conjunction with many of the municipalities and local crime prevention boards. A total of over 120,000 residents in southern Sweden during 15 years responded to the police safety surveys. The response rate has always been very high, and is believed to give an accurate picture of what the majority of the residents perceive has happened and is happening in southern Sweden. No one else, whether police, politicians, or bloggers, can speak in the name of this majority.

Analysis of measurements gives a good picture of a municipality's disorder, crime, safety, and insecurity factors. A large number of safety initiatives have subsequently been implemented by police in Skåne's municipalities over the past seven years. Working method to achieve greater safety has been visibility of police operations and focusing upon solving the major municipal problems. Low tolerance of problems and disturbances has been the main strategy and tactic. Positive results have materialized in most of the towns and villages. Improved safety in recent years has been noted in 19 of Skåne's 33 municipalities, also, in safety terms, in disputed cities like Malmö and

Landskrona. Although it is difficult to objectively assess the impact on police work in the municipalities, it remains that the police have priorities based on public information, with positive results right there and when this information was used. Perhaps successfully in half of the community policing areas. Everyday crimes have also in recent years declined in Skåne, including a lot of the most exposed municipalities, like Klippan, Landskrona, Malmö, Trelleborg, and Perstorp. The results reported for 2010 were sensational. The residents' vulnerability to everyday crimes in Helsingborg has now fallen by over 30%, and in Landskrona by over 20% since 2007, somewhat implausible figures. This civic-based approach has also led to the general public having a less critical view of police than before in Skåne. The evidence suggests that if police use safety measures and have the ability to work according to their indications, the relationship with the public improves immediately.

Community Policing in South Korea
Do Line Officers and Supervisors Feel the Same?

10

WOOK KANG
MAHESH K. NALLA

Introduction

Though the term *community policing* (CP) is widely used in policing scholarship and practice, it elicits disparate understanding about what it means. Yet, the concept has been widely embraced and accepted in many countries. The term encompasses a range of philosophical, organizational, and practical approaches to police work. At its core CP represents a set of expectations that includes work that revolves around a specific order of maintenance chores that help to bring officers close to the community. Some of these functions include handling of public nuisance calls, disputes with neighbors and family, and litter and trash issues, among others. These tasks not only consume much of the officers' time, but they are also phenomena common in many parts of the world.

A second important element of all community policing programs is an expectation for close working relationships between law enforcement officers and citizens. Citizens who are less satisfied with police are less likely to be cooperative with police officers and less willing to share information critical to making police work more efficient (Greene & Decker, 1989). Thus, a critical aspect of community policing is that police departments that have CP programs must place a greater emphasis on, and encouragement of, citizen participation in order to enhance public safety (Skogan, 2004). In this chapter we will briefly examine community-oriented policing efforts in South Korea. More importantly, in this exploratory study, we examine the extent to which the views of line officers and supervisors are similar or different regarding three aspects of community policing: views regarding the extent to which patrol officers should be concerned about community concerns that directly affect order maintenance, perceived citizen support and community cooperation with police, and support for community policing in general.

South Korean Police

As a former colony of Japan, the 20th century South Korean police history is similar to colonial experiences of former colonies from other parts of the world. That is, police organizations were structured to function primarily to protect state interests, an operational philosophy that continues in many countries, including some countries who have achieved independence from their colonial masters. Japan, which occupied the Korean peninsula until 1910, maintained tight control over Korea and used local citizens as police officers who occupied key police positions (Hoffman, 1982). Further, police substations were used to watch citizens and discourage anti-Japanese activities, and this resulted in Korean citizens perceiving police as frontline enforcers of colonization (Hwang, 2008). When Korea became independent in 1945, it continued with the Japanese national model of a centralized and highly bureaucratic style police system to control Korean citizens (Hwang, 2008). Similar patterns of a police operational philosophy are apparent in postindependent South Korea where the Korean police were involved in manipulating various elections in the 1960s and aiding and supporting undemocratic and authoritative regimes in the 1970s and 1980s (Moon, 2004).

The Korean police organization is centralized with the Korea National Police Agency as its central headquarters, and as of September, 2010, it is comprised of 16 regional police agencies (state police), 244 police stations, and 773 police substations (beat or police officers). This translates to 99,554 sworn officers, of whom 6,506 (6.5%) are women. These officers are assisted by 28,117 assistant police and 3,842 civilians. In organizations where the centrally bureaucratic line officers follow the mandate set by the central government, it may not always translate into policies tailored for local community contexts. In other words, line officers do not have much discretion to tweak national policies to adapt to the needs of the local communities (Nalla & Hwang, 2006). This situation is further exacerbated by the fact that the tenure for top police leadership is only for a short duration of time, which makes it difficult to bring about organizational changes in a sustained manner (Kim, 2000, cited in Moon, 2004). Further, unlike in the United States, these differences are further exaggerated by the separate and distinct recruitment and training methods and facilities for supervisors and line officers that result in the creation of distinct occupational cultures. For instance, there is a single training center for all officers (Korea National Police University (KNPU)) and one separate facility (Police Comprehensive Academy (PCA)) for all line officers that inculcates and fosters distinct cultural traditions.

The postindependent Korea has witnessed major police reforms. In 1991, the Korea National Police Agency (KNPA) was established to remove the police from the direct influence of the Ministry of Home Affairs, an organization that directly oversees the election administration (Pyo, 2000). These efforts were directed to minimize citizen distrust of police and enhance the public imagery of police officers. The first police reform of 1972 addressed issues of training, pay, and equipment (Lee, 2000), while the second reform (1985) focused on the creation and uniform application of policies and procedures that govern investigator recruitment and training with a goal to increase public confidence (Choi, 1985). The reform of 1999, called the grand reform, introduced a more comprehensive plan by bringing about fundamental changes to police practices and culture, and organizational changes to Korean police (Pyo, 2003). These reforms focused on promoting officers' self-confidence and professionalism, higher salaries, and a better work environment. However, the major thrust of the reforms was placed on citizen welfare as a primary mandate by creating open lines of communication with citizens (KNPA, 2004), and it appears to have had a positive impact on citizens' satisfaction with police services (Pyo, 2003). A natural outcome of the citizen-centric mandate of the grand reform was the introduction of community policing in Korea (Baek, 2000).

Community Policing Program Implementation

Korean police have used police substations to implement community policing, although ironically and historically these very police substations are ones that were used as stomping grounds by manipulative police bureaucrats serving under previous undemocratic and authoritative governments (Baek, 2000). A police substation is a branch office of a police department, and it consists of several office rooms and a conference room. Generally, local police departments have 5 to 15 police substations, which are directed by local police departments, with each police substation having its own precinct and patrols for the assigned area. Patrol officers work at police substations, and they contact citizens by visiting their homes (Hwang, 2008). In general, 20 to 40 officers work at the police substations, which are organized into three squads that cover two shifts per day. The chief officer of the police station is typically of the rank lieutenant or captain (depending on the size and number of officers assigned to the substation).

One of the goals of meeting at a substation is to improve the relationship between community and police (Baek, 2000). Meetings with community members are held at police substations because of the convenient locations, and this familiarity helps make citizens more at ease (KNPA, 2002). In 2003, there were 20,088 community meetings involving 155,600 citizens (KNPA,

2004). These meetings are similar to a beat meeting in the United States and are attended by patrol officers on duty at the time, a few team members from other shifts, detectives from the police departments, and the chief of police for the substation. Sometimes, the chief of the police department attends the meeting to receive the opinions directly from the residents, and subsequent meetings are customized to the needs of the community. For example, some police substations in cities hold meetings on weekends to make it easier for residents who work and commute on weekdays to attend. The topics covered in the meetings relate to neighborhood crimes and other law and order issues that affect residences and businesses. Police substations in rural areas focus on issues related to crimes against the environment or crimes involving safety issues. Police officers make an effort to encourage community members to attend these meetings by advertising the venue, date, and time on patrol cars. Local media such as cable TV or newspapers announce the details of the meeting and also advertise the meeting schedules. Proceedings of these meetings are shared with the local police departments as well as the community. When emerging issues have items that cross over into other jurisdictions, often joint meetings are held.

Since the grand reform in 1999, the KNPA has begun to conduct citizen surveys twice a year, a practice still existing today as one of the elements of CP in Korea. The aim of the citizen survey is to assess citizen perceptions of community problems as well as their satisfaction or dissatisfaction with police services (KNPA, 2002). Survey results, which were organized as part of a joint effort by citizens and officer foot patrols (KNPA, 2004), suggest that there was support for foot patrols as a component of community policing programs (Jaegal & Chang, 2005).

In addition, citizen police academy programs are conducted at all local police departments. These programs are conducted for a duration of six weeks and participants receive certificates upon completion (KNPA, 2004). These programs are conducted at all local police departments. The objective of the academy is not to train an individual to be a police officer but rather to inform citizens (KNPA, 2004). Participants receive three hours of training one evening each week, and they are taught the basics of criminal law, criminal procedure law, patrol tactics, as well as many other subjects. They participate in a ride-along with an officer and meet various officers, such as patrol officers and detectives. The class size depends on the local police departments, but 30 citizens is an average size. Citizens interested in the academy must complete a written application and get permission from local police departments.

It is noted that generally, in addition to partnering with local community members, local police departments that build extensive networks with other agencies are more successful at effectively solving community problems and implementing CP programs (Tilley, 2004). Accordingly, Korean police created special units that incorporate local fire departments, city governments, schools, and district prosecutors as partners of their community policing (KNPA, 2002). The members meet every month to discuss and solve community problems. As described above, the proceedings from the meetings with community members in police substations are shared with the local police departments, who in turn share these proceedings with the police headquarters. Analysts in the police headquarters compile all this information by layering it with local crime rates and identifying areas of concern, referred to as hot spots. Based on these efforts, in 2009 a total of 598 areas were designated as hot spots (KNPA, 2010), with some of these hot spots involving properties vulnerable to arson. In such instances, the local police department seeks cooperation with the local fire departments and holds a special unit's meeting. In other areas, where school safety is a concern, school principals are included in the monthly meetings and are encouraged to hire more private security guards. These are some of the examples of decisions made by special units created by KNPA (2010) as a consequence of community policing efforts.

Is There Support for Community Policing?

Researchers in other countries have examined the relationship between the demographic characteristics of the police officers and their attitudes toward community policing. Findings suggest that women and minority officers have a more positive attitude toward community policing (Paoline, Myers, & Worden, 2000; Schafer, 2001), while others have noted that gender is not significantly related to one's attitude toward community policing (O'Shea, 1999; Weisel & Eck, 1994). College education was also found to be related to attitudes toward community policing in the United States. Carter and Sapp (1989) found that officers with a college education had more positive attitudes toward community policing than those without college degrees. However, others found that an officer's attitude toward community policing is not influenced by his or her level of education (Lewis, Rosenberg, & Sigler, 1999). Paoline and colleagues (2000) reported that college educated officers are more motivated for advancement and promotion within their organizations. When they engage in effective community policing, officers are more likely to be promoted as a reward for their good performance.

Age is an important predictor of officers' support for community policing, as is years of service. Lurigio and Skogan (1994), in their research of officers who had attended CP training programs, found that those in their 50s had a more positive attitude toward community policing than did those in their 40s, 30s, or 20s, and that those officers in their 40s had a more positive attitude than those in their 30s and 20s. Research on the relationship between years of service and a positive view of CP resulted in mixed results. Paoline and his colleagues (2000) found years of service to be positively associated with an officer's attitude toward community policing; that is, more experienced officers had more positive perceptions of citizens' cooperation and more chances to be assigned to beats with favorable residents than less experienced officers. Conversely, Weisel and Eck (1994) reported that officers with less than one year in policing had the highest percentage of positive opinions regarding community policing, and that as the number of years of service increased, the opinion became less positive.

Research shows that rank was found to be a significant predictor of support for CP. Schafer (2001) and Rosenbaum, Yeh, and Wilkinson (1994) found that high-ranking officers, that is, lieutenant or captain, were more favorable to community policing than line officers. Job assignment is also related to support for CP. Patrol officers have a more positive attitude toward community policing than do detectives. This is thought to be because patrol officers have an understanding and appreciation for community policing as a result of their training programs and also favorable interactions with citizens (Lord & Friday, 2008; Paoline et al., 2000; Schafer, 2001; Wycoff & Skogan, 1994).

Prior research attempted to examine the implementation of community policing officers and citizens' views of CP programs in Korea. In a survey of 94 local police departments out of a total of 233 in Korea (Jaegal & Chang, 2005), it was found that more than half of the local police departments reported being actively engaged in community policing activities. Choi (2006) surveyed 511 patrol officers and 434 citizens and reported that more than one-third of both the patrol officers and citizens perceived community policing to be effective in the prevention of crime, while only 15% of them perceived community policing as ineffective. However, despite efforts, that community policing in Korea still has several problems, most of which stem from the vagueness of the concept of community policing and the low numbers of citizen participation (Kim & Woo, 2006).

Regarding gender as a predictor of support for CP programs, prior research in Korea did not reveal any significant findings. A survey of 1,527 officers in 47 local police departments in Korea revealed that gender is not a significant factor in predicting officers' attitudes toward community policing (Park, 2006). However, one has to keep in mind that women officers represent about 6% of the total police force. Similarly, Hwang and Woo (2009) confirmed that gender is not related to officers' perceptions of community policing in Korea. Regarding education, while Park (2006) and Moon (2006) found that education did not affect Korean officers' attitudes toward community policing, Hwang and Woo (2009) contend that an officer's education is positively related to his or her attitude toward community policing, and that highly educated officers have more positive attitudes.

Similar to Paoline et al.'s (2000) work in the United Stats, more experienced officers in Korea are found to have more positive attitudes toward community policing (Hwang & Woo, 2009). Age was also found to be a predictor of support for CP in Korea. Officers in their 50s have the most positive attitudes toward community policing, while officers in their 20s have the least positive attitudes (Park, 2006). Rank as a predictor of support for CP has received mixed findings in Korea. Moon (2006) reported that rank did not affect Korean police officers' attitudes toward community policing, while Park (2006) contends that rank is negatively associated with officers' attitudes. He reasoned that the dual and separate recruiting system in Korea may contribute to such a conclusion. However, in general, patrol officers, as compared to those assigned to other units, have a more positive attitude toward CP (Moon, 2006; Park, 2006).

While these studies offer some insights about the relationship between various demographic characteristics and support for community policing, we extended this line of inquiry by adding more context to officers' attitudes toward community policing. That is, in addition to seeking responses about their familiarity and support of community policing, we also assess their perceptions on officers' community concerns and citizen-police relationships. Effective policing involves active engagement and collaboration of citizens in the coproduction of order maintenance (Moore, Trojanowicz, & Kelling, 1988). Research suggests that citizens who are dissatisfied with the police are less likely to provide them with crime-related information and are more reluctant to cooperate with the police, which diminishes police effectiveness in controlling crime (Decker, 1985; Brown & Benedict, 2002). Literature on community policing suggests an intricate relationship between officers' orientation to order maintenance, as opposed to crime control, and the perceived citizen support. Further, public reciprocity and willingness to cooperate with law enforcement, for the most part, depend on their trust, satisfaction, and confidence in police as an organization and institution (Sunshine & Tyler, 2003). In addition to these dimensions we added an additional officer's attribute, namely, job assignment. For instance, prior research compared only patrol officers and detectives. Our study includes a third category: administrators. We believe including police administrators is important because they are not necessarily active in community policing programs and might not interact with the local community on a regular basis. Their views about community policing are important to understand, and thus in this exploratory study, we examine police officers' perceptions of community policing by rank as well as by job assignment.

The Present Study

The data for this chapter come from a survey of police officers in South Korea who attended training courses at the Korea National Police University (KNPU) and Police Comprehensive Academy (PCA). The survey was conducted from June through August 2008. Generally, the KNPU provides managers with training courses (e.g., leadership, police administration, and public relations), while the PCA trains line officers with practical programs (e.g., investigation, traffic training, and patrol). The duration of these courses range from one week to three months. It is mandatory for both police supervisors and line officers to take these training courses to get promoted to higher ranks, and on average, all officers are trained every four years. Conducting a survey at both educational facilities is a convenient way to obtain a national sample, because all police officers in Korea are trained at either KNPU or PCA. The survey instrument has a series of questions on various demographic characteristics and dimensions of community concerns that affect local citizens, police-citizen relationships, and views about community policing in general. A 5-point Likert scale response option was provided with each statement. It ranged from strongly disagree (1) to strongly agree (5) to the statements. The questionnaire was translated into Korean and was then backtranslated to check for validity and reliability.

We surveyed a total of 650 police officers who were currently attending the KNPU and PCA. Four hundred questionnaires were distributed at PCA and 250 at KNPU. The survey was conducted with the permission of the instructors and the consent of all participants. Overall, we collected 406 (176 from KNPU and 230 from PCA) of the 650 distributed surveys and the response rate was 62%.

Findings

Descriptive statistics are presented in Table 10.1. The average age of all the respondents is 39 years. Almost half of the respondents are officers aged 35, and those with more than 46 years represent 32% of the sample. Regarding years of experience, a majority of the responders have worked from 11 to 20 years and 19% of the respondents have worked more than 21 years. The average number of years of experience is 14. More than half of all the respondents have bachelor's degrees or higher. One-third of the respondents are lieutenants or higher. In Korea, the rank of lieutenant or higher is considered manager level. The rank of sergeant is between a line officer and manager, and 36% of those surveyed for this study are this rank. Some sergeants work as managers such as the chief of a patrol shift consisting of

Table 10.1 Respondents Demographic Characteristics (N = 406)

Variables	N (%[a])
Age	
1 = Less than 35	188 (47%)
2 = 36–45	84 (21%)
3 = More than 46	129 (32%)
Years of Experience	
1 = Less than 10	151 (38%)
2 = 11–20	171 (43%)
3 = More than 21	78 (19%)
Education	
0 = High school or associate's degree	199 (49%)
1 = Bachelor of arts or more	204 (51%)
Rank	
1 = Police officer[b] or senior patrol officer	125 (31%)
2 = Sergeant	146 (36%)
3 = Lieutenant or higher	133 (33%)
Job Assignment	
1 = Patrol or traffic	229 (57%)
2 = Criminal investigation	90 (22%)
3 = Police administration	85 (21%)

[a] Missing cases are excluded (i.e., valid percent).
[b] Lowest rank.

5 to 10 patrol officers, while others work as line, patrol, or traffic officers. More than half of the respondents work in the patrol or traffic division, while 22% of the respondents are investigators, with the remaining 21% of them working in administration, which includes divisions such as general affairs, general administration, public security, intelligence, national security, and foreign security.

Police officers' views on police-citizen relations and community policing are presented in Table 10.2. Although the original questionnaire employs a 5-point Likert scale ranging from 1 (strongly disagree) to 5 (strongly agree), we have collapsed them into three categories that represent strongly agree/agree, not sure, and strongly disagree/disagree.

Responses to questions relating to officers' perceptions of community concerns (i.e., matters typically considered to fall within the range of community policing concerns) suggest that for the most part, officers were either positive or at least ambivalent. Eighty percent of the respondents perceived that patrol officers should be expected to do something about a

Table 10.2 Descriptive Statistics for Officers' Views on Police-Citizen Relations and Community Policing (N = 406)

Survey Items[a]	SA/A[b]	Not Sure	SD/D[c]	Mean/SD
Community Concerns				
Patrol officers should be expected to do something about ...				
a. Public nuisance	80.3	15.7	4	3.93/0.72
b. Neighbors' disputes	53.6	28.6	18	3.40/0.95
c. Family disputes	40.1	31.4	28	3.12/1.01
d. Litter and trash	39.3	26.1	35	3.01/1.10
e. Nuisance that causes lots of problems for neighbors	68.8	19.5	12	3.67/0.89
Citizen Cooperation: Citizens ...				
a. Generally cooperate with police officers	25.9	36.9	37	2.80/.97
b. Trust police officers	15.7	49.4	35	2.75/.85
c. Often call the police if they see something suspicious	42.2	35	23	3.18/.92
d. Provide information about a crime if they know something and are asked by police	16.8	45.2	38	2.74/.84
e. Are willing to work with the police and try to solve neighborhood problems	17.5	43.1	39	2.73/.88
Community Policing				
a. I am very familiar with the concept of community policing	47.5	41.3	11	3.43/.87
b. I support community policing programs	54.6	32.9	13	3.48/.91

[a] 1 = strongly disagree, 2 = disagree, 3 = not sure, 4 = agree, 5 = strongly agree.
[b] Combine 4 = agree and 5 = strongly agree (percentage).
[c] Combine 1 = strongly disagree and 2 = disagree (percentage).

public nuisance. The Punishment of Minor Offense Act (1983, revised 2006) describes 54 minor offenses, including public nuisance. A person who commits any of these 54 minor offenses will be punished by a fine not exceeding $100. Sixty-eight percent of the respondents reported that patrol officers should be expected to do something about a nuisance that causes lots of problems for neighbors. However, only 40% of the officers perceived that patrol officers should be expected to do something about family disputes. Officers are reluctant to get involved in family disputes unless they may lead to serious crimes. In addition, 40% of the respondents reported that patrol officers should be expected to do something about litter and trash.

Regarding citizen cooperation, the officers surveyed have either negative or at best ambivalent attitudes. Korean police served undemocratic and authoritative regimes for several decades until a civilian was elected president in 1993. As noted earlier, Korean police manipulated various elections in the 1960s and suppressed democracy and freedom of expression in the 1970s and 1980s, resulting in a significant level of citizen distrust toward police officers, and resulting in the 1999 grand reform. Although the grand reform has been deemed successful, many police officers still perceive that they are not supported by the public. In our survey, only one-quarter of the respondents reported that citizens generally cooperate with police officers. Fifteen percent of the respondents perceived that citizens trust police officers, while 35% of them reported that citizens do not. Police officers also perceived that citizens are not cooperative. For example, only 16% of the respondents reported that citizens provide information about a crime if they know something when questioned by police, and only 17% of them reported that citizens are willing to work with the police to try and solve neighborhood problems. However, 42% of the respondents reported that citizens often call the police if they see something suspicious.

Despite the officers' negative perceptions of citizen cooperation, more than half of the respondents support community policing and 47% of them reported that they are very familiar with the concept of community policing, a program introduced in 1999 as part of the grand reform.

We conducted analyses of variance (ANOVAs) and F tests to assess if systematic differences exist between subgroups of police personnel by age, years of experience, education, rank, and job assignment. Mean differences on various questions representing officers' views by age are presented in Table 10.3. Findings suggest that officers who are 36 years and older are more supportive of the idea that handling a public nuisance is a patrol officer's duty than are those who are 35 years and younger. This finding is statistically significant. In addition, older officers are not only more familiar with the concept of community policing, but also more likely to support community policing than are younger officers. These statistically significant findings are similar to the conclusions drawn from Park (2006).

Officers' perceptions of community concerns, citizen-police relationships, and community policing by their years of experience are displayed in Table 10.4. Officers with work experience of 11 to 20 years have perceived negative attitudes about citizens' general cooperation and trust in police when compared to officers who have less than 10 years of experience. On the other hand, officers who have worked more than 21 years appeared ambivalent. This finding was found to be statistically significant. Regarding familiarity with the concept of community policing experience or support for community policing, officers who have more than 21 years expressed a stronger support relative to those who worked for 20 years or less. These findings are similar to research in the United States (Paoline et al., 2000), and the mean differences among groups were found to be statistically significant. This finding may be tempered by the fact that in Korea, in general, seniority is one of the important factors in determining an officer's beat

Table 10.3 A Comparison of Mean Differences (ANOVA) by Age (N = 406)

Variable[a]	Age			
	≤25 Years	36–45	≥46 Years	F
Community Concerns				
Patrol officers should be expected to do something about …				
a. Public nuisance	3.76	4	4	4.90**
b. Neighbors' disputes	3.33	3.45	3.38	0.6
c. Family disputes	3.12	3.17	3	0.78
d. Litter and trash	2.87	3.09	3.01	1.51
e. Nuisance that causes lots of problems for neighbors	3.63	3.67	3.68	0.12
Citizen cooperation: Citizens …				
a. Generally cooperate with police officers	2.77	2.76	2.9	0.71
b. Trust police officers	2.71	2.7	2.88	1.42
c. Often call the police if they see something suspicious	3.19	3.18	3.16	0.02
d. Provide information about a crime if they know something and are asked by police	2.78	2.66	2.78	1.01
e. Are willing to work with the police and try to solve neighborhood problems	2.66	2.76	2.72	0.53
Community Policing				
a. I am very familiar with the concept of community policing	3.28	3.38	3.76	8.47**
b. I support community policing programs	3.22	3.48	3.84	12.28**

+, $p < .10$; *, $p < .05$; **, $p < .01$.

[a] 1 = strongly disagree, 2 = disagree, 3 = not sure, 4 = agree, 5 = strongly agree.

assignment. Experienced officers are assigned to areas with favorable residential context, while less experienced officers get assigned to areas with a higher degree of community concerns. Thus, experienced officers have greater opportunities to implement community policing more successfully than do other groups.

The relationship between officers' education and their perceptions of community concerns, citizen cooperation, and community policing are presented in Table 10.5. Officers in general (i.e., both groups as distinguished by associate degree or less, and bachelors' degree or more) agreed that patrol officers have to do something about public nuisance complaints, neighbor disputes, and issues that cause concern to neighbors. However, they were ambivalent regarding family disputes and litter and trash. These differences

Table 10.4 A Comparison of Mean Differences (ANOVA) by Years of Experience (N = 406)

Variable[a]	Years of Experience			
	≤10 Years	11–20	≥21 Years	F
Community Concerns				
Patrol officers should be expected to do something about …				
a. Public nuisance	3.83	3.99	3.95	1.85
b. Neighbors' disputes	3.34	3.45	3.39	0.48
c. Family disputes	3.09	3.2	2.96	1.6
d. Litter and trash	2.91	3.09	2.97	1.12
e. Nuisance that causes lots of problems for neighbors	3.67	3.64	3.67	0.03
Citizen cooperation: Citizens …				
a. Generally cooperate with police officers	2.75	2.72	3	2.42+
b. Trust police officers	2.72	2.64	2.97	4.37*
c. Often call the police if they see something suspicious	3.19	3.19	3.12	0.21
d. Provide information about a crime if they know something and are asked by police	2.73	2.67	2.79	0.65
e. Are willing to work with the police and try to solve neighborhood problems	2.66	2.75	2.76	0.47
Community Policing				
a. I am very familiar with the concept of community policing	3.32	3.37	3.77	7.86**
b. I support community policing programs	3.28	3.49	3.81	8.92**

+, $p < .10$; *, $p < .05$; **, $p < .01$.
[a] 1 = strongly disagree, 2 = disagree, 3 = not sure, 4 = agree, 5 = strongly agree.

were not found to be statistically significant. Regarding citizen cooperation, officers in both groups were unsure of citizen cooperation but were slightly optimistic that they are called if something suspicious is seen. Once again, these mean differences were not statistically significant. There was some support from both groups regarding their familiarity with the concept as well as support for community policing, though the mean differences were not statistically significant.

Comparisons of mean differences within and among rank regarding officers' views regarding community concerns, citizen cooperation, and community policing are presented in Table 10.6. With the exception of issues relating to family disputes and litter, all three ranks (police officers, sergeants, and lieutenants or higher) support the idea that patrol officers

Table 10.5 A Comparison of Mean Differences (ANOVA) by Education (N = 406)

	Education		
Variable[a]	High School or Associate's Degree	Bachelor of Arts or More	F
Community Concerns			
Patrol officers should be expected to do something about ...			
a. Public nuisance	3.92	3.94	0.07
b. Neighbors' disputes	3.37	3.42	0.32
c. Family disputes	3.07	3.16	0.7
d. Litter and trash	3.02	3	0.03
e. Nuisance that causes lots of problems for neighbors	3.61	3.72	1.41
Citizen cooperation: Citizens ...			
a. Generally cooperate with police officers	2.77	2.83	0.43
b. Trust police officers	2.77	2.72	0.4
c. Often call the police if they see something suspicious	3.19	3.18	0.02
d. Provide information about a crime if they know something and are asked by police	2.69	2.77	0.98
e. Are willing to work with the police and try to solve neighborhood problems	2.69	2.75	0.5
Community Policing			
a. I am very familiar with the concept of community policing	3.46	3.39	0.54
b. I support community policing programs	3.4	3.54	2.43

+, $p < .10$; *, $p < .05$; **, $p < .01$.

[a] 1 = strongly disagree, 2 = disagree, 3 = not sure, 4 = agree, 5 = strongly agree.

should be expected to do something about community concerns. Of these concerns, the higher-ranking officers are more strongly supportive of a patrol officer's role in handling a public nuisance. The mean differences were statistically significant.

Regarding citizen cooperation overall, all officers of all ranks did not believe that citizens cooperate with police. However, compared to sergeants, both police officers and lieutenants and higher are more ambivalent about how often citizens call the police if they see something suspicious. The mean differences were statistically significant. Regarding familiarity with community policing, though all officers are familiar with the concept of community

Table 10.6 A Comparison of Mean Differences (ANOVA) by Rank (N = 406)

	Rank			
Variable[a]	Police Officer[b]	Sergeant	Lieutenant or Higher	F
Community Concerns				
Patrol officers should be expected to do something about …				
a. Public nuisance	3.78	4	3.98	3.62*
b. Neighbors' disputes	3.26	3.46	3.45	1.75
c. Family disputes	3.08	3.13	3.14	0.11
d. Litter and trash	2.98	3.09	2.96	0.52
e. Nuisance that causes lots of problems for neighbors	3.66	3.64	3.71	0.22
Citizen cooperation: Citizens …				
a. Generally cooperate with police officers	2.70	2.75	2.94	2.19
b. Trust police officers	2.74	2.70	2.79	0.37
c. Often call the police if they see something suspicious	3.18	3.33	3.05	3.07*
d. Provide information about a crime if they know something and are asked by police	2.72	2.72	2.77	0.2
e. Are willing to work with the police and try to solve neighborhood problems	2.70	2.74	2.72	0.1
Community Policing				
a. I am very familiar with the concept of community policing	3.35	3.32	3.62	5.11**
b. I support community policing programs	3.30	3.40	3.74	8.87**

+, $p < .10$; *, $p < .05$; **, $p < .01$.

[a] 1 = strongly disagree, 2 = disagree, 3 = not sure, 4 = agree, 5 = strongly agree.

policing, higher-ranking officers' perceptions reflect a higher degree of familiarity. This finding was statistically significant. We also found that while all officers in all ranks are supportive of community policing, the degree of support increased with rank. That is, compared with police officers, sergeants and lieutenants, respectively, supported community policing to a greater degree. Moon (2006) noted that rank did not affect officers' support for CP, and these findings are consistent with Park's (2006) finding and are statistically significant.

Last, we compared mean differences among officers with different job assignments and the various facets of community policing. The results are

Table 10.7 A Comparison of Mean Differences (ANOVA) by Job Assignment (N = 406)

	Job Assignment			
Variable[a]	Patrol or Traffic	Criminal Investigation	Police Administration	F
	Community Concerns			
Patrol officers should be expected to do something about …				
a. Public nuisance	3.94	3.79	4.04	2.70+
b. Neighbors' disputes	3.36	3.3	3.61	2.72+
c. Family disputes	3.16	2.98	3.18	1.17
d. Litter and trash	3	3.03	3.05	0.08
e. Nuisance that causes lots of problems for neighbors	3.67	3.59	3.74	0.62
Citizen cooperation: Citizens …				
a. Generally cooperate with police officers	2.75	2.68	3.08	4.74**
b. Trust police officers	2.76	2.64	2.83	1.11
c. Often call the police if they see something suspicious	3.29	2.92	3.19	5.40**
d. Provide information about a crime if they know something and are asked by police	2.76	2.63	2.8	0.97
e. Are willing to work with the police and try to solve neighborhood problems	2.69	2.6	2.94	3.64*
	Community Policing			
a. I am very familiar with the concept of community policing	3.51	3.1	3.56	8.80**
b. I support community policing programs	3.48	3.24	3.73	6.62**

+, $p < .10$; *, $p < .05$; **, $p < .01$.

[a] 1 = strongly disagree, 2 = disagee, 3 = not sure, 4 = agree, 5 = strongly agree.

presented in Table 10.7. Similar to other mean comparisons, officers in all job assignments support that patrol officers should do something about public nuisances, neighbor disputes, and nuisances that cause problems for neighbors. The mean differences were statistically significant only marginally. Regarding citizen support, both patrol officers and investigators do not believe citizens are generally cooperative, while officers who work in administration are more ambivalent about the issue. A similar finding was noted for citizens' willingness to work with police to solve neighborhood problems. Both findings were statistically significant. An interesting finding was observed concerning a citizen's willingness to call police if he or she sees something suspicious occurring. Among the groups, patrol officers, followed by those in administration, were more optimistic that citizens would call, while investigators appeared ambivalent.

Regarding familiarity with the concept of community policing, both officers who work in administration and patrol officers were the most familiar with it, while investigators remained ambivalent. More interestingly, however, officers who work in administration expressed the strongest support for community policing, followed by patrol officers and investigators, respectively. Mean differences for both categories were found to be statistically significant.

Discussion and Conclusion

In this chapter we explored South Korean police officers' perceptions about three important aspects that are closely tied to the overall concept of community policing. They include the extent to which patrol officers should be concerned about law and order situations, such as neighbor and family disputes and public nuisance; the extent to which officers perceive citizen cooperation with police; and in general, the officers' familiarity with the concept of community policing and support for the program. Our findings suggest that overall, all the officers surveyed believe that patrol officers should do something about public nuisance, while only about half of them feel they should be involved in neighbors' and family disputes. A majority of them either feel ambiguity about citizen cooperation in general or do not feel that citizens cooperate with police, which suggests that such perceptions impede in the successful building of partnerships between citizens and police in the community. Overall there were as many officers who strongly support community policing as there were those who are ambiguous. A comparison by groups suggests that older officers' support for CP is stronger relative to other groups, though overall all are positive about these programs. Age, which is directly tied to experience, reveals similar findings, which suggests officers who had worked for more than 21 years are more supportive of CP than less experienced officers. Though education was found to have no significant impact on the various groups of officers, rank and job assignment were significantly related to support for community policing, a finding consistent with prior research in Korea.

While this cursory examination reveals interesting findings about the differences in Korean police officers' perceptions of community policing, we believe that a more in-depth analysis of this topic with a focus on organizational and environmental factors and their relationship to officers' attitudes toward various facets of community policing is warranted. Such an examination will offer some important insights on the impact of various reforms introduced as part of the grand reform.

References

Baek, H. (2000). *The analysis of police reform*. Seoul, Korea: Police Science Institute.

Brown, B., & Benedict, W.R. (2002). Perceptions of the police. *Policing, 25*(3), 543.

Carter, D.L., & Sapp, A.D. (1989). The effect of higher education on police liability: Implications for police personnel policy. *American Journal of Police, 8*(1), 153–166.

Choi, P. (1985). *Plans for 21st century policing*. Seoul, Korea: Police Science Institute.

Decker, S.H. (1985). The police and the public: Perceptions and policy recommendations. In R.J. Homant & D.B. Kennedy (Eds.), *Police and law enforcement 1975–1981* (Vol. 3, pp. 89–105). New York, NY: AMS Press.

Greene, J.R., & Decker, S.H. (1989). Police and community perceptions of the community role in policing: The Philadelphia experience. *Howard Journal of Criminal Justice, 28*(2), 105–123. doi:10.1111/j.1468-2311.1989.tb00641.x

Hoffman, V. (1982). The development of modern police agencies in the Republic of Korea and Japan: A paradox. *Police Studies, 5*, 3–16.

Hwang, E. (2008). Determinants of job satisfaction among South Korean police officers: The effect of urbanization in a rapidly developing nation. *Policing: An International Journal of Police Strategies and Management, 31*(4), 694–714. doi:10.1108/13639510810910634

Hwang, U., & Woo, Y. (2009). Factors affecting supportive attitudes and field activities of community oriented policing among police officers. *Journal of Korean Police, 8*(1), 3–40.

Jaegal, D., & Chang, S. (2005). The role of police for the successful implementation of community policing. *Korean Association of Public Safety and Criminal Justice Journal, 20*, 415–447.

Kim, C., & Woo, J. (2006). The implications and limitations of community policing. *Korean Association of Public Safety and Criminal Justice Journal, 23*, 347–370.

KNPA (2002). *Korea police annual report*. Seoul, South Korea. Korea National Police Agency.

KNPA (2004). *Korea police annual report*. Seoul, South Korea. Korea National Police Agency.

KNPA (2010). *Korea police annual report*. Seoul, South Korea. Korea National Police Agency.

Lee, S. (2000). *The evaluation of police reforms*. Seoul, Korea: Police Science Institute.

Lewis, S., Rosenberg, H., & Sigler, R.T. (1999). Acceptance of community policing among police officers and police administrators. *Policing: An International Journal of Police Strategies and Management, 22*, 567.

Lord, V.B., & Friday, P.C. (2008). What really influences officer attitudes toward COP? *Police Quarterly*, *11*(2), 220–238. doi:10.1177/1098611108314569

Lurigio, A.J., & Skogan, W.G. (1994). Winning the hearts and minds of police officers: An assessment of staff perceptions of community policing in Chicago. *Crime and Delinquency*, *40*(3), 315–330. doi:10.1177/0011128794040003002

Moon, B. (2004). The politicization of police in South Korea: A critical review. *Policing: An International Journal of Police Strategies and Management*, *27*(1), 128–136. doi:10.1108/13639510410519958

Moon, B. (2006). The influence of organizational socialization on police officers' acceptance of community policing. *Policing: An International Journal of Police Strategies and Management*, *29*(4), 704–722. doi:10.1108/13639510610711619

Moore, M.H., Trojanowicz, R.C., & Kelling, G.L. (1988). *Crime and policing* (No. 2). Perspectives on Policing. National Institute of Justice, U.S. Department of Justice, Program in Criminal Justice Policy and Management, John F. Kennedy School of Government, Harvard University. Retrieved from http://www.ncjrs.gov/pdffiles1/nij/111460.pdf

Nalla, M.K., & Hwang, E. (2006). Relationship between police and private security personnel in South Korea. *Policing* *29*(3), 482–497.

O'Shea, T. (1999). Community policing in small town rural America: A comparison of police officer attitudes in Chicago and Baldwin county, Alabama. *Policing and Society*, *9*(1), 59–76. doi:10.1080/10439463.1999.9964802

Paoline, E., Myers, S., & Worden, R. (2000). Police culture, individualism, and community policing: Evidence from two police departments. *Justice Quarterly*, *17*(3), 575–605. doi:10.1080/07418820000094671

Park, K. (2006). What factors do explain the citizen orientation of the street-level police? *Korea Journal of Public Administration*, *44*(2), 113–148.

Pyo, C. (2000). Policing in Korea—The past, present and future. Presented at the Asian Association of Police Studies, South Korea. Retrieved from http://www.ncjrs.gov/App/publications/Abstract.aspx?id=188830

Pyo, C. (2003). The public perception of the police and various police reform initiatives in Korea: 1999–2001. *Asian Pacific Journal of Police and Criminal Justice*, *1*(1), 127–143.

Rosenbaum, D.P., Yeh, S., & Wilkinson, D.L. (1994). Impact of community policing on police personnel: A quasi-experimental test. *Crime and Delinquency*, *40*(3), 331–353. doi:10.1177/0011128794040003003

Schafer, J.A. (2001). *Community policing: The challenges of successful organizational change*. New York: LFB Scholarly Publishing.

Skogan, W.G. (2004). Community policing: Common impediments to success. In L. Fridell & M.A. Wycoff (Eds.), *Community policing: The past, present, and future* (pp. 159–167). Washington, DC: Annie E. Casey Foundation, Police Executive Research Forum.

Sunshine, J., & Tyler, T.R. (2003). The role of procedural justice and legitimacy in shaping public support for policing. *Law and Society Review*, *37*, 513.

Tilley, N. (2004). Community policing and problem solving. In W.G. Skogan (Ed.), *Community policing: Can it work?* (pp. 165–184). Belmont, CA: Wadsworth/Thomson.

Weisel, D.L., & Eck, J.E. (1994). Toward a practical approach in organization change: Community policing initiatives in six cities. In D.P. Rosenbaum (Ed.), *The challenge of community policing: Testing the promises* (pp. 53–72). Thousand Oaks, CA: Sage.

Wycoff, M.A., & Skogan, W.G. (1994). The effect of a community policing management style on officers' attitudes. *Crime and Delinquency*, *40*(3), 371–383.

11 The Weed and Seed Initiative and Police Activity Within Communities

S.E. COSTANZA
RONALD HELMS
JOHN C. KILBURN JR.
SUSAN VENDETTI KOSKI

Introduction

For nearly two decades federal officials have targeted funds to enhance law enforcement efforts through the Operation Weed and Seed program, but no research to date has used spatial modeling techniques to isolate evidence that this commitment of federal funds has provided a tangible benefit for the targeted communities. Operation Weed and Seed is a federally funded community policing initiative created by the U.S. Department of Justice that was first implemented in 1991 as an alternative approach to reducing crime in inner city areas. The administration of this federal initiative was passed off to the Community Capacity Development Office (CCDO), which has continued to oversee funding of this program in several high-crime areas since its inception.

Operation Weed and Seed has the specified overarching goal of ridding high-crime neighborhoods of violent offenders (weeding) while simultaneously implementing numerous social service programs (seeding) that are expected to improve the quality of life for citizens living in the targeted communities. An expected function of Weed and Seed zoning is that it should improve police-citizen interaction and increase citizen trust in local police (Bridenball & Jesilow, 2005).

As a policing strategy, the Weed and Seed approach has often been referred to as two-pronged. Communities granted Weed and Seed funding are directed to apply aggressive and spatially concentrated law enforcement tactics to reduce crime rates in targeted areas. While crime is being reduced in the targeted areas, steering committees are tasked with overseeing those areas and directing activities to housing revitalization, social service programs, and a broad salvo of supporting community-oriented policing activities.

There have been many criticisms of this approach, among them the concern that police are given added tools for repression while social service aspects are mostly addressed in the hypothetical rather than being fully fleshed out programs. Mann (2001) highlights a racially focused criticism, speculating that the Weed and Seed target zones allow minorities to be arrested and convicted more frequently than they otherwise would be.

Government-sponsored research surrounding the program and its localized effects has been characterized by numerous methodological shortcomings. Most studies have been commissioned reports that have examined the effect of zoning independently of sociological variables that have proven to be of significance in the study of crime, such as race, population and housing patterns, and various other social processes. Furthermore, previous research has ignored spatial overlap between error terms, a methodological problem whose effects[1] may confound linear modeling techniques. Although other studies have documented mixed, but generally supportive, evidence concerning the salutary effects of Weed and Seed zoning, they have not taken into account that spatial autocorrelation is apt to affect modeled assessments of program implementation.

The analysis that follows highlights these and other concerns surrounding implementation and evaluation of the Weed and Seed program, and seeks to overcome limitations of previous works. The principal research question is: Does Weed and Seed zoning significantly influence area police activity, when other important sociodemographic variables are held constant? In response, this research addresses the effects of the Weed and Seed initiative while controlling for spatial dependence and several variables known to be important in the prediction of police activity.

Literature Review

Previous literature on Project Weed and Seed seems to be commonly rooted in the wider community policing phenomenon. The application of Weed and Seed zoning and community policing is perhaps best understood as a political response (Helms & Gutierrez, 2007) late 1980s and early 1990s. During this time period, police–inner city citizen relations were at a low point, owing in part to violent crime having stabilized at extremely high per capita rates while drug use and instrumental criminal activities were building to a climax. Researchers such as Tonry (1994) claim that the War on Drugs mentality[2] that dominated 1980s policing promoted a war against minorities and inner city residents. Mosher (2001) emphasized that during this period, drugs were blamed for a wide range of societal problems, including poverty, family disruption, high rates of crime, as well as the proliferation of violence-prone gangs in inner cities. As a result, a more militant policing strategy emerged nationally.

During this era, arrests and imprisonment for drug offenses were expanding dramatically relative to other types of crime.[3] Developments in problem-oriented, broken windows, and community-oriented policing notwithstanding, the "professional model" (Herbert, 2006) continued to operate as the dominant policing approach. This model emphasized legal enforcement actions and all too often a disproportionate focus on aggressive policing targeted at minorities. The end result was a chasm that opened up between police and citizens, especially in the most disorganized central cities throughout the United States.

A lack of trust in, and respect for, police defined many inner city communities (Stark, 1987). Though drugs were a serious problem in many of these socially disenfranchised neighborhoods, the community-police disconnect may have worsened problems in many of these neighborhoods. Aggressive policing, random pullovers and searches, and minimal community interaction became staples of the professional model law enforcement routine (Bridenball & Jesilow, 2005).

The 1990s witnessed substantial changes in the form of federal initiatives to foster a more community-oriented policing model.[4] In 1991, the U.S. Department of Justice (DOJ) launched the Weed and Seed initiative as a coordinated effort to control crime and improve the quality of life in targeted high-crime zones. Project Weed and Seed marked the most recent sustained concentrated national effort to restore or otherwise strengthen community relations with local police agencies.

Since its inception, the Operation Weed and Seed program has been criticized on many levels. First, some commentators have articulated the concern that Operation Weed and Seed disproportionately targets minorities. Second, many researchers suspect that efforts to accomplish revitalization of urban areas through the auspices of this program have primarily resulted in displacing criminal activity, a phenomenon recently explored in a technical report by Roman, Cahill, Coggeshall, Lagerson, and Courtney (2005). A different criticism of the program is that it overemphasizes weeding at the expense of seeding—the priority centering on anticrime policing of minority neighborhoods without providing more than token social improvements for noncriminal members of those neighborhoods. Apart from these general concerns, numerous technical papers and a few research reports have put Operation Weed and Seed in their sites and provide a basic foundation for the research presented below.

Program Evaluations of Weed and Seed Zoning Initiatives

Most of the research on local Weed and Seed site effectiveness has been published by law enforcement-commissioned agencies. These technical reports, while most informative and professional, are not peer reviewed and often atheoretical. They do retain the redeeming quality of being descriptive of program features and implementation processes, and provide preliminary insights into purported effects of Weed and Seed zoning.

Commissioned evaluations of Weed and Seed effectiveness have usually found positive aspects of the strategy. Numerous formal evaluations stand out for a variety of reasons (see below) and should not go unnoticed. Evaluations of Operation Weed and Seed in Philadelphia, Pennsylvania (1997); Albuquerque, New Mexico (1999); Woburn, Massachusetts (1999); Akron, Ohio (2005); and Liberty City, Florida (2005) have each trumpeted support for the program and attainment of key goals. We review them briefly.

One of the earliest local site evaluations of the initiative was conducted by Rosenthal and Reimer (1997). The researchers evaluated Philadelphia's program, utilizing a community survey along with key informant interviews. Their report highlighted general community support for the program but also noted that police officers lacked sufficient training in community policing principles and practices. The study provided some results to support the continuation of the initiative. An evaluation of Albuquerque, New Mexico's, Weed and Seed site neighborhoods conducted in 2000 used a methodology that studied the interaction between targeted neighborhood arrests and prosecution outcomes. Morrison (2000) discovered that neighborhood participation in the court monitoring process had a positive effect on keeping criminals out of targeted neighborhoods. The findings indicated a higher number of stay-away orders, a reduction in dismissals, and an increase in the use of prison sentences for offenders arrested in the Weed and Seed sites, compared to other neighborhoods in Albuquerque.

In addition to these, some commissioned evaluations have used mapping techniques and provide more general insights regarding this program. A 1999 study of the Woburn, Massachusetts, program, prepared by the Massachusetts Statistical Analysis Center, used data taken from Weeding operations to create point maps of Woburn's hot spots (Brensilber & Krasco, 1999). The researchers concluded that mapping these areas could provide indications of possible crime displacement for local agencies, through extended use of geographic information systems.

The State of Ohio Office of Criminal Justice Services (OCJS), in an evaluation of the Akron Weed and Seed program from 2000 to 2004 (Shoaf, 2005), mapped crime at the tract level within and adjacent to Akron's Weed and Seed area. Shoaf compared the Weed and Seed area to a noncontiguous but demographically similar Akron neighborhood. The Weed and Seed area showed a greater reduction in aggravated assaults, robberies, and drug violations. Interestingly, the findings indicated that the number of murders in the Weed and Seed neighborhood did not change from 2000 to 2004, yet the number of murders in the comparison neighborhood increased. The results also documented that the comparison neighborhood had a large decrease in drug arrests and rape. To complement maps, the Akron evaluators also included the findings of a citizen attitude survey that was conducted in 2004. They concluded that community residents' satisfaction with social services provided through seeding strategies was less than that registered by residents within the Weed and Seed zones. General community awareness of specific social services was relatively low as well.

Roman et al. (2005) took a unique departure from the aforementioned technical reports by looking at potential effects of Weed and Seed zoning on crime displacement over the Liberty City, Florida, area. To measure displacement, the researchers used a weighted displacement quotient (WDQ), developed by Bowers and Johnson (2003). Their results were consistent with the overall claim that some crime may have been displaced, not eliminated by Weed and Seed efforts.

In sum, these commissioned reports relate police activity to the presence of zoning, yet do not control for other likely sociodemographic influences. In contrast to technical reports that generally show some support for the initiative, Bridenball and Jesilow (2005) offer the only peer-reviewed evaluation of the Weed and Seed program that we could locate. The researchers, who issued a survey to 1,237 Santa Ana, California, citizens, discovered that the Weed and Seed program had the latent effect of creating apathetic attitudes among many minorities within the Weed and Seed area, a result that comports with the racial disparity argument against Weed and Seed put forth by Mann (2001).

Limitations of Previous Research

Previous efforts to assess Weed and Seed have several limitations, including a lack of theoretical development and corresponding lack of controls for rival sources of police arrests and citizen requests for police service, an overreliance of citizen surveys to assess program effects, and research designs that do not allow for accurate estimates of program influences on key outcome indicators. If these can be overcome in a model that additionally overcomes problems associated with spatial autocorrelation, a pernicious problem in any area-based evaluation, we can better understand the potential of this approach to policing in the most disorganized and inhospitable neighborhoods.

Theoretical Considerations: Developing a Model of Police-Citizen Relations

Because Weed and Seed zoning is a crime policy that involves spatial variance, it is practical to use theories of area and crime that are commonly tapped to explain such variance. Insights from the social disorganization framework have been widely adapted in research on crime as well as in efforts to control it. Similarly, the routine activities (see Cohen & Felson, 1979) framework has extended understanding of the ecology of crime.

The concept of unstructured socializing activities is paramount in routine activities approaches (Osgood, Wilson, & O'Malley, 1996). Bursik and Grasmik (1993) called routine activities theory an offshoot of social disorganization theory because of its focus on ecological elements. The routine activities approach focuses on the temporal and spatial distributions of the key sustenance activities of a community (Cohen & Felson, 1979). It is related somewhat to the social disorganization model because of its ecological bias and focus on spatial patterns (Bursik & Grasmick, 1993, 65). The addition of routine activities theory to this integrated model makes it possible to focus on unstructured activities, such as single-parent households and population density, as predictors of police activity. As follows, observations of both routine activities indicators and zoning within block collection units may be useful in explaining police activity.

From the social disorganization perspective (see Byrne & Sampson, 1985; Stark, 1987), crime occurs when neighborhoods have little social or economic means to regulate the actions of residents. Weed and Seed zoning is, in part, an attempt to restore stability to such neighborhoods; nevertheless, it is expected that standard indicators of disorganization, such as transitional housing and vacant buildings, will predict some police activity regardless of zoning efforts. Observations made by numerous researchers, including Hindelang (1978), Mann (2001), and Shihadeh and Shrum (2004), also support the idea that racial composition of neighborhoods will predict some police activity regardless of zoning efforts.

Two hypotheses emerge, keeping in mind the aforementioned theoretical frameworks and the optimistic findings of previous Weed and Seed site evaluations. First, we expected that Weed and Seed zoning would significantly and positively affect local calls for police assistance in conjunction with routine activities and social disorganization indicators. Second, we expected that Weed and Seed zoning would significantly and positively affect arrests, again in conjunction with routine activities and social disorganization indicators.

In summary, this study uses insights from two broad but related theoretical frameworks to develop hypotheses about sources of citizen calls for police assistance or police arrests. Because previous research into Operation

Weed and Seed effects have not accounted for broad ecological sources of police activity, this study should add to current understanding of program influences on this important local social control agency and its level of local activities. As noted, methodological limitations in previous research have resulted in a lack of generalizable empirical results surrounding this controversial program. The analysis that follows uses a methodological approach that explicitly models spatial overlap in the dependent variable, and therefore should provide insight into influences of Weed and Seed zoning, net of widely noted ecological determinants of policing. The next section addresses more explicitly methodological considerations, after which follows a brief overview of data and indicators used in the study.

Methodological Considerations: Developing a Spatially Augmented Theory of the Weed and Seed Zoning–Police Activity Relationship

Anselin's (1995a, 1995b) methodological insights imply that efforts to predict crime within neighborhoods without explicitly modeling for spatially dependent error terms are flawed. Many researchers attempting to study the area-crime nexus using neighborhoods as their unit of analysis have ignored the importance of spatially related error terms (Doreian, 1980, 1981). We develop a model that explicitly incorporates information about spatial error relationships and so should assist in augmenting current understanding of the zoning-police activity nexus.

Weed and Seed zones have historically been placed in areas where there is a clustering of police activity. Models that assume homoskedastic variance and uncorrelated error terms ignore potential overlaps created by the placement of such zones and their relationship to spatial clustering. This relationship is problematic for macro-level researchers who seek to establish associations between zoning, which is spatially associated with disorganization, and ongoing police activity, which is partially determined by social disorganization and partially influenced by contiguous observations. To test the hypotheses stated above, we propose a model that tests for the effects of zoning and other indicators of police activity while controlling for overlap that may distort linear estimates.

Data and Methods

New Britain, Connecticut, with a population estimated at 71,538, sits 12 miles from Connecticut's state capital, Hartford. New Britain, because of its

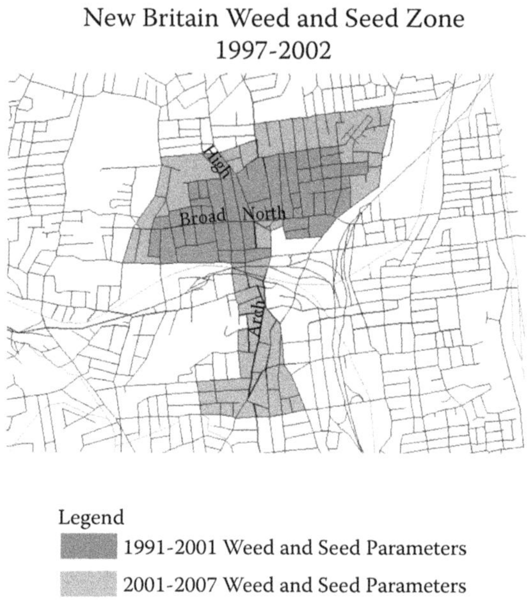

Figure 11.1 New Britain map indicating original (1997–1998) and expanded (2001–2002) Weed and Seed zoning.

rich cultural diversity and proximity to the former headquarters of the now outsourcing Stanley Tool and Dye Works, was an ideal area to test the integrated theory presented in this chapter. Figure 11.1 is a map of the entire New Britain area indicating the original Weed and Seed zone (1997–2000) and the current Weed and Seed zone (2001–present).

New Britain's Weed and Seed area (Figure 11.1), first funded in 1995, is located within the most densely populated and poorest area in the city. The median household income for the Weed and Seed area is only $25,497. The city of New Britain's median household income in 2005 was $39,303. The adult population within the Weed and Seed area without a high school diploma encompasses 23.66% of residents. The zoning area is culturally diverse, with 48.5% of residents being of Hispanic ethnicity in 2005. The high school graduation rate for the 2003–2004 school year in the Weed and Seed area was 78.2%, slightly higher than the public school system's overall graduation rate of 74.8%.

Data

Data were taken from 738 block collection units in New Britain to ascertain the relationship between zoning and aggregated police activities (calls for assistance and arrests) in the two time periods following the inception (1997–1998) and expansion (2001–2002) of the New Britain Weed and Seed

Table 11.1 Descriptive Statistics of Instrumental Variables for Block Collection Units

	Mean Across BCUS	Standard Deviation Across BCUS
Routine Activities Indicators		
Population per acre	11.60	11.25
Percent single-parent female households	8.20	10.91
Social Disorganization Indicators		
Percentage of renters	31.31	30.32
Percentage of vacant housing	6.30	10.70
Percentage of nonwhite residents	37.66	33.65
Section 8 housing per BCU	0.67	2.391
Police Activity Indicators		
Total arrests for years 1997–1998	6.78	17.91
Total arrests for years 2001–2002	6.91	17.36
Total calls for assistance for years 1997–1998	136.62	256.62
Total calls for assistance for years 2001–2002	136.69	229.72

N = 738.

zone. We observe these specific two-year time periods based on a previous examination of New Britain's Weed and Seed side (Cox, 1999), which revealed that residents felt more comfortable calling the police to report crimes after the first year of the program. Data were compiled from three official sources.

Data from the U.S. 2000 Census for block collection units (BCUs) allowed testing of variables taken from both social disorganization and routine activities theories and their possible interaction with zoning. Block collection units are the smallest unit used by the census and are viewed as representative of neighborhoods and serve as our unit of analysis. A second source of data is area-specific calls for assistance (CFAs) and arrest indicators provided by the New Britain Metropolitan Police. Finally, addresses for section 8 housing in New Britain were obtained from the Connecticut Statistical Analysis Center (SAC).

Table 11.1 displays descriptive statistics across BCUs for all variables used in the models below except for the weighted value of zoning used in the spatial models. New Britain's Police Department handles approximately 50,000 calls for assistance per year, with an average of about 136 calls per block collection unit during the observed time periods.

Based on previous findings regarding weeding and seeding in New Britain (see above), a dependent operator was created based on two two-year time periods: one immediately after initiation of the zoning efforts (1997–1998) and another following zoning expansion (2001–2002).[6] A spatial proximity variable was constructed using a computer program known as Space Stat version 1.91. In addition, data were acquired from the New Britain police on the addresses of all CFAs and arrests in the area for the two years following the Weed and Seed inception (1997–1998) and expansion (2001–2002) and were geocoded using a GIS program called Arc View. These serve as prime indicators of police activity.

A dummied indicator of Weed and Seed zoning for the two time periods was also created to assess the effects of the primary independent variable. The zoning and nonzoning indicators were coded as binary (zoning areas = 1, nonzoning areas = 0).

Instrumental Variables: Routine Activities Theory and Social Disorganization

It was assumed that the relationship between zoning and police activity would be most affected in areas with large amounts of people who cross paths on a regular basis (Cantor & Land, 1985). A general atmosphere of densely populated areas should have led to a larger proportion of people influencing police activity. From the *routine activities* perspective, there is a greater opportunity for unstructured socialization activity in areas with high population density. Population per acre therefore is expected to be an indicator of routine activities. Individuals are expected to be "easy targets" for criminals within densely populated areas. Therefore, an indicator of availability of potential victims is reflected by the value of this variable.

Counts from the 2000 census for percentage of *single-parent female households* per block collection unit are used here also as an indicator of routine activities. Work by Cantor and Land (1985), Hunter (1985), Stark (1987), and Sampson and Wilson (1995) has indicated that in neighborhoods with a great deal of family disruption, conditions conducive to crime will converge.

Work by Byrne and Sampson (1985) suggests that the new social ecology paradigm has expanded its arena of interest into at least four other factors: family disruption, physical environment, socioeconomic status, and race. What is known about race and crime comes from an understanding of William Julius Wilson's clustering theory (Sampson & Wilson, 1995). We know that nonwhites are more likely than whites to risk arrest for person crimes. Therefore, it is highly possible that *percent nonwhites* within neighborhoods contribute to police activity.

We use an indicator of the *percent renters* within block collection units to assess a social disorganization hypothesis. Since the early days of Shaw and McKay (1941), transience has been conceptualized as a positive correlate of crime (Blumstien, Cohen, & Farrington, 1988). Ownership is conversely assumed to indicate the inclination of people to invest in their immediate surroundings (Messner & Tardiff, 1985).

Percent of houses vacant in any neighborhood is another variable drawn from the social disorganization perspective. Housing vacancy should be an indicator representing a general lack of interest in neighborhoods. Work by Reiss (1986), as well as work by Blumstien et al. (1988), on neighborhood degeneration shows that one of the primary signs of neighborhoods in decay is lack of ability of citizens to repair broken windows, and another feature of neighborhood decay is uninhabited housing. Therefore, it is expected that the percent of vacant houses in a neighborhood would be closely correlated with indicators of police activity.

Methods

Using a triangulated approach adapted from Morenoff, Sampson, and Raudenbush (2001), local indicators of spatial autocorrelation (LISA) and spatial regression models were run in Space Stat to examine the potential relationship between zoning and police activity. After significant autocorrelation of the police activity indicators was observed with exploratory spatial data analysis (EDSA), it was determined that an iteration of the spatial lag model would provide the best theoretical fit in testing the proposed relationship. It was speculated that zoning was among instrumental variables associated with calls for assistance; however, ideally, the effects of crime spillover during the implementation of weeding and seeding would also prove an invaluable control variable.

A spatially augmented model was created in which police calls for assistance (CFAs) were viewed as a proxy for police-citizen relations within Weed and Seed zones. Arrests, however, were viewed more appropriately as a function of other area indicators. Since the autocorrelation across BCUs was viewed as a confounding factor, a spatial proximity variable was created in which a weighted zoning variable was held constant as an exogenous correlate. Presumably for contiguous neighborhoods (neighborhoods that are within spatial proximity of Weed and Seed zoning areas) there would be significant increases of police-citizen interaction, resulting in increased CFAs and arrests. It was expected that zoning would result in increased CFAs and possibly a decreased number of arrests across the two study samples that would become apparent in the set of cross-sectional analyses.

EDSA Analysis of New Britain Data

We began our analysis by examining the geographic distributions of CFAs and arrests across New Britain neighborhoods in an exploratory spatial data analysis (Anselin, 1988). These models were entered into a Gauss-based

Table 11.2 Global Moran Values for Instrumental Variables

Variable	*I*-Value	z-Value	Significance
Total arrests for years 1997–1998	0.13	6.94	0.00
Total arrests for years 2001–2002	0.11	5.87	0.00
Total calls for assistance for years 1997–1998	0.17	8.55	0.00
Total calls for assistance for years 2001–2002	0.08	4.06	0.00

software program dedicated to estimating regression models with spatial dependence (Space Stat). They were used to help determine whether a spatial lag or spatial error model was appropriate.[7] In testing for spatial dependence, Baller, Messner, Anselin, and Deane (2002) used Moran's *I*[8] and local Moran tests for significance of spatial autocorrelations. The Moran's *I* statistics for both local indicators of spatial autocorrelation (LISA) and global spatial autocorrelation were used to assess patterns of spatial autocorrelation (Cliff & Ord, 1973, 1980, & 1981), which is a prudent first step of any spatial analysis. Each BCU has its own *I*-value as can be seen in the tabled results. For local clustering to be significant, a cutoff point of 0.05 is required for Moran's *I*. Both global *I* and local Moran indicators (see Table 11.2) showed significant autocorrelation in the independent operators.

Figure 11.2 provides a local indicators of spatial autocorrelation (LISA) significance map (see Anselin 1995a, 1995b; Baller et al., 2002) for the 1997–1998 CFAs in New Britain, featuring high-high significance in dark gray. Figure 11.3 provides the same for CFAs during the years 2001–2002, following zoning expansion. Some tentative insights can be drawn from a visual review of Figures 11.2 and 11.3. The maps show that there is a high degree of clustering of CFAs within the zoning area, a result that anticipates later correlational evidence. The Weed and Seed zone at the year of mapping is outlined in white.

The local Moran statistic indicated that there was clustering of high-high CFAs, as expected. This is simply a function of the need to place zoning in such areas, and indicates a necessity to control for this autocorrelation within a spatially augmented model.

Clustering of arrests within the zones was further explored in Figures 11.4 and 11.5. The figures provide significance maps for arrests during the 1997–1998 and 2001–2002 time periods. High-high significance among arrests was more pronounced within the Weed and Seed zone during the years following initialization of the project.

Figure 11.5 is the most interesting of the maps, indicating that between the first time period and second time period, some changes in clustering of arrests across the BCUs arose, lending suspicions to the possibility of crime displacement (see Roman et al., 2005). Of particular interest to us are those high-high clustering values that appear directly to the east of the Weed and Seed zone.

Moran Scatterplot Map:
1997-1998 Calls for Assistance

Weed and Seed Zone Parameters
Legend
not significant
High-High

Figure 11.2 LISA map of CFAs in New Britain, 1997–1998.

A careful interpretation is necessary, however, since temporal lag is not controlled for in this paper. A secondary consideration of this research effort is that Weed and Seed zoning may affect police activity in adjacent (but perhaps not contiguous) neighborhoods. This is further discussed in the conclusions.

As is standard procedure with spatial modeling techniques, Moran's *I* was obtained, and ordinary least squares regression residuals were mapped in order to determine an appropriate model. If the correlated error terms were left unattended, there would be problems with inference. Afterward, fully weighted spatial lag likelihood models of Weed and Seed zoning were taken into account. The potential predictive relationships between zoning, proximity to zoning, and CFAs were taken into consideration while social disorganization and routine activities indicators were statistically controlled.

Anselin (1988, 1995c) put forth conditions under which the use of the spatial dependence (or spatial lag) model should be used. His work demonstrates that spatial dependence will distort linear estimation methods if not explicitly modeled. Using Space Stat software, a standardized spatial weights matrix was created by dividing each element in a given row by the corresponding row sum (see Anselin, 1995c). In the spatially weighted models, the zoning and proximity to zoning variables were held constant while exogenous factors were weighed. The adjusted R^2, as employed in a spatial

Figure 11.3 LISA map of CFAs in New Britain, 2001–2002.

model, acts as a test of goodness of fit for the models and allowed comparison between models.[11]

Analysis of SAR-ML Results for CFAs During First Stage of Zoning

Table 11.3 provides results from our analysis of CFAs during the 1997–1998 period and indicates that Weed and Seed zoning in the presence of several extraneous variables effectively predicted variation in local CFAs across block collection units. After holding constant the effects of population per acre, percent of renters, percent of vacant housing, and total section 8 housing units, the zoning indicator is a significant (z = 3.03) and positive predictor of citizen calls for police assistance. The finding that Weed and Seed zoning is a significant predictor of the CFA indicator in the two years following the start-up of Operation Weed and Seed is consistent with findings for this program presented by Cox (1999). We note that the specified model explains approximately 20% of the variance in CFAs during this time period.

Analysis of the z-values indicates that zoning and the indicator for section 8 housing (z = 5.40) were both significant predictors of CFAs. Percent

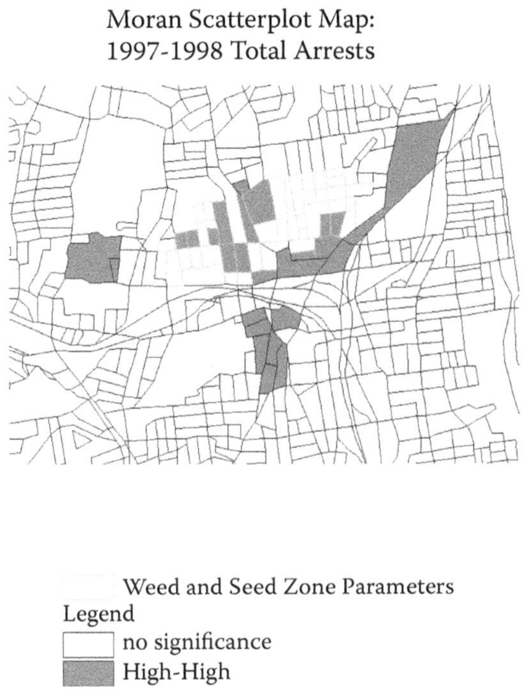

Figure 11.4 LISA map of arrests in New Britain, 1997–1998.

renters (z = 4.20) was also shown to be a positive and significant predictor of citizen calls for service in this model. We found no support for a routine activities perspective here, yet concede that it may still be useful in explaining police activity. In confirmation of our hypothesis, the tabled results indicate that zoning is closely correlated with CFAs, and by inference may be seen as a source of increased citizen trust, or at the very least confidence in the ability of police to handle problems arising locally. Additionally, the proximity variable (lagged dependent variable) proved to be significant (z = 3.25) and positive, contributing as well to the overall model fit.

Analysis of SAR-ML Effects on CFAs After Zoning Expansion

Table 11.4 is a spatially weighted lag model that indicates that zoning fails to remain a positive and significant estimator of CFAs after the expansion period. The overall model exhibits a comparable fit with the dependent variable with the adjusted R^2 explaining 21% of the variance in CFAs. Along with the value of zoning (z = 4.56), which is a strong and positive predictor of CFAs, percent renters per BCU, section 8 housing (z = 6.69), and population per acre (z = –2.93) also closely predict CFAs. The proximity measure was again significant and positive (z = 4.56).

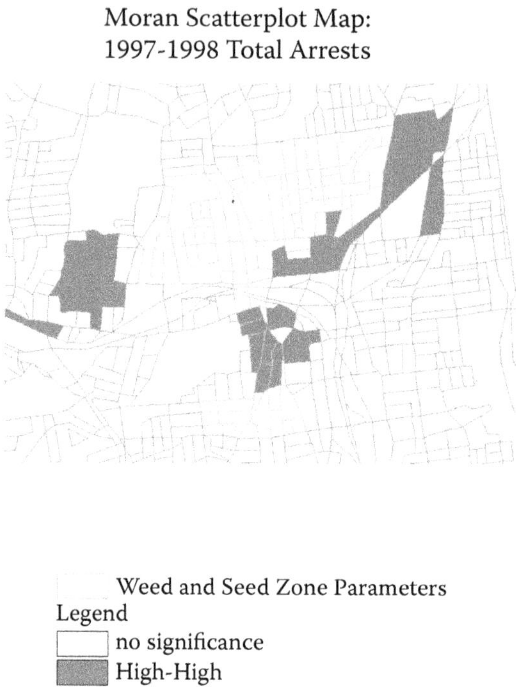

Figure 11.5 LISA map of arrests in New Britain, 2001–2002.

Table 11.3 SAR-ML Model of CFAs, 1997–1998

Predictors	z-Value	Probability
Routine Activities Indicators		
Percent single-female households	0.47	0.633
Population per acre	–2.96	0.003**
Social Disorganization Indicators		
Section 8 housing density	5.40	0.000**
Percent vacant housing	1.64	0.100
Percent renters	4.20	0.000**
Percent nonwhite	1.11	0.263
Weed and Seed Zone Area		
Proximity	3.03	0.000**
Constant	2.62	0.000**
Observations	738	

Adjusted $R^2 = 0.20$.

Table 11.4 SAR-ML Model of CFAs, 2001–2002

Predictors	z-Value	Probability
Routine Activities Indicators		
Percent single-female households	0.34	0.726
Population per acre	−2.93	0.000**
Social Disorganization Indicators		
Section 8 housing density	6.69	0.000**
Percent vacant housing	1.06	0.287
Percent renters	4.95	0.000**
Percent nonwhite	1.36	0.172
Weed and Seed Zone Area		
Proximity	−0.23	0.811
	4.56	0.000**
Constant	2.94	0.003**
Observations	738	

Adjusted $R^2 = 0.22$.

The failure of the zoning coefficient to predict CFAs during the expansion period can also be interpreted in one of two ways. First, the occurrence of a nonsignificant z-value for the 2001–2002 time period may simply be due to the geographic expansion of the Weed and Seed zone and its possible effect on limited police resources. It is important to note that the values of other indicators may not have been noticeably affected by this change. For instance, race as a predictor of calls for assistance would not theoretically be affected by the shifting geography of the Weed and Seed area.

A second and more interesting analysis of the zoning-crime relationship is that initial zoning efforts were sufficient to either displace crime from the zone area or diminish its clustering within the area. To this end, it is pointed out in the conclusion that further study of such displacement is warranted. As our LISA analyses in Figures 11.2 and 11.3 indicate, clustering of calls for assistance within the Weed and Seed zone was disrupted between the 1997–1998 and 2001–2002 time periods.

Analysis of SAR-ML Effects on Police Arrests in First Stage of Zoning

Table 11.5 utilizes the spatial lag technique to test Weed and Seed zoning effects on arrests during the first time period in the presence of the sociodemographic controls. Zoning (z = 2.08), as well as percent renters (z = 1.95) and section 8 (z = 4.38) housing, acts as a significant and positive predictor of arrests. While the model explains 16% of the variance in arrests during the 1997–1998 time period, it is important to point out that the intention of the

Table 11.5 SAR-ML Model of Arrests, 1997–1998

Predictors	z-Value	Probability
Routine Activities Indicators		
Percent single-female households	−0.22	0.82
Population per acre	−2.38	0.01**
Social Disorganization Indicators		
Section 8 housing density	4.38	0.000**
Percent vacant housing	1.64	0.093
Percent renters	1.95	0.050*
Percent nonwhite	0.63	0.520
Weed and Seed Zone Area		
Proximity	2.08	0.036*
	4.56	0.000**
Constant	2.31	0.02*
Observations	738	

Adjusted $R^2 = 0.16$.

Weed and Seed initiative was not to increase arrest rates, but provide better community police interaction. Still, the arrest rates are an important indicator of police activity and require attention since they proxy for a key element of the weeding component of Operation Weed and Seed. The population per acre indicator ($z = -2.38$) indicated negative significance, while the proximity variable remained a positive and significant ($z = 4.56$) predictor of arrests.

Holding constant the natural autocorrelation between Weed and Seed zoning and arrests, we find support for the social disorganization model toward explaining arrests. The zone itself is a significant predictor of arrests, which might be interpreted as support for the argument that there is still a tendency toward traditional reactionary policing in Weed and Seed zones. The 1997–1998 arrest rates indicate that section 8 housing and percent renters are still of importance in the presence of zoning effects.

Analysis of SAR-ML Effects on Police Arrests After Zoning Expansion

Table 11.6 presents a spatial error model that explains only 10% of the variance in arrests during the 2001–2002 expansion period. The zoning variable again loses its effect as a significant predictor of arrests. This may be due to the diminished presence of autocorrelation of the arrest indicator within the Weed and Seed zone as witnessed in Figures 11.3 and 11.4. The spatially lagged proximity variable still shows a significant ($z = 3.83$) and positive relationship to arrests.

Table 11.6 SAR-ML Model of Arrests, 2001–2002

Predictors	z-Value	Probability
Routine Activities Indicators		
Percent single-female households	−1.46	0.143
Population per acre	−3.13	0.001**
Social Disorganization Indicators		
Section 8 housing density	4.69	0.000**
Percent vacant housing	1.52	0.126
Percent renters	2.10	0.031*
Percent nonwhite	1.65	0.098
Weed and Seed Zone Area		
Proximity	−0.45	0.646
	3.83	0.000**
Constant	3.47	0.000**
Observations	738	

$R^2 = 0.10$.

What was also of interest in the model was that population per acre had a negative (z = −3.13) and significant coefficient, as was the case in the second time period for CFAs. Again, it is possible that in densely populated areas, there are social networks that develop that discourage motivated offenders. Again, percent renters (z = 2.10) and section 8 housing (z = 6.69) following the expansion period were significant and positive predictors of arrests, which speaks to the merit of the social disorganization theory. The fact that percent nonwhite population is a significant and positive (z = 1.65) predictor of arrests at the 0.10 level would also seem to provide direct, albeit weak, support for literature that focuses on the relationships between arrest and race.

Discussion

The key finding of this analysis is that Weed and Seed zoning, net of all the other variables accounted for in the analysis, was a significant predictor of police activity during the 1997–1998 time period, but experienced a decline as a significant predictor after program expansion. These results reinforce expectations that zoning is a strong correlate of police activities (arrests) and probably citizen-police relations (indicated by CFAs). Research by Helms and Gutierrez (2007) emphasized the important role that federal initiatives and targeted funding can play in stimulating local crime control initiatives. Weed and Seed represents a variation on a general model of federal support for policing initiatives and attempts to facilitate federal-local cooperation.

The results of our research provide additional tentative support for claims that such federal resourcing can be an important positive stimulus for revitalization of police-community relations and enhanced crime control.

Unfortunately, beyond the police component of the program we were unable to directly assess the subjective component of the Weed and Seed program on individual residents. One question that has been too often overlooked is whether people's lives were improved as a result of this targeted program. Certainly in terms of police arrest activity we can infer from the statistical results that Weed and Seed zoning resulted in heightened arrest initially, followed by a reduction in arrest activities after several years operation of the program. If weeding was effective, this pattern would be expected. We note in this context that the overall rate of crime dropped throughout this period for the city of New Britain (see Cox, Costanza, & Ruffolo, 2007), a trend that mirrored national crime patterns. This may have been a contributing factor in the decline in arrest activities in the zoning areas during the later phase of the program's operation.

The findings allow for a somewhat optimistic interpretation of the program's effects during its initialization period; however, since these findings do not persist during the second time period, a dilemma arises. In the face of reduction in crime overall and reduced police arrest activities, the significant link between zoning and CFAs indicates to us that citizens were confident during the 1997–1998 time period that police were a capable institution for handling community social control problems. While this redounds well to the credit of the operating program, it does not account for the loss of zoning significance in the 2001–2002 models. Also, we cannot know whether the seeding programs were directly influential in causing initial improvements in more general social relations beyond police-citizen relations. Future research might tackle this aspect directly and thereby begin to formulate needed answers to questions surrounding this aspect of Weed and Seed. While our results remain tentative and inferential, we believe that the evidence proffered here is consistent with claims that federal cooperative programming can indeed provide key benefits to local police agencies and the communities they serve as they continue to seek out innovative and progressive solutions to local crime.

Two variables in the models seemed to defy traditional logic about CFAs and police arrest activity; these are percent nonwhite per BCU, which does not prove to be a significant predictor of CFAs, and population density (population per acre), which continually shows a negative and significant relationship with CFAs. It is possible that the lack of significance in racial composition can be explained by the weeding component of Weed and Seed zoning. It is speculated that even within the presence of a Weed and Seed zone there is still some mistrust between the police and minorities.

The negative and significant relationship between CFAs and population density is elusive, but explainable by one of two concepts. First, there is the simple probability that more densely populated areas are characterized by poverty clustering. In this context suitable targets may be in short supply due to social factors that place more people in positions where informal (and generally speaking, unintentional) controls become operative. Put differently, there may be informal networks of social control that develop in areas where people who are economically marginalized are clustered closely together. As an example, a motivated offender would have more difficulty committing a burglary in an apartment complex when a disproportionate number of neighbors are likely to be home.

Findings by Cox et al. (2007) indicate that crime rates went down in the zoning area during the period between initial zoning and expansion. But there are several questions that have yet to be addressed that cannot be addressed by the data that were used here. Among them is the question: Were peoples' lives made substantially better in those areas that were initially targeted by Project Weed and Seed?

Data acquired from the New Britain police allowed mainly tests to the weeding component of the program.[12] It is important to note that among the fair criticisms of the Weed and Seed initiative is that weeding dominates seeding. Seeding in these areas could not be measured with the data acquired in this analysis, but it is possible to make certain inferences about the benefits of the initiative from the data analyzed here.

As predicted, there was an overlay of the New Britain Weed and Seed area with overall police activity as measured through CFAs and arrests during the initial weeding and seeding phases of the program. The implementation of Weed and Seed zoning is supposed to enhance police-citizen interaction within these areas. However, whether that is a good thing for residents in various neighborhood areas can only be tested through qualitative measures such as surveys that are structured to assess whether citizens are living with less fear of crime. Findings from Exploratory Data Spatial Analysis (EDSA) also revealed a great deal of autocorrelation of arrests within the initial Weed and Seed zone that was somewhat dispersed between the two examined time periods.

Future analysis should seek to ascertain whether the diminished clustering of arrests in these areas was a direct result of zoning.

Among the more interesting findings of this analysis was the fact that population density proved to be a negative and significant predictor of calls for assistance and arrests in both time periods. It was suggested that a general atmosphere of densely populated areas, paired with Weed and Seed zoning in these areas, leads to a larger proportion of people influencing police activity; however, dense populations may provide an extra measure of social control. One of the unanticipated results of this analysis is that evidence would seem to support claims that informal guardianship in economically and socially marginalized areas may be a contributing factor in reduced reliance on formal social control measures.

Another interesting finding is the persistent positive significance of the section 8 housing and percent of renters indicators. Both of these reinforce insights from the social disorganization perspective. But the fact that they remained significant in the presence of the other indicators included in our models also has implications for Weed and Seed zoning and police activity. Specifically, zoning does not negate the effects of neighborhood deterioration on police CFAs or arrests.

Conclusion

This research makes a contribution to our understanding of not only Weed and Seed zoning, but also the variables that may potentially be linked to community policing activity. The most important contribution of the research, however, is that it provides some support that Weed and Seed zoning is a working predictor of police activity, net of various important sociodemographic variables. However, a decline in effectiveness of expanded zoning efforts might indicate that the federal stipend was too meager to accommodate the needs of the expanded zoning area. The proposition that zoning is an important predictor of police activity (as measured here), of course, does not necessarily allow us to conclude that Weed and Seed works the way it was intended to. The idea that Weed and Seed promotes police-citizen trust while reducing crime cannot be tested with quantitative data alone. We suggest further analysis of the New Britain Weed and Seed zone with a survey instrument of some sort as a test of this.

Models seem to converge on three major points. First, Weed and Seed zoning acts as a significant and positive predictor of police activity. Second, section 8 housing and percent renters always act as significant predictors of police activity. Third, population density is a negative predictor of police activity.

Weed and Seed zoning, in the models, predicts police activity within neighborhoods regardless of sociodemographic context. By these standards, Weed and Seed appears to have had a decided effect. Of these findings, we express concern about the double-edged nature of Weed and Seed success as proposed by its initial critics. While the objective of the Weed and Seed Project was to foster police-citizen interaction and provide a safe environment for residents to live (Dunworth & Mills, 1999), it is noteworthy that zoning has also been a positive predictor of arrests within the area it intends to serve.

Weed and Seed is an engaging concept, and it is backed by intuitive logic. But its implementation, as noted in a variety of research reports, has been uneven, and perhaps incomplete since less emphasis has been placed on any of the spectrum of pro-social inputs (the seeding) that might result in positive developments in the community. One conclusion that could be argued with some persuasion is that police may not be the most appropriate institution for the steering and implementation of such complex community programming. Giving police a larger role in the community may actually work in the wrong direction since, as Kraska (2001) and others emphasize, police may focus on enforcement matters more than community matters. Coercion and its threat may not be the most efficacious instruments to gain public support and build resilience in the community. Police agencies, with their unique powers to use coercion, may lack the requisite restraint and related skill set to be successful in building strong communities. It may make sense to direct resources to institutions whose primary *raison d'être* is centered on community capacity building, and not divert these critical resources to an institution whose primary instrument is coercion and whose dominant tactic involves suppressing the community's most threatening elements.

The results bear other implications for social policy. Local Moran's *I* maps indicate a visible reduction of police activity clustering within the zone between the two time periods. While we interpret such a reduction as a sign of a functional program, it is important to remember that at the heart of the zoning activities is a desire to stop crime, not to displace crime. We suggest a further study of the specific patterns of crime detected in our maps in order to better understand the extent to which crime was displaced as a result of the program's operation.

Future research is required into the zoning-crime nexus. One step toward a better understanding of Weed and Seed is to break calls for assistance into categories (i.e., drug violations, public order offenses, etc.) and rerun the models. It is possible that zoning may explain greater variance in police activity in models regressed upon specific crimes. A more reliable assessment would also involve including an indicator of SES at the block collection level, and for validity, we propose attitudinal surveys of long-term residents of the zone,[13] assessing their perceptions of the program.

New Britain forfeited its Weed and Seed funding in 2007 and would currently only be eligible to renew if a different area was selected for the site.

Displacement of police activity also could not be covered in full by the simple exploratory analysis covered in this research. We suggest that, along with a qualitative analysis of the LISA maps presented above, a replication of the WDQ developed by Bowers and Johnson (2003) should be attempted in New Britain. Further examination of the patterns of clustering might expand current insights into the ways Weed and Seed zoning affects opportunities for offending.

Notes

1. Serial spillover refers to auroregressive spillover of the dependent variables across space. The use of the maximum likelihood spatial lag model in this chapter is based largely on the idea that significant spillover of police activity is an undesired effect of the Weed and Seed initiative. Statistics derived from spatial error modeling also indicate the use of the lag specification as proper.
2. Here, we are referring to the proactive policing component of the War on Drugs. For further discussion of proactive policing related to the War on Drugs see Charles Faupel's (1991) seminal research.
3. The scale of increase is captured in a 1999 U.S Department of Justice report that showed the proportion of state and federal inmates incarcerated for drug offenses had increased more than 300% between 1986 and 1992. This Bureau of Justice Statistics (BJS) prison study included a table indicating the increases in sentences for each type of crime. Incarceration for drug-related offenses increased from 19,000 in 1980 to near 170,000 in 1992. This information is readily available as public information on the BJS website.
4. For a more detailed discussion of the shift from proactive policing to community policing, see Senna and Seigel's introductory criminal justice textbook (1998).
5. While there are a scant few peer-reviewed papers relating to the initiative and its outcomes, we have found only this one reviewed paper that models Weed and Seed zoning as an independent operator.
6. We chose to run a nonstandardized two-year indicator of police activity based on findings in pervious literature that indicated that notable effects did not immediately follow zoning. We did not use a rate, but instead controlled for population per acre within the model.
7. A central theme in most spatial modeling research is whether or not a specification of the spatial lag or spatial error model is appropriate. We view such a discussion as redundant given the multitude of previous seminal material comparing and contrasting the two methods. Suffice to say mapping of the residuals, along with the significant values of the Wald statistic in the error model, justified the use of a spatial lag model.
8. The derivation of Moran's I is given by the formula $I = \Sigma I \Sigma j\ wij(\mathrm{p}i - \mathrm{P})(\mathrm{p}j - \mathrm{P}) / \Sigma i(\mathrm{p}i - \mathrm{P})^2$, where wij is an element of a row-standardized spatial weights matrix, p is the police activity of individual block collection units, and P is the average indicator of police activity in the sample (see Doreian, 1981). I is treated as a standardized normal deviate and the test for autocorrelation is based on a variance between expected and observed frequencies.
9. Further information in this study may be referenced through the following link: http://www.ccsu.edu/ccsunews/ccsu_scene/NBPDevaluation.htm.
10. With regard to the addition of the Breusch-Pagan test, spatial dependence in the overall model was expected and does prove significant. However, it is important to note that the models used here attempt to control for that dependence within our primary indicator of police activity. Although some spatial models of dependence do not include the result of the B-P statistic, we did so here, as a significant value confirms the specification of a spatial model as a proper

technique. The model also includes a spatial lag term that does not vary across BCUs, meaning that the spatial process is assumed to be uniform across the entire New Britain area.

11. It should be noted that results from the Breusch-Pagan test for heteroskedasticity indicated that even after full weighting some spatial dependence persisted. With this caveat in mind, we note that the specified model explains approximately 20% of the variance in CFAs during this time period. Also, when Akaike info criterion (AIC) and likelihood scores from the spatial lag estimation procedure were compared, they produced a better fit than ordinary least square (OLS) and spatial error modeling.
12. Although it could be argued that CFAs are indirect measures of the seeding component of the program, insofar as they might indicate improved police-citizen relations, the possibility of ecological fallacy exists in so broadly interpreting the nature of CFAs. It is suggested in the conclusions that a more direct approach is needed to gauge actual citizen response to the nature of police-citizen relations. Official data simply do not allow for that sort of assessment.
13. In 1994, Jan Roehl of the National Institute of Justice (NIJ) created a survey instrument for gauging the effectiveness of Weed and Seed programs within targeted communities. The survey instrument in its original form contained several questions to be posed to citizens regarding their attitudes after experiencing two years of Weed and Seed-oriented policing activities. Unfortunately, Roehl's pioneering survey instrument has rarely been used in its original format, despite the fact that other commissioned reports used similar instruments and research designs to gauge community attitudes about the Weed and Seed program.

References

Anselin, L. (1988). *Spatial econometrics: Methods and models*. Dordrecht: Kluwer Academic.

Anselin, L. (1995a). Local indicators of spatial association—LISA. *Geographical Analysis, 27*(2), 93–115.

Anselin, L. (1995b). *New directions in spatial econometrics*. New York: Springer Press.

Anselin, L. (1995c). *Spacestat version 1.80: User's guide*. Morgantown: West Virginia University.

Baller, R.D., Messner, S.F., Anselin, L., & Deane, G. (2002). The interchangeability of homicide data sources: A spatial analytical perspective. *Homicide Studies, 6*(3), 211–227.

Blumstien, A., Cohen, J., & Farrington, D. (1988). Longitudinal and criminal career research: Further clarifications. *Criminology, 26*(1), 57–74.

Bowers, K.J., & Johnson, S.D. (2003). Measuring the geographical displacement and diffusion of benefit effects of crime prevention activity. *Journal of Quantitative Criminology, 19*(3), 275–301.

Brensilber, D., & Krasco, K. (1999). *Analysis of police activity and programming in the Woburn, Massachusetts Weed and Seed area.* Technical report prepared by the Massachusetts Executive Office of Public Safety Programs Division Statistical Analysis Center.

Bridenball, B., & Jesilow, P. (2005). What matters: The formation of attitudes toward the police. *Police Quarterly, 7*(2), 151–181.

Bursik, R., & Grasmik, H. (1993). The use of multiple indicators to estimate crime trends in American cities. *Journal of Criminal Justice, 21*(5), 509–516.

Byrne, J., & Sampson, R. (1985). Key issues in the social ecology of crime. In J. Byrne & R. Sampson (Eds.), *The social ecology of crime: Theory, research and social policy,* New York: Springer-Verlag, 1–22.

Cantor, D., & Land, K.C. (1985). Unemployment and crime rates in the post-World War II United States: A theoretical and empirical analysis. *American Sociological Review, 50,* 317–332.

Cliff, A.D., & Ord, J.K. (1973). *Spatial autocorrelation.* New York: Methuen Press.

Cliff, A.D., & Ord, J.K. (1980). On statistical models for spatial diffusion processes. *Geographical Analysis, 12,* 12–21.

Cliff, A.D., & Ord, J.K. (1981). *Spatial and temporal analysis: Autocorrelation in space and time, quantitative geography: A British view.* Routledge & Kegan.

Cohen, L.W., & Felson, M. (1979). Social change and crime rate trends: A routine activities approach. *American Sociological Review, 44,* 588–607.

Cox, S.M. (1999). *Final report of the evaluation of the New Britain Weed and Seed program.* Commissioned report submitted to the New Britain Weed and Seed Steering Committee.

Cox, S.M., Costanza, S.E., & Ruffolo, L. (2007). *Evaluation of the New Britain Weed and Seed program.* Prepared by the CCSU Institute for the Study of Crime and Justice. Technical report submitted to the New Britain Police Department.

Doreian, P. (1980). Linear models with spatially distributed data: Spatial disturbances or spatial effects. *Sociological Methods and Research, 9,* 29–60.

Doreian, P. (1981). Estimating linear models with spatial distributed data. In S. Linehardt, *Social methodology.* London: Jossey-Bass Publishers, 359–388.

Dunworth, T., & Mills, G. (1999). *National evaluation of Weed and Seed Salt Lake City case study: Research report.* Technical report prepared by J. Greene, H. Frank, & K. Jacoby for the National Institute of Justice, U.S. Department of Justice.

Faupel, C. (1991). Shooting dope: Career patterns of hardcore heroin users, Gainesville, FL: University of Florida.

Helms, R., & Gutierrez, R. (2007). Federal subsidies and evidence of progressive change: A quantitative assessment of the effects of targeted grants on manpower and innovation in large U.S. police agencies. *Police Quarterly, 10*(1), 87–107.

Herbert, S. (2006). Tangled up in blue conflicting paths to police legitimacy. *Theoretical Criminology, 10*(4), 481–504.

Hindelang, M. (1978). Race and involvement in common law personal crimes. *American Sociological Review, 43*(1), 93–109.

Hunter, A. (1985). Private, parochial, and public social orders: The problem of crime and incivility in urban communities. In G. Suttles & N. Mayer, *Citizenship and institutions: Building modern society.* Norwood, NJ: Ablex Publishing.

Kraska, P. (2001). Militarization and policing—Its relevance to 21st century police. *Policing*, 1(4), 501–513.

Mann, E. (2001). Building the Anti-Racist, Anti-Imperialist United Front: Theory and practice from the L.A. Strategy Center and Bus Riders Union. *Souls: A Critical Journal of Black Politics, Culture and Society*, *3*(3), 87–102.

Messner, S., & Tardiff, K. (1985). The social ecology of urban homicide: An application of the routine activities approach. *Criminology*, *23*, 241–267.

Morenoff, J.D., Sampson, R.J., & Raudenbush, S.W. (2001). Neighborhood inequality, collective efficacy, and the spatial dynamics of urban violence. *Criminology*, *39*(3), 517–559.

Morrison, C. (2000). *Albuquerque, New Mexico's Weed and Seed site neighborhoods.* Technical report: Weed and Seed Evaluation Final Report. Albuquerque, NM: University of New Mexico Institute for Social Research Statistical Analysis Center.

Mosher, C. (2001). Predicting drug arrest rates: Conflict and social disorganization perspectives. *Crime and Delinquency*, *47*, 84–104.

Osgood, W., Wilson, J., & O'Malley, P. (1996). Routine activities and individual deviant behavior. *American Sociological Review*, *61*, 635–655.

Reiss, A.J. (1986). Communities and crime. In A.J. Reiss & M. Tonry, *Communities and crime*. Chicago: University of Chicago Press.

Roehl, J. (1994). *Evaluation of the Weed and Seed initiative in the United States.* Computer file, ICPSR version. Alexandria, VA: Institute for Social Analysis [producer], 1995. Ann Arbor, MI: Interuniversity Consortium for Political and Social Research [distributor], 1998.

Roman, C.G., Cahill, M., Coggeshall, M., Lagerson, E., & Courtney, S. (2005). *The Weed and Seed initiative and crime displacement in South Florida: An examination of spatial displacement associated with crime control initiatives and the redevelopment of public housing.* Noncommissioned technical report. Justice Research and Statistics Association (JRSA).

Rosenthal, S., & Reimer, H. (1997). *Final evaluation report for the Philadelphia Weed and Seed Project.* Prepared by the Center for Social Police and Community Development, School of Social Administration.

Sampson, R., & Wilson, W.J. (1995). Toward a theory of race, crime, and urban inequality. In J. Hagan and R. Peterson, *Crime and inequality.* Boston: Allyn and Bacon, 37–54.

Shaw, C.R., & McKay, H.D. (1941). *Juvenile delinquency and urban areas.* Chicago: University of Chicago Press.

Shihadeh, E., & Shrum, W. (2004). Serious crime in urban neighborhoods: Is there a race effect? *Social Spectrum*, *24*(1), 223–241.

Shoaf, L.C. (2005). *Evaluation of the Akron Weed and Seed program 2000–2004; State of Ohio.* Technical report. State of Ohio Office of Criminal Justice Services (OCJS).

Siegel, L., and Senna, J.J. (2008). *Introduction to Criminal Justice*, 8th edition. Beverly, MA: Wadsworth.

Stark, R. (1987). Deviant places: A theory of the ecology of crime. *Criminology*, *25*, 893–909.

Tonry, M. (1994). Racial politics, racial disparities, and the war on crime. *Crime and Delinquency*, *40*(4), 475–494.

12 The Survival of Community Policing in a Remilitarized Police Approach

A Paradoxical Case of South Africa

SETLHOMAMARU DINTWE

Background

The majority of police institutions in different democracies have opted for community-oriented policing. This is evident in the statement of Morash and Ford (2002, 277), who submit that what currently dominates most police agencies is the overriding theme of adopting the community policing philosophy. This reform and choice can be attributed to a number of factors. In South Africa, for instance, the police had to cease use of excessive force and cooperate with the communities in an endeavor to deal with the epidemic proportions of crime. The police also had to redress the past imbalances in which the police were seen as oppressors. Isolated use of police tactics, techniques, and methods without incorporation of community involvement in trying to solve the crime problem has also proved to fruitless over the years. Successful policing includes the cognizance that the other informal means of dealing with crime, such as obtaining information from the members of the community, can complement other strategies of policing. The design and redesign of the South African Police (SAP), including changing the SAP into the South African Police Services (SAPS), redefining the functions and ideologies, as well as engaging the community members, emanated from this desire to embrace community policing. Due to the atrocities committed against human rights during the past regimes, the SAP assumed different images and ideologies over various periods.

The history of South African Police[*] depicts an interesting evolution and different ideologies adopted by the SAP over various periods. This was influenced by a number of factors, including a need to transform

[*] See http://www.sahistory.org.za.

the police institution in such a way that it could deal with the challenges encountered over a particular period. In certain instances, the crisis of legitimacy came as a result of a deep-rooted institutional complicity or organizational deviance as submitted by Nel and Bezuidenhout (2003, 61). For instance, after the Anglo-Boer War in 1902, the SAP was mainly military in nature and was involved in a number of wars. Since the early 1900s and past 1910 the police function was characterized by continuous involvement in military actions to quell disorders such as labor disputes, strikes, as well as rebellions. These included the miners' strike of 1913, the Indian Passive Resistance Campaign, the railway and mines strikes of 1914, as well as the Rand Rebellion of 1922, to mention but a few. An interesting development came into effect with the Defence Act of 1913, which assigned certain powers relating to national defense to the SAP. Throughout the 20th century, particularly during the apartheid years, the SAP portrayed itself as an independent servant of the law. However, the regulation of the edifice of segregationist and apartheid laws undermined the image of the SAP as an apolitical nonpartisan body (Saunders & Southey, 2001, 134).

Although the paramilitaristic approach dominated the police for many years, other developments came to the fore after the disbanding of political parties in South Africa. According to Burger (2007, 70), the National Peace Accord and the Ready to Govern documents of the African National Congress (ANC), which is now the ruling party in South Africa, opted for community-oriented policing. Chapter 3 of the National Peace Accord contained important principles aimed at a serious adjustment of the police approach and the following abstract is a testimony to that effect:

> In recognition of the need to promote more effective policing, a commitment to sound policing practices and a co-operative relationship between the police and the communities is necessary. (Hough & Du Plessis, 1994, 59)

The preceding discussion effectively means that the police approach after the first democratic elections in South Africa in 1994 was largely influenced by the principles of community policing. According to Burger (2007, 97), although the development and implementation of community policing was certainly not limited to the period 1994–1996, this was the time during which policing in general was dominated by the principles and terminology of community policing. In support of that, the SAP came to be known as the South African Police Service (SAPS), with civil ranks such as superintendent, inspector, director, and others.

Rationale for the Study: The Paradox

In 2009, Deputy Minister of Police Fikile Mbalula said that he wanted the police transformed into a paramilitary force, with military ranks and discipline, which effectively meant a reversion to an apartheid era conceptualization of the police. In addition to that, Minister of Police Nathi Mthethwa argued to the cabinet that the military ranks would herald a return of discipline and command and control aspects that "flew out of the window" when the police demilitarized at the end of apartheid (Duncan, 2010, 20). This announcement was implemented in April 2010, 15 years after the police demilitarized in 1995 and moved from a paramilitary police force to a civilian police service. This, although not explicit at the time, was seen by many, and as pessimistically argued by the deputy minister, as a way to instill more discipline and enable the police to react more vigorously to crime. It is therefore clear that this move by the government was a result of the opposing dilemmas that the police faced. This dilemma was characterized by high levels of crime, including violent crimes on one hand and a need for a more civilized police approach consistent with the constitution of the country on the other hand. Although there were no directives or clear communication from the police management that they were remilitarizing the police, the minister of police was quoted by Politicsweb (2010, 1) as having stated:

> Police forces around the world are referred to as the Force and their ranks are accordingly linked to such designations. We have taken a stance as this government of fighting crime and fighting it tough. The rank changes are therefore in line with our transformation of the force, not only in terms of a name-change but change in attitude, thinking and operational duties.

The choice of organizational dynamics of the police at any given time was influenced by factors such as the political climate, the levels of crime, discipline, and many other variables. For instance, the SAP was functioning in paramilitary mode because of the outbreak of different unrests, including strikes and rebellions. But the SAP also purported to be civil because the politics of the day, particularly the National Peace Accord and the Ready to Govern documents, mandated cooperation between the police and the community. In addition, the democratic government, which came into parliament in 1994, had to mitigate the bad image that the police created over the years. This perception was also exacerbated by the past divisions and imbalances that characterized the South African society for decades. This is echoed by Burger (2007, 60), who asserts that the name change from the force to the service can be closely linked to the development of community policing, but also seems to be part of the desperation of the police to make themselves more presentable in view of the severe criticism leveled against them.

It is against this background that this research attempts to clarify the links between dealing with crime and the policing paradigm at any given time. The chapter intends to depict a threefold causal link between civilian police, paramilitaristic police, and the levels of crime in South Africa. Hypothetically, the civilian police approach is often a product of community policing. On the other hand, high levels of crime demand a more vigorous policing approach, which is beyond a mere cooperation between the police and the community. The crux of this erudition is therefore to establish whether community policing can survive in a paramilitary police environment or whether a paramilitary police environment can potentially hamstring the relationship between the police and the community. This chapter examines how the paramilitaristic police can impact on the success or failure of community policing.

The Concept of Community Policing

Community policing has been described in many ways, although its principles remain universal. For the purpose of this research, community policing refers to a philosophy of policing that emphasizes a cooperative approach between the police and other citizens, focusing on solving community problems and improving the quality of life in the community (Cox & Wade, 1998, 104). From this definition, one can deduce that crime is one of the community problems. The most interesting facet of this philosophy is that it will not only focus on the problem but also further seek remedial measures in an endeavor to improve the quality of life of the community, thereby going beyond a mere resolution of crime. This definition further asserts that although there can be arguments on whether community policing is a success, it still remains an integral part of modern and democratic policing in South Africa and elsewhere in the world.

Fox, Fourie, and Van Wyk (1998, 186) summarize the important principles of community policing as follows:

- It is dedicated to broad, focused, problem-oriented policing.
- It relies on organizational decentralization and reorientation of patrol tactics to create informal dual channels of communication between the police and the community.
- It expects the police to be sensitive to the needs of the community.
- It requires the necessary dedication to support neighborhood watches or similar initiatives in helping themselves. The police must be the catalyst of such initiatives.

The principles of community policing are clearly in line with the definition tendered earlier. Even if it is viewed in different contexts, its central theme is cooperation and partnership, which demand a conducive environment in which this partnership can take place. A distinction will always be inevitable if one looks at community policing practiced under either civilian or military police environments. This distinction has led to a plethora of arguments about whether community policing was a success in South Africa. Although this is not identical to the theoretical foundation of this research, this issue is worth reflection. Some people believe that the philosophy of community policing, whether understood as a police style, a practice, or a strategy, was not a success at all. According to Burger (2007, 142), community policing has failed in the United States, the United Kingdom, and South Africa as well.

Community policing, if implemented correctly, can provide a number of answers to today's problems, particularly the high levels of crime with very low detection rate, as well as assist the police in gaining legitimacy in the eyes of the communities (Nel & Bezuidenhout, 2003, 62). The philosophy and practice of community policing requires a transformation not just on organizational structures and procedures, but on the way in which the police think about their role and relationships with the community and how they provide their services. In essence, what is required is a transformation from a militaristic force toward a culture devoted to service ethos (Stevens & Yach, 1995, 76).

Difference Between Civilian Police and Military Institution

There are many differences between the civil police institutions and the paramilitary police or a military institution in general. These differences are found on the premise that these institutions perform different tasks, in a different manner, and with different resources. The most important difference between these institutions in the context of this research is that a military institution is known to be bureaucratic, hierarchical, and biased toward unconditional obedience. This is supported by Kleinig (1996, 39), who further submits that the police often work alone or in pairs and very seldom in compact bodies, which are characteristic of combat soldiers. Apart from that, the other difference between civil police and paramilitary police is with regard to approach, purpose, and accountability (Thackrah, 2004, 19). In a military culture, the low-ranking officials are expected to follow the orders blindly, even if those orders transgress the rights of the community they claim to serve. Military policing is normally characterized by brutality and lack of empathy. A list of comparative elements tendered by Burger (2007, 61–62) carries a meaningful tone, especially as far as the survival of community policing is concerned. These elements are:

- The functions of the police are different from those of the military.
- Unlike the military, the civilian police are only lightly armed.
- Police training, although often including military drill exercises, is focused on the preparing of recruits to perform police, and not military, functions.
- There are important differences between police and military doctrines. For example, the police act according to the doctrine of minimum force, while the military doctrine is maximum force. Whereas the police doctrine is to search and arrest, the military doctrine is to search and destroy.
- Police members are trained to act alone, while soldiers act and train in unison.

Threats to Community Policing

The rationale of this research is to establish if community policing can be successful if a conducive environment exists to permit such a mode of functioning. Literature suggests that community policing is dependent on a healthy partnership between the police and the community. In South Africa, community policing was only implemented during transition to democracy and the principles of community policing were clearly opposite from a traditional policing characterized by paramilitarism, as pointed out by Murray (2005, 447). The following section interrogates different factors that are associated with paramilitary police in order to establish their suitability or incompatibility to community policing.

Authoritarian Behavior

Bayley (1994, 104) views community policing as a sound attempt to formulate the purpose and practices of policing along professional models. It is clear that a strict enforcement of law that includes operationalization of police actions and arrests undermines the principles of community policing. An authoritarian approach emphasizes arrests, with less emphasis on the causes of crime, advice given by the community, and the professional discretion in dealing with the community problems. An example of an authoritarian police is the "strike hard" campaigns that were launched in China from 1983. The strike hard policing, as pointed out by Zhong (2009, 160), was characterized by catching criminals, cracking cases, and severe punishment.

It is most probable that an excessive use of authority to deal with what affects the community without their inclusion can only create tensions. This is confirmed by Zhong (2009, 162), who argues that the police-public relations deteriorated substantially as a result of strike hard policing. In South Africa, an authoritarian police was not a solution. Although some of the police managers believe that a change in management style associated with community policing has apparently brought about a loss of authority (Prinsloo & Bradshaw, 2010, 89), there is no doubt that a paramilitary management of the police did not bring about success in dealing with community problems.

Coerced Compliance

In a military environment, compliance is an order of the day. It is common cause that soldiers prescribe to the rule that "you comply with an order and complain later." Traditional policing that is paramilitary in nature expects officers to work with established rules and regulations. This culture, as submitted by Murray (2005, 354), leads the police to be regimented to act on direct orders with the assumption that the rank-based authority ensures not just compliance, but also efficiency and effectiveness. Forced compliance and strict following of rules and regulations cannot be conducive to community policing. In executing the duties by the book, there is a possibility that the soft community issues, such as unemployment, financial inactivity, and lack of entertainment, as well their impact on levels of crime, will be overlooked. This will therefore have an adverse impact on the survival of community policing. According to Cox and Wade (1998, 105), community policing differs from paramilitary policing in respect to attempting to identify and address underlying problems rather than responding to calls or incidents, as is the case with paramilitary police.

An example of strict compliance to rules and regulations in executing the police duties is the arrest of people for minor offenses. These arrests may have a long-term effect on people, leading to a negative impact on police legitimacy as well as a criminogenic effect on the arrestees (Sherman, 1998, 259). An extreme impact of coerced compliance is when the community loses confidence in the police. This may also prevent the members of the community from sharing critical information with the police. Police operations cannot succeed in isolation but need to be complemented with the support of the community in an endeavor to deal with myriad issues pertaining to crime.

Exclusivity

Community policing cannot survive in an environment where decisions are made with reference to "us" and "them." This state of affairs leads to an exclusion of the community in the decision-making process, portraying an attitude that the police know what is best for the community. Excluding the community from the decisions that affect them can only be poisonous to partnership and cooperation, which are central to the successful implementation of community policing. According to De Vries (2008, 128), the character of the police prior to 1995 was molded by decades of war, rebellion, and civil conflict, giving the SAP its quasi-military role and rendering it vulnerable to extraordinary political influences. Since the police were seen as oppressors of the majority of the civilian population (De Vries, 2008, 128), the police saw themselves as "us" and the community as "them," and vise versa.

This "us" and "them" labeling of two parties who are supposed to be working together in order to achieve a common goal is an established setback in any partnership. The police will continue to focus on their planned operations to deal with the scourge of crime, while the community will withhold critical information that could assist in both crime prevention and detection. The crime statistics will soar while two supposed partners are locked in suspiciousness, mistrust, and isolation. According to Marks, Shearing, and Wood (2009, 145), the tensions and ambiguities that the police feel about their current place in the world are evident in a broad narrative they express through their policy statements, media presentations, and public commitments. In South Africa, police cling to the idea of policing monopoly and prove reluctant to exhaust possibilities for sharing the load of creating safety (Marks et al., 2009, 145).

Police Management Style

The way in which the police institution is managed is greatly influenced by either militaristic or civilized connotations. For instance, the police used the term *commander* prior to 1995, which was associated with more compliance and high levels of discipline, while the term *manager* was used after democracy. The latter had characteristics of democracy and engagement in managing the police institution. According to Prinsloo and Bradshaw (2010, 88), a prominent change that occurred during the transformation process was the change in rank structures from commanders to managers at the station level. The latter, for example, had to take cognizance of the police officers' rights as employees, whereas the former were regarded as very militaristic.

The traditional managerial style of the SAP was influenced by the political climate and did not recognize the human rights of the majority of South Africans. The policies aimed at dealing with crime did not bother to include the community, and this soured the relations between the police and the community. This argument is echoed by Cawthra (1993, 1–8), who generally feels that since the 1960s, the nature of the liberation struggle by the African Nationalists was used in arguments to further militarize and politicize the old SAP. Researchers on public administration issues have continuously pointed out that the actions of the operational members of any organization mirror the management of that institution. It is common cause that the beliefs, feelings, and thoughts of the management are always traceable in the policies of that institution. It is also a common cause that the success of community policing is determined by the management style of the police managers. The more militaristic these managers are, the less the cooperation between the police and the community. Research has established with no doubt that traditional policing is more biased toward a paramilitaristic managerial style, which is characterized by authoritarianism, forced compliance, and rigid bureaucracy, among others (Auten, 1981, 68).

Police Subculture

According to Kotze, Mthembu, and Khashane (2007, 801) bureaucracy has a tendency of resisting change, with an example being that of a military that may epitomize resistance to institutional change, for it tends to focus on traditions of seniority, previous military successes, and past comradeship. There is no doubt that in South Africa, owing to historical developments, the police culture is more bent toward paramilitarism. A police culture is best defined by Reiner (1992, 21) as the values, norms, perspectives, and craft rules that inform police conduct. The police subculture is therefore an essential element of the police's reaction toward crime, dealing with any other issues pertaining to their mandate, as well as the level of cooperation and partnership between the police and the community. A creation of an environment fertile enough to allow for germination of police-community partnerships is therefore reliant on the values, norms, and perspectives of the police or, in a nutshell, the police subculture.

The positive aspects associated with subculture, such as social cohesion and teamwork, cannot be ignored. However, a bias toward a more regimental operation cannot do community-police partnership any justice. Burger (2007, 146) asserts that like the military, the police institution is a lawful coercive force, authorized to use physical force, including deadly force against citizens when required. In the same breath, like the military, the police are sometimes expected to work under dangerous conditions. These submissions, coupled with the recent announcement by the ministry of the police to remilitarize the police, go a long way in showing that the police may be reluctant to demilitarize, and that paramilitarism will remain part of the police subculture for years to come.

The success of community policing is dependent on police subculture. This means that if the subculture is a negative one accompanied with a fearful community, community policing is bound to fail. The manifestation of a fearful community in a hostile police subculture may not be a cause for concern for police officials because the majority of police officials were recruited, trained, and socialized in a traditional law enforcement orientation and may be supportive of the status quo (Roberg, 1994, 252). It can be deduced therefore that less progress will be registered until such time that the police subculture is reengineered in accordance with the spirit and aspirations of the constitutional law of South Africa.

In the final analysis, the findings of Steyn and De Vries (2007, 1) indicate a slow pace, or a total absence thereof, of a move toward a transformed police subculture. Their research found that most of the SAPS Basic Training Institutes, excluding the Bisho SAPS Basic Training Institute, only served to either maintain or strengthen newcomers' attitudes in support of police culture of solidarity, isolation, and cynicism. Although this is not the focus of this research, it is upsetting that the training of the new recruits in the SAPS is doing little in transforming the police subculture in line with the principles of human rights and democracy.

Nascent Prognosis: Conflict Between Paramilitarism and Community Policing

This chapter acknowledges arguments that community policing did not succeed as a police philosophy in many countries, including South Africa, the United States, and the United Kingdom (Burger, 2007; Williams, 2003; Reiner, 1992). However, partnership with the community remains a practiced dogma in many democratic societies. This chapter is not concerned with the level of success of community policing over years, but attempts to interrogate the environment in which community policing is supposed to flourish. An alternative argument will therefore be that whether successful or not, community policing defined the policy formulation and implementation of many police institutions, particularly that of South Africa. Burger (2007, 97), in supporting this argument, states that Chapter 3 of the National Peace Accord advocated that the police shall endeavor to obtain the cooperation of the public, whose partnership in the task of crime control and prevention is inevitable. In addition to that, Section 221 of the Interim Constitution of the Republic of South Africa, Act 200 of 1993, legitimized the legislative value of community policing by advocating for the establishment of community policing forums (CPFs). It is therefore clear that the concept of community policing has been elevated to a status of legislation, which requires compliance and mechanisms to ensure its success.

The crux of this discussion is therefore that community policing must be observed in letter and in spirit. However, the environment is contaminated largely by the police subculture, which tends to be biased toward paramilitarism. Paramilitarism is a serious threat to community policing, and the purported failures and challenges are directly attributable to it. The recent remilitarization of the police, whether it was fully blown or not, will hamper the development of community policing, which was supposed to be gaining momentum after being adopted after democratization of South Africa. In China, for instance, the "mass line" policing of 1949 to 1980 recognized the fact that policing relies on the masses and on the mobilization of the masses, as well as the police function, to gain the support of the population (Zhong, 2009, 158). It is empirical that this research took a different stance compared to other research. It is the conclusion of this research that instead of preaching the failures of community policing without a proper prognosis, there should be remedial measures that will assist or at least resuscitate community policing, which cannot be absent in any democracy.

It is concluded that the policy regarding the South African Police services is not conducive for partnerships (Marks et al., 2009, 146). More than that, paramilitarism, as recently announced by the Ministry of Police, may instill discipline and place police officials in a position to deal with crime in a more vigorous way. However, the price to be paid far exceeds the advantages of paramilitaristic policing operations. This abstract from Marks et al. (2009, 151) summarizes the paradox pertinent to this state of affairs:

> It may seem that what is being suggested represents a retreat from community policing, a step backward towards professional, disassociated policing. To the contrary, we are trying to explore ways of making community policing work better and to avoid a situation where people in places like South Africa throw up their hands and say that it is simply a failed colonial import. We also want to move beyond a community policing narrative that the police own and control, towards a model that accounts for police limitations and the range of alternative policing sources that are already out there.

Remedial Measures: A Calculated Model for the Future

There are many criticisms leveled against community policing. Although there are many authors who have written on the shortcomings of community policing, Barak (2007, 84) summarizes these criticisms as follows:

- Community policing is soft on crime or deflective of true crime fighting because of its policies of employing counseling and other community-based social work methods of dealing with noncomforting behavior.

- Community policing may have unintended consequences of broadening policing reach and power into the domain that is better handled by the families and the community.
- Because of lack of consensus over what constitutes community policing, it has been difficult to evaluate community policing programs to determine its effectiveness.

The biggest justification tendered by the critics of community policing is that community policing philosophy did not prove sufficient in dealing with rising levels of crime, low morale among the police officials, lack of discipline, and lack of command. In reaction to these purported illnesses, it is recommended that the police institutions across the world acknowledge that a shift from traditional policing to community policing needs a major transition in both managerial and cultural terms (Murray, 2005, 354). Instead of remilitarizing the police, it is suggested that the police reinforces the unit management, as is being implemented in the Department of Correctional Services in South Africa. Unit management will mean that there will be specific units in the police that will deal with the policing of soft community problems and foster relations in the process. The unit management as implemented in correctional services in South Africa is slightly similar to sector policing as currently utilized by the police. It is, however, critical that certain aspects of sector policing need to be revised to embrace a total engagement and involvement of the community. The other units, such as the current task force in the South African Police, can then focus on more violent and serious crimes and deal with these crimes in a combination of operations and other police tactics. There is a task force already, and it passes all military tests, as it is heavily armed, trained in a militaristic way, and deals with crimes considered somehow beyond the capabilities of other police officials. As a word of caution, though, these specific mandates must not happen in silos, as the task force will still need to be given necessary information by other units that are able to interact with the community on a more regular basis.

There is no need to remilitarize the whole police institution with the aim of reducing epidemic levels of crime. To date, no research has guaranteed that paramilitarism reduces crime. Instead, paramilitarism involves police actions that equate to another crime in many democracies, such as police brutality, interrogations, and extractions. In a paramilitary institution, evidence is normally obtained illegally and through means that undermines the basic human rights of those suspected of a crime. This is surely against human rights and remains a challenge to the police oversight bodies across the world. It is therefore recommended that the thinking and position of the police in the society is reassessed and a necessary change is effected. These changes will have to deal with the police attitudes, police stereotypes, police image, paramilitaristic subculture, and reorientation of the police management style. Although SAPS is not the only role player in handling of crime, the continued high levels of violent crimes emphasize the fact that leadership and clear ideological direction have failed to materialize (Prinsloo & Bradshaw, 2010, 93).

Summary and Conclusion

Community policing is a better option than traditional policing in any democratic dispensation. Its principles are geared toward mitigating the human rights abuses pertinent to older regimes associated with paramilitarism and creation of fearful communities. It is upsetting if the police who are a smaller portion of the entire society think that they know what is best for the community, which is generally in the majority. The principles of community policing emphasize community-police partnerships, which have proved to be a driving force behind successful policing. Although there is a feeling that community policing did not succeed in many countries, the deduction from this research is that community policing is a policy issue clearly advocated for in the legislation of South Africa and other countries.

This research looked at the concept of community policing and the principles that define this concept. At a later stage, the threats to community policing were also analyzed. Throughout this process, it became clear that that all threats that were identified resulted from the paramilitaristic approach of the police. It is therefore a general feeling that a paramilitaristic approach may yield a desirable level of discipline but at a huge cost of bitter relations between the community and the police.

References

Auten, J.H. (1981). The paramilitary model of police and police professionalism. *Police Studies*, *4*(2), 67–78.

Bayley, D. (1994). *Police for the Future*. New York: Oxford University.

Barak, G. (2007). *Battleground criminal justice*. Westport, CT: Greenwood Press.

Burger, J. (2007). *Strategic perspectives on crime and policing in South Africa*. Pretoria: Van Schaik.

Cawthra, G. (1993). *Policing South Africa: The South African Police and the transition from apartheid*. London: Zed Press.

Cox, S.M., & Wade, J.E. (1998). *The criminal justice network: An introduction*. Boston: McGraw-Hill.

De Vries, I. (2008). Strategic issues in the South African Police (SAPS) in the first decade of democracy. *Acta Criminologica*, *21*(2), 125–138.

Duncan, J. (2010). *Voice, political mobilization and repression under Jacob Zuma.* Paper delivered at the symposium on a Decade of Dissent: Reflections on Popular Resistance in South Africa, Johannesburg.

Fox, W., Fourie, M., & Van Wyk, B. (1998). *Police management in South Africa.* Kenwyn: Juta & Co. Ltd.

Hough, M., & Du Plessis, A. (1994, July). *Selected documents and commentaries on negotiations and constitutional development in the RSA: 1989–1994.* ISSUP Ad Hoc Publication 31. Pretoria: University of South Africa, Institute for Strategic Studies.

Kleinig, J. (1996). *Handled with discretion: Ethical issues in police decision making.* Lanham, MD: Rowman & Littlefield Publishers.

Kotze, E., Mthembu, O., & Khashane, E. (2007). Psychological empowerment in the military. *Journal of Public Administration, 42*(8), 798–815.

Marks, M., Shearing, C., & Wood, J. (2009). Who should the police be? Finding a new narrative for community policing in South Africa. *Police Practice and Research, 10*(2), 145–155.

Morash, M., & Ford, J.K. (2002). *The move to community policing: Making change happen.* Thousand Oaks, CA: Sage Publications.

Murray, J. (2005). Policing terrorism: A threat to community policing or just a shift in priorities? *Police Practice and Research, 6*(4), 347–367.

Nel, F., & Bezuidenhout, J. (2003). *Policing and human rights.* Lansdowne, South Africa: Juta & Co. Ltd.

Politicsweb. (2010). *Military ranks for SAPS to take effect April 1—Mthethwa.* Retrieved October 5, 2010, from http://www.politicsweb.co.za

Prinsloo, M., & Bradshaw, D. (2010). The experience of transformation by police officers: Findings from a qualitative study conducted in Cape Town, South Africa. *Acta Criminologica, 23*(1), 84–95.

Reiner, R. (1992). Policing a postmodern society. *Modern Law Review, 55*(6): 761–781.

Roberg, R.R. (1994). Can today's police organizations effectively implement community policing? In D.P. Rosenbaum (Ed.), *The challenge of community policing: Testing the promises.* Thousand Oaks, CA: Sage.

Saunders, C.C., & Southey, N. (2001). *A dictionary of South African history.* Claremont: David Phillip Publishers.

Sherman, L.W. (1998). *Policing for crime prevention.* National Institute of Justice. Retrieved October 6, 2010, from http:www.ncjrs.org.work/index.htm

South African History Online. Retrieved October 6, 2010, from http://www.sahistory.org.za/pages/governance-projects/organisations

Stevens, P., & Yach, D.M. (1995). *Community policing in action: A practitioner's guide.* Kenwyn: Juta and Co. Ltd.

Steyn, J., & De Vries, I. (2007). Exploring the impact of the SAPS Basic Training Institutes in changing the deviant police culture attitudes of new recruits. *Acta Criminologica, 20*(1), 1–34.

Thackrah, R. (2004). *Dictionary of terrorism.* New York: Routledge.

Williams, E.J. (2003). Structuring in community policing: Institutionalizing innovative change. *Police Practice and Research, 4*(2), 119–129.

Zhong, L. (2009). Community policing in China: old wine in new bottles. *Police Practice and Research, 10*(2), 157–169.

13

Community Policing in the Netherlands

A Continuously Changing Constant

ARIE VAN SLUIS
LEX CACHET
PETER VAN OS
RUTH PRINS
PETER MARKS

Introduction

Nineteen seventy-seven was an important year for the Dutch police, as it was then that a seminal strategy document called "A Changing Police" was published that would set the course for the next three decades. The writers of the report felt that for the police to bridge the growing gap between them and the society they serve, they would have to be innovative, and think outside of their usual security paradigms. They found their solution in community policing, and the strategy document laid out the framework for community policing (COP) in the Netherlands. This document was widely considered a milestone in the development of Dutch policing (see Cachet et al., 1998).

However, by 2005, the Dutch Board of Chief Commissioners felt it necessary to publish a new strategy document to once again map out the future of Dutch policing. After nearly three decades, the Dutch police was again in need of a shared philosophy that would serve as a foundation for its mandate. This new document was titled the "Police in Evolution" (PIE), but it stayed true to the values of COP by once again focusing on the local community and stressing community policing.

In this chapter we explore the establishment and development of Dutch COP. We look at several distinct phases in the long-term development of Dutch COP, and examine the factors that explain the shifts that have taken place in the way Dutch COP is carried out. We ask also about the prospects of Dutch COP in the future.

The chapter consists of four sections. In the first section, we examine the historical roots and the development of Dutch COP since its inception in 1977. In the second section, we look at the current state of affairs for COP in the Netherlands. In the third section, we put forward several explanations for the significant shifts that have taken place over the course of the COP's 30-year history. In the fourth section, we discuss the prospects for Dutch COP in the coming years. The final section presents our conclusions.

Distinct Phases in the Development of Dutch COP

The concept of Dutch COP is neither clearly defined nor static. Nonetheless, we follow from Terpstra (2010, p. 217) in assuming that the strategy has five central ambitions:

1. Reducing the rift between the Dutch police and citizens
2. Maintaining a keen focus on a range of problems in the neighborhood
3. Taking a preventive approach and a proactive work style in addition to a reactive one
4. Cooperating with other agencies
5. Encouraging citizen involvement

While the main aims of COP have not changed over the years, the shape and feel of the COP effort have varied significantly during different phases of its development. As we will show in subsequent sections, there seems to have been a constant balancing and adjusting of three basic orientations that are simultaneously fundamental to modern policing.

State, Community, and Profession

The first of this is the traditional view of the police as the strong arm of government. Under this orientation, the police are state centered and their work is geared toward the tasks associated with state control, including repression (Punch, 2010, p. 203). The focus under this orientation is not only on crime control, but also on the maintenance of order on a large scale and the management and prevention of large-scale incidents. Key terms associated with this orientation are the state, vigilance, vigor, repression, centralization, uniformity, and hard policing.

The second orientation impacting the shape and form of Dutch COP is that of the police as a service to the (local) community. This orientation is usually associated with community-oriented policing. Key terms associated with this second orientation are the local community, responding to local needs and demands, citizen involvement, legitimacy, tailor-made solutions, fragmentation, soft policing, and prevention. While the state-centered perspective focuses on hard policing or the grave matter of catching crooks, the service orientation uses soft policing, which refers to the broader social tasks within the community.

While the two orientations appear seemingly opposite, both exert significant pressures on the form and function of the Dutch police force. The police are viewed both as the strong arm of power, belonging to a strong, central government, and as the protectors of the rights and freedoms of ordinary citizens in the community.

The third orientation is that of the police as a profession. The PIE document from 2005 states that while the police are subordinate to the police authorities, they have the professional authority to claim an autonomous role in the formulation and implementation of police policy. Key terms under this perspective are the police organization, competence, professional autonomy, discretion, and police education.

As stated above, the three perspectives exist simultaneously, with each coming to the fore at different times depending on the political and social climate. An exclusively state-oriented and state-controlled police cannot meet the requirements of a democratic constitutional state, nor does it ensure that policing is done according to high professional standards. At the same time, a police force geared exclusively to local needs and wants of citizens results in a powerless police that lacks the authority and independence to act in conflicts between societal groups. Similarly, neglecting the third orientation of the police as a professional body can lead to poor training, incompetence, and policies that are difficult to implement, while overly stressing the police's status as a professional group may lead to the undervaluing of their democratic accountability and reduce the focus on local needs. This may then increase problems of legitimacy.

Below, we identify five successive phases in the evolution of Dutch COP based on shifts in its position with regard to these three basic orientations.

Phase 1: Fighting for Existence (1970s and Early 1980s)

The first major shift in the direction of Dutch policing after the Second World War arose in the 1970s. It was at this time that the traditional (professional) model of policing was viciously attacked for being incapable of dealing with the more complex and dynamic problems faced by Dutch society.

Before 1977, the role of a police officer was primarily to enforce the law and to make arrests. Police discretion was neither acknowledged nor accepted and tasks were simplified and standardized by the use of standard operation procedures. Specialized units were created to handle more complicated problems. There was a degree of concern about the professionalism of the police, but this progressed largely through the use of technology. For example, squad cars replaced surveillance on foot and citizens were seen merely as recipients of professional police services (van Sluis, 2002). The police in this era acted clearly as the strong arm of government. This state-centered force was a distant, highly centralized, and strongly technocratic form of policing that had its roots in an earlier time when society had much confidence in technology and social engineering and progress.

But the 1960s left the Dutch police with gigantic losses in their legitimacy. The rigid and repressive style adopted during the student protests of the period resulted in particularly bitter criticism of the police. The Dutch police found it necessary to reintegrate themselves into the society and regain the trust of their citizens. In looking for ways to reestablish their mandate, the Dutch police found inspiring examples from the United States.

It took the better part of the decade, but the new philosophy was crystallized in the 1977 strategy document "A Changing Police." The document clearly stipulated that police work should be done by well-educated policemen oriented toward the good of the community. Such policemen should work both individually and in teams under the framework of a horizontal, decentralized organization.

After 1977, Dutch police started experimenting with COP. The first community police officer was a beat constable working in a limited area with the broadly defined task of keeping the neighborhood safe and quiet and restoring contact with citizens (Punch et al., 2002). Not surprisingly, the first beat officers met with a lot of criticism from their colleagues for not being "real policemen." At the same time, they were criticized by the public for being too soft, for always being alone, and were accused of lacking any authority. This initial criticism resulted in the creation of neighborhood teams that aimed for both external integration between the police and the public and integral integration between departments of the police organization.

Phase 2: COP as the New Orthodoxy (Late 1980s and Early 1990s)

Despite the introduction of COP in 1977, by the early 1980s, most police forces had failed to implement neighborhood teams. Even when they were implemented, things were not always smooth sailing. For example, the city of Delft had a medium-sized force that was designated a COP pioneer in 1980. However, its pilot program ended prematurely because both the detectives and the uniformed officers felt threatened and opposed the intended changes. Further, the chief of police himself showed himself to be ambivalent in his support of the pilot project, and the public prosecutor openly expressed his doubts about the quality of crime control under this new model (van Os, unpublished paper).

While their experiment was doomed to failure because of the poor support of key figures, other forces had greater success. The municipal police of Haarlem successfully adopted and implemented neighborhood teams in three areas. And once the municipal police of Amsterdam (which is the leading police force in the Netherlands) adopted COP, many other police forces followed soon after. By the beginning of the 1990s, nearly all forces in the Netherlands had adopted teams based on "A Changing Police." COP become the standard way of delivering basic policing and became the new orthodoxy of policing (Punch et al., 2008).

Phase 3: Competing Perspectives on Policing (1990s and Early 21st Century)

Just as COP became the dominant policing model, the social and international environment changed. While the shift toward the COP model was triggered primarily by concerns over the loss of police legitimacy, its implementation coincided with major changes in the social climate in the Netherlands.

New developments took place in the field of public order in the late 1980s, specifically that the squatter movement grew significantly and presented a new challenge to the police, as did football hooliganism and a vast increase in the number of petty crimes. In the 1990s, the Netherlands also experienced the emergence of more professionally organized and more international forms of crime, all of which served to undermine the predominance of the COP. It became clear that while a COP perspective was important, the police had to be able to serve their old role as the strong arm of government to an extent if they were to achieve their primary goals of crime control and public order maintenance. These developments stimulated the growth of a new degree of professionalism in law enforcement and the reestablishment of specialized units to deal with complex new forms of crime, first at the regional level and later at the national level.

As a result of these pressures, by the 1990s, COP had gradually lost its status as the dominant policing model and as a remedy for all diseases. Zero tolerance policy became a feature of Dutch policing in the big cities, as did broken windows policing and hot spot policing. Just as COP itself was inspired by the U.S. experience, the move toward these more hard-line approaches was also inspired by American and British experiences of criminal activity. The shift in focus occurred also against the backdrop of a growing sense that the Dutch tradition of tolerance had gone too far and police had to focus on catching criminals again (Das et al., 2002; Punch et al., 2002).

Phase 4: COP as Area-Bound Policing (After the 1993 Police Act)

Just as it appeared that COP was beginning to take a back seat to the new initiatives, it was unexpectedly revived in 1993 when a new police act came into being. The act merged the 148 Dutch municipal police forces and the state police into 25 regional police forces. This regionalization and the upscaling of the police were aimed at improving police performance, especially in crime control, but shortly after regionalization, area-bound policing was introduced in almost all regions (Beumer, 1997). New community officers were introduced who, unlike the beat constables, were not ordinary cops. These new community officers were made responsible for organizing security in their area in a much wider and more permanent sense. They were called area managers or neighborhood directors and they were supported by their colleagues in specialized departments (Punch et al., 2002).

During this period, the COP movement was characterized by the need to restore the balance between centralizing tendencies (as seen by a drastic increase in scale of police forces) and decentralizing tendencies (specifically the wish to strengthen the bonds between the police and local communities).

The shape of COP in the 1990s reflects important shifts in local safety policy in the Netherlands and the ever-changing role of the police. From the early 1990s on, the central government puts a lot of effort into stimulating local authorities to develop their own local safety policies.

As a consequence of this, the police found themselves having to rethink their core tasks and role in the chain of collaboration with other parties (De Kimpe and Cachet, 2008). Gradually, the role of the police in local safety programs became less and less dominant as the rise of independent local safety plans and the concomitant introduction of a variety of local supervisors gave the police an opportunity to dispose of certain policing tasks that they considered improper as well. In summary, this period was defined by the movement away from the earlier overwhelming emphasis on the profession and on scale enlargement and a reprioritization of the community.

Phase 5: New Realism, Pragmatism in Policing (2005–)

The early 21st century saw more changes in the shape of Dutch COP. The new vision of COP was articulated in the strategy document called the "Police in Evolution" (PIE). This document arose with the backdrop of the events of 2001. While earlier community officers were seen almost as social workers, the new officer is clearly a visible force in the streets. He engages in criminal investigations, order maintenance, and law enforcement. Once again, he serves as the traditional strong arm of the government. But he is more than that. He participates actively in citizen networks and cooperates with professional agencies such as schools and municipalities as well. He is a generalist who performs all policing tasks, except the ones that require specialist expertise. When such expertise is called in or new initiatives are introduced by the local government, the community officer provides valuable information and supports them.

The push toward a more assertive and firm enforcement led to a stronger involvement of community officers in crime fighting and in "hard policing." To close the gap between COP and crime investigation, PIE emphasizes a hybrid approach of COP in which the focus is on hard policing as well. But the community policeman or woman is also a professional whose knowledge and expertise has to be taken seriously by local administrative authorities. In this way, PIE also lays the foundation for enhancements of the professional competence of community officers.

The Current State of Affairs: Dutch COP in Practice

According to Straver et al. (2009) the Dutch police are reasonably well integrated in neighborhoods, professional networks, and local government. Such local integration also contributes to generally satisfactory levels of police legitimacy. From this perspective, the basic goals of COP appear to have been met rather well. However, an examination of recent literature published on this topic demonstrates that the overall picture is less straightforward. While the results are generally satisfactory, Dutch COP clearly faces a number of key challenges. We will discuss some of the discrepancies between the ambitions and achievements of the Dutch practice of COP in the following section (Stol et al., 2004, Stol, 2009; Terpstra, 2008, 2010; van der Torre, 1999; 2007; Bervoets et al., 2009; Straver et al., 2009; Vlek and van der Torre, 2010).

COP as the Leading Principle

Although COP is the guiding principle used in the day-to-day police work of all 25 Dutch regional police forces, there are major differences between and even within the forces with regard to the organization and practice of COP. Some of the differences are greater than what would be expected purely from the perspective that local police units need the freedom to establish tailor-made solutions. For example, while in most forces community officers are part of the basic unit, in others they operate as rather isolated individuals or as part of a neighborhood team. Another common difference is that in some forces community officers only perform specific community policing tasks, while in others their job includes criminal investigations and emergency assistance (Terpstra, 2008).

Further, each force has its own denomination for community officers and position in the hierarchical structure. There are also significant differences in the working styles of community officers across forces in different neighborhoods (Terpstra, 2008; Straver et al., 2009).

Balancing Uniformity and Variety

This broad range of implementation styles has not gone unnoticed and the Dutch board of police chiefs now aims to end the proliferation of diverse styles. To this end, they have developed a national program for the development of area-bound policing. The board has opted for the further development of COP as the basic concept for the organization and practices of the whole police force, and their vision is of relatively small-scale teams constituting the core of the organization and that support the community officers. Such a team is responsible for public safety and the integral exercise of the police function in its area. The board has rejected the idea of COP as a separate function that complements basic police services, crime investigation, and other specialized services organized at the district level.

The national program now being rolled out contains a referential framework with nine facets or standards for the COP. These facets refer to the breadth of police services, the scale of the basic units, the position of the community officer, the management of community officers, the process-oriented practice, planning and control, information, integral public safety, and leadership style (van Os, 2010). These nine facets are also seen as interrelated and, depending on how they are implemented, can strengthen or weaken COP. Each year, audits are conducted to determine the degree to which police forces meet the criteria established, and the board of police chiefs regularly discusses the results (van Os, 2010).

This strategy fits the ambition of the chiefs of police, which is to unify the Dutch police into one concern and to enhance professional competence through the implementation of national standards for specific policing domains. This aim is backed up by a number of educational programs provided by the Dutch Police Academy (Vlek & van der Torre, 2010). In addition, all forces appear to be increasing their number of community officers with financial support from the Minister of Internal Affairs and the Ministry of Kingdom Relations. The overall aim is to have 1 community officer per 5,000 inhabitants. However, to date no police force has yet been able to achieve this or fully comply with stipulations related to the nine COP facets outlined above.

Changing Image of Dutch COP

Over the years, the image of COP has changed substantially. Community officers are now seen more as police officers and not as social workers. They contribute to law and crime investigation by taking on criminal investigations, enforcement, and emergency services, as well as by working on prevention and problem solving. Intelligence-led policing has also become a big part of the community officers' duties. According to "Police in Evolution" community officers not only have to act as sources of information for criminal investigations, but they have an important "signal and advice" function in that they are responsible for providing administrative authorities with information and early warnings about significant societal trends, emerging problems, signs of terrorism, and radicalization.

Role Conflicts

In their empirical study on policing on the streets Stol et al. (2004) observed that community officers not only perform soft policing tasks, but also take more repressive actions. They frequently deal with social disorder caused by youth, road safety issues, and petty crime. Terpstra similarly observed in 2008 that rule enforcement has become an important part of their work. As a result, Stol says, their soft image no longer fits the way they actually do their job

The new role of community officers in intelligence-led policing sometimes comes into conflict with their mandate to solve problems by cooperating with representatives of the community (Bervoets et al., 2009). Their role as law enforcers means that they are obliged to pass privileged and sensitive information to other police departments for purposes often outside of why it was provided to them (de Kool, 2007). Community officers often report that this dual role harms the relations they have developed in their neighborhoods as it muddies trust. Sometimes community officers also experience difficulties with the new repressive demands that are made upon them, for example, writing tickets in order to meet arbitrary performance targets.

Finding the Balance Between Community Policing and Crime Investigations

As outlined above, a long-standing problem faced by Dutch police is that of balancing community policing, emergency responses, and criminal investigations. According to "A Changing Police," all members of a community policing team cover the whole spectrum of police work. However, in practice, criminal investigation tends to be neglected by neighborhood teams because of a lack of necessary expertise and competences. Community officers are sometimes unable to feed detectives with knowledge of local perpetrators.

As crime control was once again designated a core task of police work in the 1990s, new specializations appeared and old specializations like that of the juvenile cop and the vice squad were reinstated in order to increase the level of professional competence in crime control. However, modernizing the process of criminal investigation alone was not sufficient. Many criminal cases (160,000 by some estimates) were not pursued by the police and eventually shelved, even though case screenings demonstrated sufficient indications for a follow-up. Community officers thus had to participate in criminal investigations in one way or another, in order to fill this void.

The quest for a sensible balance between both disciplines has gone on for years, and a number of means of balancing the two have taken years with experiment, including colocating different units in the same building, functionally integrating detectives in neighborhood teams, and having community officers work temporarily in investigative units (Zoomer, 2006).

Special crime investigation units have also been created in most police districts in order to improve the current level of collaboration and exchange of information between specialists and community officers, as well as to deal with all kinds of petty crime. This approach better integrates criminal investigations with community policing. However, there are some specific demarcations between the roles of the community officer and specialists. As a rule, neighborhood teams only deal with criminal offenses that don't require imprisonment (so-called six-hour cases); however, community officers also serve as experts in community affairs during criminal investigations. Despite these initiatives, it remains that only a disappointing 12% of the community officer's time is spent on criminal investigations. This is far less than would be expected given the current "crisis" in crime investigations (van Os and Gooren, 2010).

Finding the Balance Between Community Policing and Emergency Response

According to "A Changing Police," emergency responses should be integrated into the work of community officers. However, this has proven to be less than feasible because community officers do not typically spend as much time on the streets as would be required for them to effectively meet this role. Furthermore, emergency response is discipline in and of itself, and it is aimed at immediate problem solving. It requires a different disposition than that required to deal with structural problems in the community.

Following from the original concept of community policing, the work of the community officer in the neighborhood would take the front seat. Because of their key role community officers can call upon other officers for emergency responses as well as for support and backup during criminal investigations. However, in practice community officers lack the necessary power and authority to play such a role well (van der Torre, 2007). What's more, police managers tend to see emergency responses as being more critical for gaining the trust of the public than community policing, and so tend to prioritize it accordingly.

Emergency response is thus organized in separate units, outside of neighborhood teams, and is directed out of a central (integrated) control room. A dispatcher prioritizes the requests for assistance from the public and directs available surveillance cars accordingly. Priorities are based on written policy, and requests that are less critical are left to the neighborhood teams so as to regulate public demand for police assistance. In practice, assistance calls are rarely passed on directly to community officers in the streets (van Os and Gooren, 2010). Instead, the community officer is involved as a way of filling up the gaps in the duty rosters of the emergency response teams.

Time Spent in the Neighborhood

Another area in which the COP has fallen slightly short of its ambitions is in the area of time spent on community policing. The intentions outlined in the COP's original framework state that community officers should spend about 80% of their time on community policing. However, Bron et al. (2010) observes that community officers spend only about 65% of their work hours on neighborhood-related activities. The major part of their non-neighborhood-related actions (32%) consists of emergency response, surveillance, and order maintenance that they do outside of their designated neighborhood, as well as administrative tasks like maintaining contact through e-mail or writing a weblog to keep in contact with their neighborhood. About 3% of the remaining time is spent on attending briefings.

Professional Autonomy and the Management of COP

The autonomy of the professional community officer was an important element in the original conception of community policing. Community-oriented policing and problem solving (COPPS) demanded a nonbureaucratic way of management, and it was thought that the traditional hierarchy and structure of responsibility had to be turned around (van Sluis, 2002) for this purpose.

Despite these noble intentions, the practice of granting professional autonomy to community officers is not particularly popular among researchers studying community policing. Writers in this area find that such an approach has resulted in officers having too much elbow room to do things their own way. Internal instructions lack precision as a result of such autonomy, and this creates a number of significant shortcomings (for example, Bervoets et al., 2009; van der Torre, 2007).

While the researchers draw on studies of the behavior of community officers in coming to this conclusion, the officers themselves vehemently disagree. Officers themselves report that they often feel overruled by their managers in setting their priorities and executing their roles. This prevents them from spending more time on tasks they see as critical to the security of their neighborhoods.

The Impact of the Traditional Police Culture

The preoccupation with the management of COP has its roots in the perceived lack of professional competence of community officers. Despite its 30-year history, community policing as a profession can still be said to be in its infancy relative to the culture of the more established or more traditional police force. "Street cop" culture is still dominant, and community officers remain reactive and incident focused. Systematic problem solving is not a common practice, even though it is said to be an indispensable tool for community policing (van Sluis, 2002). Terpstra (2010) states: "Community policing is, despite its ambitions, largely reactive and ad hoc. The analyses of local problems of crime and disorder made by community officers are often rather unsystematic and lack explicitness. To a large degree they are based on quite tacit, practical knowledge."

Part of the explanation for this is that community officers tend to favor direct immediate action and rely more on information they receive from personal contacts with citizens (street knowledge) than on information gained by research and science. Their own information and personal experience in the police practice are seen as superior to knowledge from central databases. Their actions are thus primarily practice based, not evidence based (Terpstra, 2008). This tendency is furthered by the fact that community officers tend to distrust standardized instruments that are developed by their colleagues in the police force, including the rather successful Crime and Disturbance Area Scan that is currently being implemented.

To address this problem, the Dutch Police Academy has recently developed a standard program to educate community officers. Before, each police force had its own course at the police academy, but the newly developed program aims to integrate training across police forces and deliver community officers at two levels, the highest being that of inspectors with bachelor's degrees.

Cooperation With Other Agencies, Although With Little Attention Being Paid to Citizen Participation

Another feature of current Dutch COP is the cooperation between agencies involved in local security. Much of this cooperation is initiated by the community officers themselves. Although they do well with other agencies, community officers have greater difficulties supporting or even appreciating undertakings by citizens. The role of citizens appears to be limited in their view to the initiative of providers of information (the eyes and ears of the police) (Terpstra, 2008). Despite all efforts to comply with the official police policy that considers safety a joint effort between the police and the citizens, community officers are still rather police centered in their orientation (van Os, 2010).

Integration Into the Local Community?

Integration into the local community is one of the central ambitions of Dutch COP, but its importance seems to be slowly eroding. Police forces have tried to bring more "blue" back by increasing area-bound policing, despite the fact that many cities have installed enforcers of their own. These are nonpolice personnel with limited responsibilities and tasks, but who are controlled exclusively by the local government. This trend was furthered by the retreat of the police to their core tasks and by a tremendous growth in the use of local administrative sanctions for nuisances and minor offenses (van der Vijver, 2004). This rather chaotic proliferation of guards, watchmen, wardens, stewards, and others (the extended policing family) has led to increasing debate in the Netherlands about reinstating a kind of local police.

A recent survey among members of local councils showed that a majority (55%) were in favor of the return of a local police force, despite their overall satisfaction with the work of the regional police forces (van der Torre et al., 2009). Part of the reason for this is that councilors are pessimistic about their influence on police policies under the current structure. They fear that an increase in central or national steering of the police will be detrimental for the local determination of police work. A local police force could both strengthen the local influence on policing and put a stop to the chaotic proliferation of nonpolice enforcement and surveillance.

Analysis: Shifts Explained

What factors explain the shifts that Dutch COP has undergone? The following are key factors that have been identified as impacting the face of the Dutch COP over various phases of its existence.

The Dutch Aversion Toward Centralized State Power

The Dutch attitude toward the police and the power of the state has always been ambiguous. This ambiguity is reflected in the state structure (the Netherlands is a decentralized unitary state), in which there is no room for a strong, centrally managed police apparatus. Aversion to a strong, centralized police apparatus was initially fueled by the French domination of the state and local police forces a long time ago, as well as German occupation during the Second World War. The current decentralized police system reflects the broadly shared view that the police should be oriented primarily toward delivering services to the public and should serve as the strong arm of central government to a lesser degree. It was this view that made the Netherlands fertile ground for COP in the first place, although the shape of the COP has changed constantly since its inception.

The Impact of Managerialism

In its current form, Dutch COP appears to have been stripped of the more radical elements inherent in its original framework. For example, there was the initial requirement to overturn the traditional police organization and to empower rank-and-file officers in the development of strategic police policy.

This revolutionary potential of COP was successfully neutralized by an increase in the level of top-down steering. Police managers are now again more inclined to see rank-and-file officers merely as implementers of policies formulated by the top that are controlled by the use of standard operation procedures and statistical analysis, such as that available through Compstat management. This has undoubtedly led to less professional autonomy for community officers (Van Os, 2010, 267), but part of the reason for this rise despite the noble intentions for COP was the community officers' poor performance in the fight against crime.

Above all, this shift meant a comeback of the professional model of policing that was dominant in the 1960s and early 1970s, and a further inhibition of the development of postbureaucratic ways of organizing.

Changes in the Political and Social Climate

The growing popularity of the reform model among Dutch policy makers and police managers reflects not only a shift in COP practice but also a major shift in Dutch safety policy of the last 15 years. The shift has been primarily toward a harsher, stricter policy with extensive use of penal sanctions (Das et al., 2002; Terpstra and van der Vijver, 2006). Such a penal rationale has permeated virtually all measures of crime prevention, and prevention now means only proactive intervention on the basis of risk profiles. The focus is primarily on street crime (van Swaaningen, 2005, 303).

Moving to and fro Between Hard and Soft Policing

A regression toward hard-line enforcement (Punch, 2010, 201) threatens the very survival of the COP. But the pressures to reform were real and insistent. The 1990s saw strong pressures exerted on the police to be more effective in the fight against crime, and to focus less on delivering services to the public. It has also led to the emergence of alternatives to the COP model, including the zero tolerance movement. As a result, the police became more visible on the streets and were more assertive, and there were clear signs of a new élan among police officers (Punch, 2006).

The Impact of Police System Reforms

Since the Police Act of 1993 came into force, regional police forces have become larger and more complex organizations. The reorganization of 1993 was inspired by the larger discontent with police performance and caused a fundamental break with the COP philosophy. It thus heralded a partial return to the professional model of policing, which is based on larger, centralized police forces and greater distance between the police and the public. In retrospect, however, this shift can be said to have been a temporary one. COP was soon reintroduced in the form of area-bound policing, and this served to balance somewhat against the growing detachment and centralization (Cachet et al., 1998).

Innovation Dynamics Within the Police

Innovations in Dutch policing often have a high turnover rate (Hoogenboom, 2006). New ideas and concepts alternate quickly, whereas real shifts in the way police officers think and act take much more time to enact, and the many new models initiated by management have not changed the community officers' day-to-day activities significantly (Terpstra, 2010, 228). For example, some elements of the zero tolerance or reassurance policing have crept into their day-to-day activities, but this has been a very slow development in the work of the community officers. COP has remained the guiding principle over the years, even though it too had a slow start and has changed over the years. There has been an almost invisible incorporation of other concepts that continue to come and go in a complex process of change (compare Pollitt and Bouckaert, 2009).

Unifying Tendencies Within the Dutch Police

The term *community policing* has suffered as a result of its abstract conceptualization, as this has hampered the development of a shared interpretation and implementation. However, in recent years, the further development of COP has been made part of a systematic program run by the Board of Chiefs of Police, and this has been backed up by the educational program introduced by the Dutch Police Academy. These efforts are further supported by a national referential framework for COP.

The Future Prospects of Dutch COP

Any assertion one could make about the future of Dutch COP would be speculative in nature. Nevertheless, certain trends can be extrapolated and several key threats and challenges identified. Many of these challenges are far from new, such as the continuing need to involve citizens more actively into COP, the need to balance COP with emergency response and crime control priorities, and the need to reconcile the many claims that are made upon community officers. The board of police chiefs has now formulated a vision of policing that more clearly guides the process of COP implementation. A new challenge likely to come up in the near future is that of serious budget cuts. Such cuts have already been announced and are likely to add significant obstacles to the development of COP.

A Strategy for the Diffusion and Adoption of COP

National standards for the organization and execution of community policing have been set in place, as have educational foundations. These illustrate the growing unity of the Dutch police. However, although significant progress has been made, community policing is still not fully developed as a profession.

Nonetheless, the referential frame for COP and the support given to it by the program manager are invaluable to the serious practitioner. With these in place, there is less risk of COP remaining an abstract concept, and being interpreted in different ways across and within police forces. However, while uniformity and compliance with protocol are important, they are not targets in themselves. These goals have to be weighed against the need for solutions that are more closely targeted to the needs of the local community.

While the referential frame for COP is invaluable, it is best regarded as a seed for planting than as a plant for potting. Specifically, it is the view of these authors that it should not function as a mere blueprint. Rather, it needs to be adopted in a way that facilitates learning and the establishment of policing best practices. This addresses the current problem of poor adherence to practices that have proven their value in other police forces.

A positive side effect will be that the sometimes heavily debated concept of professional autonomy will be guided by professional norms and standards instead of individual discretion (Van Os, 2010). This process would be analogous to the development of the criminal investigations process that has gone on in the Netherlands. While there is always room for solutions that are tailor-made based on the information and experience of community officers, these are best created under a framework where deviations from evidence-based practices have to be clearly articulated and justified. It may take up to 10 years for this development to be fully implemented. If seriously adopted, this may just be the latest and most important development in the constant quest to pursue professional excellence while balancing the focus on local communities.

Increasing Quality and Professionalism

An easy way to increase the quality and professionalism would be to increase the number of community officers on the ground. While increasing the number of community officers may do wonders for the effectiveness of the COP, numbers alone may not significantly increase the amount of time devoted to neighborhood-related activities. This would require serious parallel efforts in improving the manpower situation in other parts of the police force, implementing adequate administrative support for area-bound policing efforts and increasing the level of professionalism among community officers.

A second way to improve professionalism and quality is to reintroduce a focus on problem-oriented policing (POP). This model seems to have fallen behind and it would be good for it to catch up. The ideal scenario is for POP to become an integral part of the repertoire of the professional community officer. However, this may be too optimistic a goal (compare Braga and Weisburd, 2006). It would be good at least to increase the problem-solving skills of community officers, as this would position the community officer more firmly within the broader safety program of the local government.

The necessary tools, like the Crime and Disturbance Area Scan, are already there. However, in addition two shifts seem to be required: first, a shift from a primarily practice-based work style toward a primarily evidence-based one, and second, a shift from a police-centered approach toward one in which the police play primarily a supportive role and act as the last resort (Straten, van Sluis, Thaens, & Bekkers, 2010).

Two other changes that would be necessary to make are increasing the participation of citizens and improving the professional skills of the community officer in the area of crime investigation. These will be even more indispensable for successful community policing in the future than they are at present (see Tops, van Duin, van Os, & Zourides, 2010).

In part, these changes require that the Dutch police return to the inspiration behind "A Changing Police" and its original plea for greater use of the knowledge, creativity, and problem-solving capacity of rank-and-file officers whose core business is professional problem solving, and to ensure cooperation with a variety of internal and external strategic partners. But for such a strategy to work, it would require leadership styles and management performance systems that recognize and reward problem-oriented policing.

Information-Led Cops

More than in the past, community officers have to have a clear image of the concrete results they want to achieve and perform their job accordingly. This is necessary if they wish to avoid unrealistic expectations and demands from their partners and the public. To this end, detailed information about what is going on in communities is crucial. This is especially so in efforts to fight radicalization and terrorism. Community officers are the first link in the safety chain because they have ample access to community intelligence and it is through them that COP can effectively be combined with hard policing.

Fine-Tuning Police Strategies

Given the multiple demands on the police, to be effective, in the future COP has to better integrate the multiple policing models and strategies, such as reassurance policing, "fixing broken windows" policing, and POP. COP also needs to be better tuned to other seemingly incomparable popular models, such as Compstat, so that the two complement rather than oppose each other's effects (see, for example, Willis et al., 2010).

COP in a Centralized Dutch Police System

As outlined above, the Dutch police have been subject to more and more direct political control by the minister of the interior and kingdom relations. Recently, the trend toward an even more centrally and nationally organized police force has become unmistakable. The Rutte cabinet that came into power in October 2010 has made the unambiguous choice to have a single, unified national police force that is spread across a consolidated number of regions (10 vs. the existing 25). In a more centralized system of policing, the balance between central national and regional tasks will be much harder to maintain.

The question that arises then is whether Dutch COP will be resilient enough to counter the strong centralization tendencies and if there will be enough room within its bounds to safeguard the provision of tailor-made local policing.

Conclusions

Despite great changes in Dutch society and the many policing innovations that have come and gone, COP has continued to be a key feature of Dutch policing for the last three decades. The police and police authorities have had to strike a balance between the different demands of state, community, and profession, and COP had to mold and remold itself accordingly. Among other things, the Dutch COP had to come to grips with policing models that, at various times, are more oriented toward either the state or the police as a profession. Needless to say, the organization and implementation of Dutch COP has not been without obstacles, and it continues to be a work in progress. Despite these constant assaults, Dutch COP has proven itself to be the most enduring and integrative platform that has managed to successfully survive the many changes in the public and professional view of police work.

References

Bervoets, E., et al. (2009). *Bij de tijd: Wijkagenten in Hollands Midden. Beschrijving en analyse van dagelijkse praktijken*. Den Haag: COT, Boom Juridische Uitgevers.

Beumer, R.J. (1997). *Gebiedsgebonden politiewerk: Een verkenning.* Den Haag: Ministerie van BZK.

Braga, A., & Weisburd, D. (2006). Problem-oriented policing: The disconnect between principle and practice. In D. Weisburd & A.A. Braga (Eds.), *Police innovation: Contrasting perspectives.* New York: Cambridge University Press.

Cachet, A., van der Torre, E.J., & van Natijne, W. (1998). *De blijvende betekenis van Politie in Verandering.* Den Haag: Elsevier.

Das, D., Huberts, L., & van Steden, R. (2002). The changing "soul" of Dutch policing. Responses to new security demands and the relationship with Dutch tradition. *Policing: An International Journal of Police Strategies and Management, 30*(3), 518–532.

De Kimpe, S., & Cachet, L. (2008). Police and local safety policy. In L. Cachet et al. (Eds.), *Governance of security in the Netherlands and Belgium* (pp. 209–234). The Hague: Boom Legal Publishers.

de Kool, W. (2007). Mission Impossible? Het signaleren van islamitisch radicalisme en terrorisme door Nederlandse wijkagenten. *Het Tijdschrift voor de Politie, 69*(3), 4–8.

Hoogenboom, A.B. (2009). Dingen veranderen en blijven gelijk. *Justitiële verkenningen, 35*(1), 63–77.

Pollitt, C., & Bouckaert, G. (2009). *Continuity and change in public policy and management.* Cheltenham: Edward Elgar.

Punch, M. (2006). *Van 'alles mag' naar 'zero tolerance': Policy transfer en de Nederlandse politie.* Apeldoorn: P&W Verkenningen.

Punch, M. (2010). COP's vulnerability to paradigm swing. *Cahiers Politiestudies, 10-3*(16), 199–214.

Punch, M., Van Der Vijver K., & Zoomer O. (2002). Dutch "COP." Developing community policing in the Netherlands. *Policing: An International Journal of Police Strategies and Management, 25*(1), 66–79.

Punch, M., C. van der Vijver, C., & Hoogenboom, A. (2008). Community policing in the Netherlands: Four generations of redefinition. In T. Williamson (Ed.), *The handbook of knowledge based policing: Current conceptions and future directions.* Chichester, UK: Wiley.

Stol, W.Ph. (2009). Veranderingen in politiestraatwerk in Nederland: 1991–2005. Cahiers *Politiestudies, 2009-4*(13), 199–227.

Stol, W.Ph., van Wijk, A.Ph., Vogel, G., Foederer, B., & van Heel, L. (2004). *Politiestraatwerk in Nederland. Noodhulp en gebiedswerk: Inhoud, samenhang, verandering en sturing.* Politie en Wetenschap 14.

Straten, G.J., van Sluis, A., Thaens, M., & Bekkers, V. (2010). *Informatiegestuurde politiemensen.* Erasmus Universiteit, Politie en Wetenschap.

Straver, R., et al. (2009). *Integratie van Nederlandse politie in wijken, netwerken en lokaal bestuur.* Dordrecht: Stichting SMVP Producties.

Terpstra, J. (2008). *Wijkagenten en hun dagelijks werk.* Politie en Wetenschap 46.

Terpstra, J. (2010). Community policing in the Netherlands and the use of other related police models: Problem-oriented, disorder and reassuring policing. *Cahiers Politiestudies, 10-3*(16), 215–232.

Terpstra, J., & van der Vijver, C.D. (2006). The police, changing security arrangements and late modernity: The case of the Netherlands. *German Policy Studies, 3*(1), 80–111.

Tops, P., van Duin, M., van Os, P., & Zourides, S. (2010). *Sleuren of Sturen, Gemeenten en de sturing van veiligheid en politie.* Apeldoorn: Politieacademie.

van der Torre, E.J. (1999). *Politiewerk: Politiestijlen, Community Policing, Professionalisme Politiewerk.* Alphen aan den Rijn, Samson.

van der Torre, E.J. (2007). *Lokale politiechefs. Het middenkader in de basispolitiezorg.* Politie en Wetenschap 38. Den Haag: Elsevier Overheid (typologie van wijk-teamchefs en van operationele chefs).

van der Vijver, C.D. (2004). Kerntaken, sturing en professionaliteit. In B. van Stokkum and L. Gunther Moor (Eds.), *Onoprechte handhaving? Prestatiecontracten, beleidsvrijheid en politie-ethiek.* Dordrecht: Stichting Maatschappij, Veiligheid en Politie, 35–55.

van Os, P. (2010). Community-oriented policing in the Netherlands: A process with many obstacles. *Cahiers Politiestudies, 10-3*(16), 261–268.

van Os, P., & Gooren, W. (2010). *Operationalisering referentiekader gebiedsgebonden politie; de tweede oogst.* Apeldoorn: Politieacademie.

van Sluis, A. (2002). *Van "planning and control" naar strategische beleidsvorming. Een onderzoek naar beleidsvorming bij de politie.* Doctoral thesis, Erasmus University, Rotterdam

van Swaaningen, R. (2005). Public safety and the management of fear. *Theoretical Criminology, 9*(3), 289–305.

Vlek, F., & van der Torre, E.J. (2010). De Nederlandse politie sinds 1993: Een wereld van verschil. Beelden over en uit de praktijk. *Cahiers Politiestudies,* 2009-4(13), 229–286.

Willis, J.J., et al. (2010). Recommendations for integrating Compstat and community policing. *Policing: An International Journal of Police Strategies and Management,* 30, 237–256.

Zoomer, O. (2006). *De opsporingsfunctie binnen de gebiedsgebonden politiezorg.* Kerckebosch: Zeist.

Index

J

O

P

Q

R

S

IPES History

The International Police Executive Symposium (IPES) was founded in 1994. The aims and objectives of the IPES are to provide a forum to foster closer relationships among police researchers and practitioners globally, to facilitate crosscultural, international, and interdisciplinary exchanges for the enrichment of the law-enforcement profession, and to encourage discussion and published research on challenging and contemporary topics related to the profession.

One of the most important activities of the IPES is the organization of an annual meeting under the auspices of a police or educational institution. To date, meetings have been hosted by the Canton Police of Geneva, Switzerland (Police Challenges and Strategies, 1994), the International Institute of the Sociology of Law in Onati, Spain (Challenges of Policing Democracies, 1995), Kanagawa University in Yokohama, Japan (Organized Crime, 1996), the Federal Police in Vienna, Austria (International Police Cooperation, 1997), the Dutch Police and Europol in The Hague, The Netherlands (Crime Prevention, 1998), and Andhra Pradesh Police in Hyderabad, India (Policing of Public Order, 1999), and the Center for Public Safety, Northwestern University, Evanston, Illinois, USA (Traffic Policing, 2000). A special meeting was cohosted by the Bavarian Police Academy of Continuing Education in Ainring, Germany, University of Passau, Germany, and State University of New York, Plattsburgh, USA, to discuss the issues endorsed by the IPES in April 2000. The Police of Poland hosted the next meeting in May 2001 (Corruption: A Threat to World Order), and thereafter the annual meeting was hosted by the Police of Turkey in May 2002 (Police Education and Training). The Kingdom of Bahrain hosted the annual meeting in October 2003 (Police and the Community).

The 2004 meeting in May of that year (Criminal Exploitation of Women and Children) took place in Chilliwack, British Columbia, Canada, and it was cohosted by the University College of the Fraser Valley, Abbotsford Police Department, Royal Canadian Mounted Police, the Vancouver Police Department, the Justice Institute of British Columbia, Canadian Police College, and the International Centre for Criminal Law Reform and Criminal Justice Policy. The next meeting (Challenges of Policing in the 21st Century) took place in September 2005 in Prague, The Czech Republic. The Turkish National Police hosted the meeting in 2006 (Local Linkages to Global Security and Crime). The 14th IPES was held in Dubai on April 8–12, 2007 (Urbanization and Security). The 15th annual meeting (Police without Borders: The Fading Distinction between Local and Global) was hosted on May 12–16 in Cincinnati, Ohio by the City of Cincinnati Police and the Ohio Association of Chiefs of Police in Cincinnati. The Republic of Macedonia hosted the 2009 meeting (Tourism, Strategic Locations, and Major Events: Policing in an Age of Mobility, Mass Movement and Migration) in Ohrid, Macedonia on June 9–14. There will be a Special Meeting of IPES in 2010 (November 2–6) on the theme of Community Policing. In the following year 2011 (June 26–July 1) the City of Buenos Aires, Argentina, will host the 18th (20th with two Special Meetings included) Annual Meeting on the topic of Mass Action, Violence, and Crime: Policing Disorder and Discontent.

The majority of participants of the annual meetings are usually directly involved in the police profession. In addition, scholars and researchers in the field also participate. The meetings comprise both structured and informal sessions to maximize dialog and exchange of views and information. The executive summary of each meeting is distributed to participants as well as to a wide range of other interested police professionals and scholars. In addition, a book of selected papers from each annual meeting is published through CRC Press/Taylor & Francis Group, Prentice Hall, Lexington Books and other reputed publishers.

The IPES fulfills its mission with the cooperation of a global network of Institutional Supporters.

IPES Institutional Supporters

APCOF, The African Policing Civilian Oversight Forum, (contact Sean Tait), 2nd floor, The Armoury, Buchanan Square, 160 Sir Lowry Road, Woodstock Cape Town, 8000 South Africa. Email: sean@apcof.org.za

Australian Institute of Police Management, Collins Beach Road Manly NSW 2095, Australia, (contact Connie Coniglio) Email: cconiglio@aipm.gov.au

Cliff Roberson, Police Practice and Research: An International Journal, Managing editor: Email: managingeditorppr@gmail.com

Cyber Defense & Research Initiatives (contact James Lewis), LLC, PO Box 86, Leslie, MI 49251, USA. Tel: 517-242-6730. Email: lewisja@cyberdefenseresearch.com

Defendology Center for Security, Sociology and Criminology Research (Valibor Lalic), Srpska Street 63,78000 Banja Luka, Bosnia and Herzegovina. Tel and Fax: 387-51-308-914. Email: lalicv@teol.net

Department of Criminal Justice (Dr. Harvey L. McMurray, Chair), North Carolina Central University, 301 Whiting Criminal Justice Bldg., Durham, NC 27707, USA. Tel: 919-530-5204, 919-530-7909; Fax: 919-530-5195. Email: hmcmurray@nccu.edu

Department of Psychology (Stephen Perrott), Mount Saint Vincent University, 166 Bedford Highway, Halifax, Nova Scotia, Canada. Email: Stephen.perrott@mvsu.ca

Edmundo Oliveira, Prof. Ph.D. 1 Irving Place University Tower Apt. U-7-A 10003.9723 Manhattan – New York, New York, Phone 407-342-2473. Email: edmundooliveira@cfl.rr.com

Fayetteville State University (Dr. David E. Barlow, Professor and Dean), College of Basic and Applied Sciences, 130 Chick Building, 1200 Murchison Road, Fayetteville, North Carolina, 28301 USA. Tel: 910-672-1659; Fax: 910-672-1083. Email: dbarlow@uncfsu.edu

International Council on Security and Development (ICOS) (Andre Souza, Senior Researcher), Visconde de Piraja 577/605, Ipanema, Rio de Janeiro 22410–003, Brazil. Tel: (+55) 21-3186-5444. Email: asouza@icosgroup.net

Justice Studies Department, San José State University, 1 Washington Square, San José, CA 95192-0050 (Mark E. Correia, Ph.D, Chair and Associate Professor), 408-924-1350. Email: mcorreia@casa.sjsu.edu

Kerala Police (Jacob Punnoose, Director General of Police), Police Headquarters, Trivandrum, Kerala, India. Email: JPunnoose@gmail.com

Molloy College, The Department of Criminal Justice (contact Dr. John A. Eterno, NYPD Captain-Retired), 1000 Hempstead Avenue, PO Box 5002, Rockville Center, NY 11571-5002, USA. Tel: 516-678-5000, Ext. 6135; Fax: 516-256-2289. Email: jeterno@molloy.edu

National Institute of Criminology and Forensic Science (Mr. Kamalendra Prasad, Inspector General of Police), MHA, Outer Ring Road, Sector 3, Rohini, Delhi 110085, India. Tel: 91-11-275-2-5095; Fax: 91-11-275-1-0586. Email: director.nicfs@nic.in

National Police Academy, Japan (Suzuki Kunio, Assistant Director), Police Policy Research Center, Zip 183-8558: 3-12-1 Asahi-cho Fuchu-city, Tokyo, Japan. Tel: 81-42-354-3550; Fax: 81-42-330-1308. Email: PPRC@npa.go.jp

Royal Canadian Mounted Police (Helen Darbyshire, Executive Assistant), 657 West 37th Avenue, Vancouver, BC V5Z 1K6, Canada. Tel: 604-264-2003; Fax: 604-264-3547. Email: helen.darbyshire@rcmp-grc.gc.ca

School of Psychology and Social Science, Head, Social Justice Research Centre (Prof. S. Caroline Taylor, Foundation Chair in Social Justice), Edith Cowan University, 270 Joondalup Drive, Joondalup, WA 6027, Australia. Email: c.taylor@ecu.edu.au

South Australia Police (Commissioner Mal Hyde), Office of the Commissioner, South Australia Police, 30 Flinders Street, Adelaide, SA 5000, Australia. Email: mal.hyde@police.sa.gov.au

The Faculty of Criminal Justice and Security, (Dr Gorazd Mesko), University of Maribor, Kotnikova 8, 1000 Ljubljana, Slovenia. Tel: 386-1-300-83-39; Fax: 386-1-2302-687. Email: gorazd.mesko@fvv.uni-mb.si

UNISA, Department of Police Practice (Setlhomamaru Dintwe), Florida Campus, Cnr. Christiaan De Wet and Pioneer Avenues, Private Bag X6, Florida, 1710 South Africa. Tel: 011-471-2116; Cell: 083-581-6102; Fax: 011-471-2255. Email: Dintwsi@unisa.ac.za

University of Maine at Augusta, College of Natural and Social Sciences (Mary Louis Davitt, Professor of Legal Technology), 46 University Drive, Augusta, ME 04330-9410, USA. Email: mldavitt@maine.edu

University of New Haven (Dr. Richard Ward, School of Criminal Justice and Forensic Science), 300 Boston Post Road, West Haven, CT 06516, USA. Tel: 203-932-7260. Email: rward@newhaven.edu

University of South Africa, College of Law (Professor Kris Pillay, School of Criminal Justice, Director), Preller Street, Muckleneuk, Pretoria. Email: cpillay@unisa.ac.za

University of the Fraser Valley (Dr. Darryl Plecas), Department of Criminology & Criminal Justice, 33844 King Road, Abbotsford, British Columbia V2 S7 M9, Canada. Tel: 604-853-7441; Fax: 604-853-9990. Email: Darryl. plecas@ufv.ca

www.ingramcontent.com/pod-product-compliance
Ingram Content Group UK Ltd.
Pitfield, Milton Keynes, MK11 3LW, UK
UKHW010956180926
475701UK00004B/389

* 9 7 8 0 3 6 7 8 6 6 7 6 1 *